S407

THE SPALDING TRUST

FRONTISPIECE. Henry Norman Spalding in the sitting room at 'Bell Cliff', Lyme Regis, April 1936.

The Spalding Trust and the Union for the Study of the Great Religions

H. N. Spalding's Pioneering Vision

EDWARD HULMES

M͏C

© Edward Hulmes, 2002

First published in 2002 by
The Memoir Club
Whitworth Hall
Spennymoor
County Durham

British Library Cataloguing-in-Publication data
A catalogue record for this book is available from the British Library

ISBN 1 84104 040 1

The descriptions of events, incidents and characters featured in this book
are true and correct according to the recollections of the author

Designed and typeset by Carnegie Publishing, Lancaster
Printed in the UK by Bookcraft, Bath

'It is not enough today for mankind to seek to avoid a Third World War, necessary as that is; we must prepare for—must lay the foundations of—the First World Renaissance that mankind has ever known ... God reveals Himself in many ways, depending on the social circumstances of the various peoples. It is man's task today, while adhering to the inessentials so far as they still help him, to look within and to see the essentials—the Divine Nature and man's Way of Return to It. As we all draw nearer the One, though from many different and it may be distant points, we shall all draw nearer to one another. A knowledge and love of the One God will bind the sons of God together in the Kingdom of God. Union with Him and with all things in Him is the goal of mankind and of the universe here and hereafter.'[1] (H. N. Spalding, born 1877)

'For me the most important spiritual experiences are connected with the fact that gradually and with pauses of years and decades I found the same interpretation of human life among the Hindus, the Chinese, and the Christians, I was confirmed in my intuition of a central problem, which I found expressed everywhere in analogous symbols. These experiences supported more strongly than anything else my belief that mankind has a meaning, that human need and human searching at all times and throughout the whole world are a unity. It is unimportant from the point of view whether we regard, as many do today, the religious-philosophical expression of human thinking and experience as something outmoded, an exercise of an epoch now outdated. It does not matter to me if what I am here calling 'theology' is transient, a product of one stage of human development that someday will be superseded and left behind. Art too and even speech are perhaps means of communication that are appropriate only to certain stages in human history and they also may become obsolescent and replaceable. But at each stage nothing will be so important to men, it seems to me, in their search for truth, nothing will be so valuable and comforting as the realization that beneath the division in race, colour, language, and culture there lies a unity, that there are not various peoples and minds but only One Humanity, only One Spirit.'[2] (Hermann Hesse, born 1877)

---

1. H. N. Spalding, 1958, *The Divine Universe* (published posthumously as a sequel to his *Civilization in East and West*, Oxford University Press, 1939). The extract quoted here is to be found on pages 353–4.
2. Hermann Hesse, '1932, A Bit of Theology', in *My Belief* (Triad Paladin Grafton Books, 1989), translated from the German by Denver Lindley, pp. 203–4.

Contents

Abbreviations

BNC	Brasenose College, Oxford
CEW	H. N. Spalding's *Civilization in East and West: An Introduction to the Study of Human Progress*
HFP	Henderson Family Papers
HNS	Henry Norman Spalding
IPL	H. N. Spalding's book, *In Praise of Life*
JMKS	John M. K. Spalding
KDDH	Kenneth D. D. Henderson
NUSGR	K. D. D. Henderson's *News Letters* for members of the Union for the Study of the Great Religions
OCA	Oriel College Archives, Oxford
SFP	Spalding Family Papers
STP	Spalding Trust Papers
TDU	H. N. Spalding's book, *The Divine Universe, or the Many and the One: A Study of Religions and Religion*
USGR	The Union for the Study of the Great Religions

List of Illustrations

Acknowledgements

For their invitation and encouragement to write this book I am grateful to my Spalding Trust colleagues, Dr John Spalding, his wife Dr Elizabeth Spalding, their daughter Miss Anne Spalding MA, Professor J. A. Emerton, Professor C. E. Bosworth, Dr Michael Loewe, Dr Julius Lipner, and Dr Humphrey Fisher. The book is respectfully dedicated to Dr John Spalding and his wife. It has been my privilege to enjoy their friendship for the past thirty years. They, more than anyone else, have provided me with detailed information about the life and career of Dr H. N. Spalding, and the history of the Spalding Trust.

I would also like to record my thanks to Mr David Henderson MA for providing me with access to the papers of his father, K. D. D. Henderson CMG, MA, the first and last General Secretary of the Union for the Study of the Great Religions (USGR) and Secretary of the Spalding Trust from 1953 to 1986. I also pay tribute to the late Professor Mary Lago of the Department of English in the University of Missouri, whose biography of Edward John Thompson—a man for whom H. N. Spalding provided the funding for a Senior Research Fellowship at Oxford in the 1930s at my own College, Oriel—opened up several interesting lines of enquiry.

For her help in directing me to unpublished material about H. N. and K. J. Spalding in the archives of Oriel College and Brasenose College, Oxford, I am grateful to the Archivist, Mrs Elizabeth Boardman. My wife, Mrs S. D. L. M. Hulmes, and my daughter, Mrs Rosalind P. Kenrick BA, have offered constructive comments throughout. Others have offered information, criticisms, and counsel. Their assistance is acknowledged in appropriate places in the text.

For their help in bringing the book to publication I wish to thank the staffs of the Memoir Club and Carnegie Book Production; also the Steward, Administrative Staff, and Porters of Oriel College.

Edward Hulmes,
Oxford, 2002

Foreword

In the early years of the twentieth century the study of the great religions of the world was neither as well established nor as fashionable in this country as it is today. The promotion of interest in this important area of human knowledge and experience was the task to which Henry Norman Spalding devoted his life at the end of the First World War.

Spalding's pioneering venture led to the founding of the Trust that bears his name, and which continues its work to this day by providing limited financial assistance for scholars working in the field of Religious Studies. His vision of the essential unity that lies beneath the outward differences of name and form in the religions of the world led him shortly before his death in 1953 to found the Union for the Study of the Great Religions (USGR), with its representatives and area committees in different parts of the world.

This book gives an account, based on hitherto unpublished sources, of the origins and development of the Spalding Trust and the Union, but more importantly perhaps, it gives an account for the first time of the lives of Spalding (who was almost universally known as 'HN') and K. D. D. ('Bill') Henderson, who shared HN's vision and sought to implement his ideals. They, without question, were the leading figures in the history of both organisations. Spalding was an Oxford scholar, philosopher, poet, and bene-factor who, with the constant support of his wife, used his talents and resources in the service of his ideals. Henderson, who took over the day to day running of the Trust and the Union in the year of Spalding's death, brought to the task his experience in the Sudan Political Service as an administrator and a provincial Governor.

Both Spalding and Henderson were Oxford men to the core. Several Oxford colleges (Oriel among them) benefited from Spalding's generosity. In the years shortly before the outbreak of the Second World War he financed a Research Fellowship in Indian Studies at the College, and for a number of years he enjoyed a personal friendship with a former Provost, Sir David Ross. Only last year a file of correspondence about the promotion of the study of world religions in Oxford and elsewhere, especially the religions of the East, was discovered by the author of this book in the archives of Oriel.

Other Oxford colleges, notably Brasenose and Pembroke, were helped in many ways as a result of Spalding's generosity. However, the best known benefaction he and his wife made to Oxford must be the resources they provided for the establishment of the Spalding Chair in Eastern Religions and Ethics, the first occupant of which was Sir Sarvepalli Radhakrishnan. This unique position is associated with a fellowship at All Souls College. With personal donations and gifts, but above all with his tireless and powerful advocacy, Spalding sought to encourage other universities, colleges, institutions, and individuals in many different parts of the world to promote the study of aspects of religious belief and experience.

The cause to which Spalding devoted his life took on still more significance and, indeed, urgency as the twentieth century moved on. The peoples, nations and religions who in the early twentieth century seemed far away from each other are in our modern world brought much closer together by modern communications, modern means of travel and, most of all in the West, by the increasing amount of immigration during the second half of the twentieth century. At no time in modern history has it been more urgent to encourage the study and greater understanding of the great religions, whose adherents are now (and to an unprecedented extent) neighbours, and at no time has it been more urgent to bring to bear on the world's problems and needs the common insights of these religions concerning the worth of humanity, human rights, a just sharing of the world's resources, and a new concern for the poor of the world. The urgent need that Spalding identified in the troubled world of the first half of the twentieth century is as urgent in this new century. Spalding was indeed a pioneer who could not have fully realised the increasing importance for succeeding generations of what he sought so earnestly and tirelessly to foster and encourage.

I am delighted and honoured to welcome and commend this excellently researched and delightfully written book by Edward Hulmes, who is a distinguished member of Oriel College.

The Revd Professor Ernest W. Nicholson, DD FBA
Provost's Lodgings,
Oriel College, Oxford
June 2002

Preface

In 1948 a small book with the title *Two Quiet Lives* was published by Constable. The author was the Oxford don, Lord David Cecil, who described the subjects of the book—Dorothy Osborne and Thomas Gray—as 'complex enough to deserve a closer analysis and a more extended interpretation than they have up to now received.'[1] The pages that follow are about two notable individuals—Henry Norman Spalding and Kenneth David Druitt ('Bill') Henderson—about whose lives and careers little has yet been published Humanly speaking, their lives may have been quiet, but their achievements were far from insignificant. The fact that they were able to influence the lives of countless others, not only in this country but far beyond its shores, is a sufficient reason for bringing their work to the notice of a wider public. Put simply, they sought to promote the study of what Spalding called 'the Great Religions', at a time when it was far less common (or fashionable) to do so than it is today. It is true that neither he nor Henderson sought to promote this study for its own sake. Neither man was interested in adding another 'subject' to an already crowded curriculum. The advocacy of such study was explicitly intended by both men to serve what they believed to be a vital purpose, namely, that of helping to promote unity and peace in a world convulsed by dissension and violence. They believed that beneath the outward differences of religious names and forms there lies a unity of religious experience and aspiration. To study the religions of the world (so they believed) is first to sense and then to reveal this unity.

To discover this unity (so they averred) is to make human conflict less likely. Both men had good reason to hope that this was so because both had witnessed how the world wars of 1914–18 and 1939–45 had threatened humanity. The two men certainly shared a vision about how the world might be made a better place to live in, but they were realists. They took practical and effective steps to develop and advocate their plans, conscious of the fact that some critics would inevitably dismiss their efforts as naïve and misguided. It was Spalding, who fashioned the instruments for implementing these plans and for directing their use. The Union for the Study of the Great Religions and the Spalding Trust were his creations. They were the charitable foundations for which he provided not only leadership and direction but financial support. Spalding planned, and Henderson subsequently guided, the work of these foundations for sixty five years, from 1923 to 1988. From 1923 until his death in 1953 Spalding was the dominant figure. From 1953 until his death in 1988 Henderson organised the Union and the Spalding Trust as the faithful steward of Spalding's legacy. Neither man could have achieved what he did without the willing help of many others, as this book will show, but there are two people who deserve special recognition. The first is Spalding's wife, Mrs Nellie Maud Emma Spalding. The second is Spalding's younger brother K. J. Spalding. Both remained in the background, but each played an influential supporting role. An account of the work of the Union and the Spalding Trust would be far from complete without an acknowledgement of their different and complementary contributions to the success of Spalding's efforts.

A Personal Tribute

At the fifty-second annual general meeting of the Spalding Trust, held in Robinson College, Cambridge on Saturday 13 May 2000, the Trustees met under the chairmanship of Dr John Spalding, the son of the founder. He and his wife, Dr Elizabeth de Carteret Spalding, had already informed their colleagues that after many years of service—in his case, almost forty years, nearly thirty of them as Chairman—they had decided to retire. In addition to their efforts on behalf of the Trust, Dr John Spalding and Dr Elizabeth Spalding have each enjoyed a distinguished career in the medical profession. John Spalding, DM (Oxon) and a Fellow of the Royal College of Physicians, is a neurologist who dealt with disorders of the brain, the spinal cord, and the peripheral nerves. In collaboration with some of his colleagues he wrote a number of influential books on these subjects. He was one of the first to help design, build, and operate, an artificial respirator for patients whose breathing muscles were affected. After a paediatric appointment in Oxford he worked in London in general medicine and in a neurological hospital. He then returned to Oxford to work with the neurologist Dr Ritchie Russell. In 1955 he was elected as a Senior Research Fellow at St Peter's College, Oxford, and he spent the rest of his career as a Consultant in Neurology in the city, retiring in 1977.

Dr Elizabeth Spalding's mother was a gynaecologist in London at a time when there were comparatively few women doctors (and women surgeons, in particular). Elizabeth Spalding (*née* Falle) completed her pre-clinical training at University College, London (UCL), and her clinical training at the West London Hospital in Hammersmith. Her training suffered from the chaos of wartime London, but she benefited from the varied practical

Dr John M. K. Spalding, son of the founder of the Union and the Trust.

Dr Elizabeth de Carteret Spalding.

experience she was able to gather in that situation. Having gained her Membership of the Royal College of Physicians, the postgraduate qualification in Medicine, she was appointed senior registrar at her own teaching hospital in Hammersmith. After marriage and the arrival of the two children, Anne and Susan, her time was fully occupied with the family and the management of the seven households at Shotover Cleve. The word 'seven' is not a mis-print. Life at Shotover Cleve was often hectic. The complex of dwellings built by H. N. Spalding was large enough to accommodate several families. Coping with the close proximity of guests and temporary residents called for considerable tact and strength of mind. Elizabeth Spalding provided both. Even so, she found time and energy to work for the Family Planning Association. This was an exciting and innovative time for those involved in this work, when the contraceptive pill and the intra-uterine loop were being introduced. She was soon involved in helping to integrate the family planning service into the National Health Service, and to assist with counselling for some of the psycho-sexual problems that presented.

Towards the end of the meeting in Robinson College, when tributes had been paid and presentations made, the Trustees unanimously elected Miss Anne C. Spalding to succeed her father as Chairman. The leadership of the Trust was thus handed on to the founder's granddaughter. The Trustees also decided at that meeting to commission a memoir about H. N. Spalding, K. D. D. Henderson, and the work to which both men were committed for so many years. Having been associated with the Trust since 1974, first as Assistant Secretary, and then as a Trustee, I was invited by my colleagues to write the book. It is intended to be an affectionate, though not uncritical, tribute to the work of the two principal figures in the history of the Union and the Trust. In a book of this size it has not been possible to consider the contents of more than a selection of the papers that have accumulated over the years. The book does not pretend to offer a comprehensive history of either the Union or the Trust. The usual exchanges of information, comment, and response between the Trustees about the numerous applications for financial assistance, which they have to consider each year, make rather dull and repetitive reading. They are of little general interest in any case. Moreover, the discussions about these applications, and the decisions taken by the Trustees, are confidential and ought to remain undisclosed.

Sources

The primary sources for the details contained in this book are four. The first is the information provided by H. N. Spalding's son, Dr J. M. K. Spalding, about the life and career of his father. Dr Spalding became a Trustee in 1953 and served as Chairman of the Trust from 1971 to 2000. His knowledge is

a unique source of information about the history of the Trust and of the
deliberations of the Trustees. The second source is the substantial collection
of papers assembled for some fifty years by the Secretaries of the Trust,
notably by Henderson. Many of these Spalding Trust Papers (STP) carry the
marks of his organisation and careful annotation, although the cataloguing
of the whole collection is far from complete. The third source is the collection
of Henderson family papers (HFP) to which the author has been given access
by Henderson's son, David. The fourth source of information is arguably
the most important. It consists of the published and unpublished works of
H. N. Spalding himself. Many passages from this source are quoted in the
following pages. Additional information has been discovered in the Bodleian
Library, Oxford and in Oriel and Brasenose Colleges, Oxford. A number of
references to H. N. Spalding's work were located in the libraries of the
University of Bristol, the University of Durham, and the London School of
Economics.

Note

1. Dorothy Osborne (1627–95) married the English diplomat and essay writer Sir William
   Temple (1628–99) in 1655, after her family, staunch Royalists, had opposed the marriage
   for seven years. Her place in English literature rests on the letters she wrote to her future
   husband before their marriage. The English scholar and poet, Thomas Gray (1716–71),
   is best known, perhaps, for his poem 'Elegy Written in a Country Churchyard' (1751).

CHAPTER ONE

The Partnership

Names and Initials

In adult life Henry Norman Spalding was known almost universally as HN. His first two initials became his name, although his wife seldom used the abbreviation. She usually shortened his second name, Norman, to its first syllable, retaining the dissyllabic Christian name for more formal occasions. The abbreviation stuck, however. People who knew him more by reputation than through personal friendship also called him HN. His younger brother, Kenneth Jay Spalding, came to be known as KJ far beyond the family circle. Kenneth David Druitt Henderson, the man who was appointed Secretary of the Spalding Trust shortly after HN died, was often known as KDDH, although to most of his colleagues, friends and acquaintances he was usually called 'Bill'. The reason why a man with three perfectly good baptismal names should come to be known as 'Bill', a name that was not linked to any of them, will be described in a later chapter. His wife preferred to call him Kenneth. It will come as no surprise to readers of the following pages that these abbreviations, HN, KJ, and KDDH, appear frequently.

Spalding and Henderson

The phrase *Spalding and Henderson* looks a little like the name of a small family business to be found somewhere in the shires or the remoter parts of the country, but the partnership thus named had little to do with business or commerce. It was a partnership of spirit and it had everything to do with the world of religious beliefs and values. The result was an enterprise whose purpose was to promote the study of religion and religions, especially in the West, where the horrors of war no less than the corrosive effects of critical thinking had already started to undermine the once secure foundations of religious conviction and practice. The two men first met at breakfast one day in Oxford in 1922. This book tells how their friendship flourished during the following four decades. The work that HN started almost eighty years ago continues to the present day, though on a much more modest scale. At the beginning of the twenty-first century it is appropriate to consider what he achieved and then to ask questions about how and why the work he pioneered is to proceed in circumstances very different from those that obtained in the aftermath of the First World War.

'The study of religion and religions' is the phrase that HN chose to use about his work. He lived and worked for much of his life in the university city of Oxford. In 1925 he built 'Shotover Cleve' on Shotover Hill, about three miles from Oxford's city centre. Some years later he moved to number 9 South Parks Road, where he lived until his death in 1953. The house is no more. It has been replaced by a University laboratory. Kenneth Henderson was a man who spent thirty years in the Sudan Political Service. In 1926 he went as a Probationer to Khartoum. He went on to hold a succession of increasingly responsible posts in the Service, ending with his appointment as Governor of Darfur Province in 1949. He served in that capacity until he retired from the Service in 1953. Only a few months after his retirement he accepted the invitation to became General Secretary of the Union for the Study of the Great Religions and Secretary of the Spalding Trust. The pioneering venture in which both men were involved was to assume a far from local reputation and significance. It was built upon at least a century of work undertaken by a host of scholars, Eastern as well as Western, who had devoted themselves to the study of religion. The findings of these eminent researchers were clearly of considerable interest to a comparatively small number of specialists in the field, but the task was to promote the study of religion on a much broader front, in schools, colleges and universities.

The nineteenth century, in particular, had seen the growth in the West of real interest in the religions of the East. These religions were revealed as the cradles of rich civilizations and spiritual insights. For centuries Hinduism and Buddhism, no less than Judaism and Christianity, had promoted and sustained the religious faith of millions. At a time when religion in the West appeared to be in decline, the continuing resilience of Eastern religions was worthy of note. Spalding and Henderson never claimed to be scholars in a strictly academic sense. They were scholarly men, certainly, but they always deferred to those whose reputations for scholarship in this field were clearly established and well deserved. In consequence both men were deeply indebted to those who were authorities in what had come to be called *Comparative Religion*. They were always scrupulously honest in acknowledging their indebtedness to the work of others. The record shows that they did much to encourage and to promote further scholarly research in this wide and widening field, but the subject of Comparative Religion was not just one of many possible intellectual options for them. In a much more profound sense they believed that the study of mankind's religious experience could provide an answer to the most intractable problems facing humanity. This was the conviction that guided what they set out to do. They believed that the scholarly study of religion should not be undertaken or promoted just for its own sake. Religion, they averred, is not just one 'subject' among many others. Religion may lend itself to 'objective' investigation—from the outside, as it were—as one of many possible intellectual pursuits, but neither Spalding nor Henderson was ever convinced that the inner secrets of the religious experience of mankind are revealed to the merely intellectually curious.

Both men were concerned that the unique importance of religion in human affairs was in danger of being overlooked in an increasingly secularised and secularising Western world. They believed that a more comprehensive and personally engaged approach to the study of religious experience could help to prevent this dimension of human existence from being further neglected in the West. They argued that a purely (or a predominantly) cerebral approach to religion stultifies the spirit and induces a sickness of the soul. They were convinced that a *malaise* of this nature was developing in the West in a way that was unknown (or at least less harmful) in the East. What prescription might help to cure this distressing human condition? Some spoke with approval about what the decadent West could learn from the East. Others used the phrase 'the soul of the East for the mind of the West' as a *mantra*. This was too simplistic a prescription, but the phrase contained a grain of truth that both men thought was useful. Their conviction about the unique importance of religion in human affairs invested their efforts with an element of advocacy, which some critics viewed with distaste as evidence of a proselytising spirit. It was true that both Spalding and Henderson consistently urged and defended the cause in which they believed, but neither man was insensitive to the reality of religious and cultural diversity. They sought to change attitudes by persuasion, principally through education. They appealed to teachers to widen the curriculum so as to include teaching about the great religions of the world. In doing so they were among the first in Britain to advocate changes that were not only desirable but necessary.

H. N. Spalding (1877–1953) was a man whose vision, scholarly ability and exemplary determination, initiated the enterprise. The task to which he committed himself in the third decade of the twentieth century was specifically *religious*, although he was never to define it as such in an orthodox Christian sense. K. D. D. Henderson (1903–1988) devoted his energies in 'retirement' to carrying on the work started by Spalding. The task was to challenge the decline of theism in the Western world by promoting renewed interest in the great religions of the world, especially those of the East. What Spalding meant by the phrase 'the great religions' will be considered later. Needless to say, the phrase included the religions of Judaism and Christianity for which he had a profound respect. His vision of a world, in which 'the great religions' reveal discrete yet complementary insights about ultimate reality, and thus point to the common source of a universal life-enhancing wisdom, provided the initial impetus for the task he undertook. Henderson's administrative gifts were complementary and used to organise and to extend the influence of Spalding's vision world-wide.

Although he was never what might be called an orthodox Christian, HN never wavered in his conviction that of all the world's religious teachers and spiritual masters, Jesus of Nazareth—especially in the figure of the redeeming victim, resurrected and glorified—was the one whose message could not finally be denied, despite the repeated failure of the Christian Church (or churches) to interpret His teaching. Theological niceties about the distinction between the Jesus of history and the Christ of faith did not feature in his thinking, however. Consider, for example, one of HN's 'Sonnets of Ascent', which carries the title, *The Church.*

> Not priest, not prelate, but the sons of man,
> These are the Church of Christ: he gave the keys
> That ope the Paradisal mysteries
> Not to a saint, but to a fisherman,
> Snob, coward, traitor: yet 'twas he who ran
> First to the Sepulchre; and it did please
> Wisdom as on a rock on him, on these,
> To found the Kingdom will'd ere time began.
> Then let us, Peters tho' we be, go on
> Toward that Kingdom builded in the Heaven
> Wherein man's longing shall be satisfied:
> Men are we; yet Christ's Church shall stand upon
> Poor human nature, Deified, forgiven:
> Peter denies; Christ will not be denied.[1]

Spalding was a man with a vision of the potential unity of mankind in what he called *the Divine Universe*, but he was more than a dreaming visionary. He planned his work in a meticulous and practical way, although a number of the highly ambitious schemes he devised proved to be impracticable. His plans, his achievements, and his failures will be considered later. He was a prolific writer of prose and poetry, of memoranda, articles, and letters. Much of his poetry was privately published. He was dismissive of its quality, but many readers did not, and would not, agree with him. His ability to recall apparently insignificant detail became the subject of affectionate family amusement and even irritation.

He could remember exactly what happened, and when. He is said to have been able to tell you what [the members of the family] did and said (for instance) three years and four days ago ... Along similar lines,

I gather he noticed when the chronology in books did not fit ... HN's copies of P. G. Wodehouse [are] annotated in the margins with comments along the lines of 'It can't be Thursday; there have only been two days since Sunday'.[2]

Henderson was also a prolific writer, who shared Spalding's vision and sought to interpret and express it. His two major works of scholarship were written about the Sudan.[3] Apart from them he wrote reports of the many conferences he attended in different parts of the world. His unique *News Letters*, written for circulation among the members and friends of the Union for the Study of the Great Religions, will also be considered later in the book. Throughout his career he corresponded regularly and fully with friends and associates all over the world. Some of these friends like to remember that he also wrote verse of a kind that was often amusing and satirical. It was never intended for publication. A few pieces survive in private collections. They were a source of whimsey and amusement for friends, yet the author sometimes sounded a serious note. The following example is typical. It was written as part of his Christmas greeting to H. N. Spalding in 1946, and sent in an Air Letter, typed in red ink capitals. The postmark is Khartoum, where Henderson was serving as Assistant Civil Secretary (Political).

> *Eheu Fugaces*
> Ah Postumus Ah Postumus, the years fly on apace
> And no amount of noble thoughts
> Drive wrinkles from one's face;
> But Oxford never alters, and, changeless now and then,
> Amid her ageless buildings walks, agelessly, H.N.
>
> The day we met at breakfast in nineteen twenty-two;
> The evenings round the wine-glass talking with one or two;
> Old age will find the memories in glad confusion mix
> With dinner at the Eastgate in nineteen forty-six.
>
> I wondered as I listened, and the same old genial glow
> Came from his conversation's enthusiastic flow,
> Whether a new foundation was being subtly laid
> For such another friendship as in Longwall was made;
>
> Whether his new young listener would find as time went by
> The same unchanging interest to hearten him as I;
> And as the years rolled backward and I thought of what I'd done
> To implement in action the dreams of twenty-one
>
> I wondered just how much I owed to one who never ceased
> To feel the dreams had substance till some came true at least.[4]

In a way that tends to be overlooked (or misunderstood) today, both Henderson and Spalding were *scholarly* men. Both, as was more common in their day than now, read Greats (Classics) at Oxford. Neither man excelled in the Schools, but both acquired an extensive knowledge of philosophy, literature and the Classics. They read widely and had retentive memories. They were articulate in conversation, receptive to new ideas, and above all sensitive to *style* in the written and spoken language. Schooled in the manner of Greek and Latin authorities, they were familiar with the masters of English verse and prose—Shakespeare, Milton, Tennyson, Gibbon, Bacon, Burke, Hume, Macaulay, Matthew Arnold, the translators of the King James version of the Holy Bible, and many more. To these august names they came to add yet more from the Near and Far East, from the ancient philosophies and sacred texts of Hinduism, Buddhism, Chinese and Japanese religions, and from the Islamic world. Both men were undoubtedly opinionated to a degree, but they were also ready listeners. Both were men of discriminating taste and aesthetic sensibility. Both were capable from time to time of self-deprecation, and both had a sense of humour. Henderson's characteristic roaring laughter was felt as much as heard, whenever a conversation among friends provoked his mirth. On these occasions his face would assume a contorted wrinkled aspect as he struggled to control the mirth that he could not prevent shining out of his eyes.

Henderson had a keener ear for poetry and the spoken word than for music. From a well-stocked memory he was able to draw inspiration and consolation from his favourite poetry and prose, often quoting long passages with facility and appositeness. He kept in his head much of his *Commonplace Book*, his store of the passages of prose and verse that he particularly admired. Others committed their own favourite selections to writing. Henderson published one such collection in tribute to his chief mentor in the Sudan Political Service, Sir Douglas Newbold.[5] In other ways Henderson was a prolific writer of papers, notes and letters. This was in addition to his substantial scholarly works on the history of the Sudan. The records of the Trust are filled with examples of his world-wide correspondence. From February 1954 to Autumn 1982 he produced thirty-nine News Letters for circulation to the members and supporters of the Union for the Study of the Great Religions. They constitute an unique record of the Union's activities, frequently enlivened by the editor's literary skill, his philosophical reflections, and his perceptive observations. Sometimes they record his moods as well. The length of these News Letters varies considerably. Some are quite short. As he grew older they became more discursive. The contents were sometimes controversial. He acknowledged this and included in subsequent issues the criticisms he received. He had an eye for detail, and sometimes pursued the points he wanted to make with dogged persistence.

Henderson and Spalding shared the same vision of a world in which religion had a decisive role to play in the promotion of racial harmony, justice, and peace. Neither man was ever wholly satisfied with the phrase 'comparative religion', or even 'the comparative study of religion'. They did use these terms on occasions, but preferred to avoid using words that could possibly imply invidious comparisons. Neither man was ever directly involved as teacher or administrator in an academic community in which these discrete areas of scholarly investigation and research were being developed. In 1972 Henderson wrote:

> What Spalding hoped for was a peacefully co-existing world which would share certain ethical principles and certain basic beliefs in what Julian Huxley called the stuff of divinity; a culture co-terminous with humanity but including a rich variety of faiths and traditions and local patriotisms, a cross-pattern of loyalties which are not always subject to logical explanation or susceptible of classification. I myself am Scots by birth and English by upbringing. Circumstances have led me to regard Australia as my second home. I have many personal ties with the U.S.A. and few with France, yet I can share a Frenchman's European view of America and Australia. I am a European and a Christian, but two of the closest friends I ever had were non-English-speaking Afro-Asian Muslims. In my eyes, therefore, nothing in the way of integration-cum-differentiation should be ruled out as impossible.[6]

If Spalding was the visionary with an almost irresistible capacity for persuading individuals from different backgrounds, religions, and cultures, to join him in the pursuit of an ideal, Henderson was the imaginative and competent administrator. He could be tetchy at times, given to exaggeration, and forthright in the expression of his own opinions. At 6′ in height Spalding was the taller of the two, bespectacled, and slightly stooping in old age. He bore himself with unassuming dignity, and had the gift of making others feel at ease in his company. Henderson's frame was sturdy, the result of vigorous athletic activity in his earlier years, but progressively gnarled by arthritis. His expressive face creased, his eyes twinkled behind spectacles, and his moustaches twitched when he was amused (which was often). Both men took pleasure in the company of friends and the stimulus of vigorous debate. Both were men of unimpeachable integrity.

Mrs Nellie Maud Emma Spalding

HN was supported throughout his endeavours by two other influential, if less well-known, figures. The first was his wife, Mrs Nellie Maud Emma Spalding. It is doubtful that he would have started on his course of action, or at least sustained it for long, without her help and encouragement. She was the quiet but by no means inactive partner in the venture. From the time of their marriage in 1909 until his death in 1953, many individuals and groups benefited from the couple's joint acts of generosity. Mrs Spalding (*née* Cayford) was comfortably provided for not long before the marriage by her father, Ebenezer Cayford. He died shortly after reluctantly agreeing to the marriage of HN and his daughter. It was she whose inherited wealth made it possible for her husband to leave paid employment and to devote himself to a prolonged exploration and exposition of what he called *The Divine Universe*. With his wife's full approval, HN assumed the responsibility for managing the family's finances. For the rest of his life he was to discharge this responsibility with scrupulous care. In this respect he acted as an assiduous steward, regarding himself as a trustee of the family finances, and playing the active role in their management. At every stage he consulted his wife about the major decisions to be made, especially with regard to gifts for charitable purposes.

For her part, Mrs Spalding resisted any suggestion that she and her husband should have separate bank accounts. She did keep shares in a phosphate company and in Houlder Brothers, a successful shipping and trading company, in both of which her father had once had interests. The personal gifts and benefactions donated by the Spaldings took different forms, and were made for different purposes. For obvious reasons details about many of these gifts and benefactions remain unknown. After her husband's death in 1953, it was she who invited Henderson to carry HN's work forward. Disinclined to run the Trust herself, and knowing that the two men had shared the same ideals for many years, she was convinced that Henderson was the right person for the task When he agreed to act as Secretary to the Trustees and to accept responsibility for co-ordinating the work of what she called 'the Movement' [7] (that is, the newly constituted Union for the Study of the Great Religions), she was delighted, describing him as 'an old friend who understood HN's ideals perfectly'. In the course of the letter she wrote to Tom Knox-Shaw, then the Master of Sidney Sussex College, Cambridge, and the senior Spalding Trustee, Mrs Spalding wrote:

> I think the appointment of Mr K. D. D. Henderson C.M.G., will be a great help to all of us. It certainly will relieve my mind tremendously. Before Norman [H. N. Spalding] died he discussed the question of the work being carried on and I feel sure that he would be extremely pleased at this appointment. We shall none of us have to explain H. N. to Bill Henderson! They knew one another for thirty years and Norman was so much interested in the work he was doing in the Sudan and had a great feeling for him personally.

I hope that you and John [her son, J. M. K. Spalding] and Mr Veale [Sir Douglas Veale,[8]] have discussed the question of salary. I have only talked over this with John. It should be adequate for what I know he will undertake to do, and although he has his pension, he has three children to educate and when he takes up this work he will be relinquishing a Government job in London after he has done two things they want from him, namely a memorandum on the health of those living in the commonwealths (*sic*) and also of the education in the commonwealths. I hope that he will come to us soon, even if he has to finish this work during part time. I have had masses of letters from all parts of the world expressing deep interest in the Movement, and I am longing for someone to answer them.[9]

Mrs Spalding died suddenly in the afternoon of Saturday, 27 April 1957. She had been unwell for several weeks, but seemed to be making a good recovery. For some years she and her husband had taken a personal interest in the development of Oriental Studies at the University of Durham. Only a few hours before she died she sent a telegram congratulating the University authorities on the award of a grant of £60,000 from the Gulbenkian Foundation. The money was to be used to build the first wing of the Oriental Museum at Elvet Hill. This interest in the plans to develop Oriental Studies at Durham went back to the years following the Second World War. She and her husband made grants to establish at Durham a lectureship in Indian Studies and a lectureship in Chinese Studies. They also helped with grants for Professor T. W. Thacker's work in Middle Eastern Studies. Thacker was to become a Spalding Trustee in due course. In 1951 the University awarded HN the honorary degree of DCL in recognition of his scholarly and philanthropic activities. Henderson's eighth USGR News Letter includes the following obituary paragraph of a remarkable woman.

> Mrs Spalding not only took an intense interest and an active part in the work of the Trust and Union. She provided a personal link with eminent men and women all over the world, whose desire to see her again brought them inevitably from time to time to South Parks Road [10] and so to renew their contact with the Movement.[11] The sense of loss which they have expressed in their many letters cannot help being even heavier for those who met her every day and talked over with her current projects and problems.[12]

Kenneth Jay Spalding

The second influential figure behind the scenes, as it were, was HN's younger brother, K. J. Spalding. The close personal relationship between HN and KJ should not be overlooked in assessing the former's life and work. KJ exercised a powerful influence on his brother, who often solicited his advice and acknowledged him in print as 'Master'. HN repeatedly expressed his gratitude for his brother's help in terms of which the following, to be found in the Preface to *Civilizations in East and West*, his most ambitious religio-philosophical work, are typical: 'Without him—brother in the flesh, father in the spirit—the book could not have been written'.[13] KJ was considered by some members of the family to be the most intellectually gifted among their number. He was HN's junior by two years, born on 17 March 1879. He died at Woodcote, Churt, in Surrey on 20 January 1962. He was educated briefly at St Servan in Normandy before being sent to Eastbourne College, a small public school on the south coast of England.[14] From school he went as a Commoner to Balliol College, Oxford. He left Balliol in 1902 and took up a post as a teacher of French at Culham College near Oxford.

In 1905 he became Lecturer in Logic at King's College London. Four years later he was elected Professor of Classical Literature and Philosophy at what was to become Queen Elizabeth's College, London. During the First World War he served as a temporary civil servant In 1928 he took up a Senior Research Fellowship in Philosophy at Brasenose College, Oxford. HN and his wife had made a grant to the College to make the move possible. KJ's wife died on 15 March 1932. From that date he took up residence in Brasenose. In 1949 he became a Supernumerary Fellow and continued to live in College until 1952. Strictly speaking, he had no tutorial responsibilities at Brasenose as Senior Research Fellow. He was a devoted teacher, however, so the College gladly used his pedagogical gifts to the full. He was particularly successful with the less able—better, perhaps, the less philosophically engaged—students in a College which at that time was 'a College of vigorous athletes and hard-headed lawyers'.[15] He made a special study of Immanuel Kant's *Critiique of Pure Reason*. During the Second World War he served the College as Senior Tutor and edited *The Brazen Nose*, a College magazine. After World War II he produced two works, *The Philosophy of Shakespeare* (1953) and *Essays in the Evolution of Religion* (1954), but found the modern trends in Oxford philosophy not to his liking—'this subject alone being capable of moving him to anger.'[16]

His obituary notice in *The Brazen Nose* includes a notable tribute. 'If a vote had ever been taken in Common Room as to who was its best-loved member, KJ's name would have been on every voting paper.'[17] He was quietly spoken, something of an introvert, and rarely voiced his opinions. The original Spalding Trust Deed dated 16 January 1923 provided for 'the promotion of the study, teaching and development of the principles set forth in the works of, and taught by, Kenneth Jay Spalding and in particular of his cardinal principle that the happiness of man consists in the knowledge and love of

Nature, spirit and God'. It went on to specify more general aims in the field of Oriental, Biblical, and Greek, literature and philosophy 'whether in translation or in the original language and whether or not in association with the principles set forth in the works of, and taught by, the said Kenneth Jay Spalding. He will be remembered as a gentle and courtly person, who found it difficult to refuse or oppose any application for help.[18]

Imperial Echoes

In late Victorian times HN's copy of a world atlas would have included maps showing large expanses of land coloured in pink. Born in 1877, the year in which Queen Victoria was proclaimed Empress of India, he grew up at a time when the British Empire was already extensive, gaining still more territory, and apparently unassailable. In comparison with many other countries Great Britain was rich and powerful, yet within half a century of the death of the Queen in 1901 the picture was to change. Doubts about Britain's role in the world were beginning to be voiced at home. Demands for independence from British imperial and colonial rule were becoming increasingly strident overseas. The importance of religion in Britain was more openly disputed. The influence of the Christian churches on social, moral, economic, and political, decisions was subjected to increasingly critical scrutiny. At the same time there was a significant awakening of interest in the religions of the East. India, in particular, was to become a focus of scholarly interest and attention. India was the jewel in the imperial crown. Britain's imperial power had helped to open up the East to Western exploration and exploitation. In the process the English language was imposed on the sub-continent in the 1830s, serving as an acceptable *lingua franca* and contributing over the years— not least, to the enrichment of literature written in English by Indians. Rabindranath Tagore (1861–1941) was awarded the Nobel Prize for Literature in 1913. Knighted in 1915, he resigned the honour in 1919 in protest against British policy in the Punjab. He was comparably fluent and imaginative when writing in the vernacular.[19] Many other Indian writers of English followed him in the twentieth century, including more recently R. K. 'Malgudi' Narayan, Dom Moraes, A. K. Ramanujan, and Arvind Krishna Mehrotra, although their work shows little interest in the religious vision espoused by Tagore himself.

In his Introduction to a book of Rudyard Kipling's short stories—tales that gave millions of readers the world over a vivid, if idiosyncratic, picture of Indian life—W. Somerset Maugham reflected on Britain's nineteenth-century imperial, industrial, and economic power.

The mother country was immensely rich. The British were the world's bankers. British commerce sent its products to the uttermost parts of the earth, and their quality was generally acknowledged to be higher than those manufactured by any other nation. Peace reigned except for small punitive expeditions here and there. The army, though small, was confident (notwithstanding the reverse on Majuba Hill [20]) that it could hold its own against any force that was likely to be brought against it. The British navy was the greatest in the world. In sport the British were supreme. None could compete with them in the games they played, and in the classic races it was almost unheard-of that a horse from abroad should win. It looked as though nothing could ever change this happy state of things. The inhabitants of these islands of ours trusted in God, and God, they were assured, had taken the British Empire under his particular protection.

There is irony in the way that Maugham uses the words 'to the uttermost parts of the earth' (cf. *Acts* 1.8) in connection with the export of material goods rather than the sharing of a spiritual treasure to which the words originally referred. But this description of a successful and buoyant empire was far from complete. At home there was a darker side to the picture, as Maugham himself noted.

It is true that the Irish were making a nuisance of themselves. It is true that the factory workers were underpaid and overworked. But that seemed an inevitable consequence of the industrialisation of the country and there was nothing to do about it. The reformers who tried to improve their lot were regarded as mischievous trouble-makers. It is true that the agricultural labourers lived in miserable hovels and earned a pitiful wage, but the Ladies Bountiful of the landowners were kind to them. Many of them occupied themselves with their moral welfare, sent them beef tea and calves-foot jelly when they were ill and often clothes for their children. People said there always had been rich and poor in the world and always would be, and that seemed to settle the matter.[21]

The economic and industrial strength of nineteenth-century Europe supported exploration and colonialisation in many parts of the world. Boundaries were often re-drawn in the new colonial territories to suit European interests, bringing disruption as often as not to the religious and cultural organisation of local communities. European administrators, merchant venturers, and Christian missionaries were given opportunities to use their talents and energy in distant lands. Their motives were very different. Many went in order 'to serve', taking with them (as they believed) the light of European civilisation. Others went for personal gain. Many felt called to the service of Christian mission, responding to the dominical command of Jesus to take the Gospel to the 'uttermost parts of the earth'. There were other things to be discovered beside the deprivation, the disease, the ignorance and the poverty, which were undoubtedly to be seen in foreign parts. Religious traditions of great nobility and antiquity were to be discovered as well. These discoveries promoted questionings about the claims of Christians that Jesus is 'the Way, the Truth, and the Life' in a universal or even cosmic sense.[22] The suggestion that Christianity was (and is), merely one of many different paths to blessedness was (and remains) disconcerting to many Christians. The *particularity* of Christianity was not in question, but the *uniqueness* of Christianity was vigorously challenged from several quarters in Europe in the nineteenth century.

'The Death of God'

In 1900 the philosopher Friedrich Nietzsche died in Weimar in the south-eastern part of Germany. Growing insanity clouded his last ten years of life, during which he was cared for by his sister. The son of a Lutheran pastor, he became a passionate opponent of civilisation, West as well as East, regarding it as decadent. As far as Western civilisation is concerned he went further, asserting that the cause of this decadence was the 'slave morality' fostered by Christianity. He hurled defiance at the religion preached by Jesus. In its place he advocated a new heroic morality, exemplified by the *Übermensch*—'the superman'—a human being capable of living beyond the conventional standards of 'good' and 'evil'. The creative powers of this new race of superior beings would distinguish them from 'the herd' of inferior beings which made up the rest of humankind. A later generation of Nietzsche's countrymen were quick to adapt his doctrines of national and racial superiority for their own purposes in Europe between the years 1933 and 1945. He wrote the parable of the Madman to express in words of terrifying defiance his conviction that God is dead.

> Have you not heard of that madman who lit a lantern in the bright morning hours, ran to the market-place and cried incessantly: 'I am looking for God! I am looking for God!' As many of those who did not believe in God were standing together there he excited considerable laughter. 'Have you lost him then?' said one. 'Did he lose his way like a child?' said another. 'Or is he hiding? Is he afraid of us? Has he gone on a voyage? Or emigrated?' Thus they shouted and laughed. The madman sprang into their midst and pierced them with his glances. 'Where has God gone?' he cried. 'I shall tell you. *We have killed him*—you and I. We are all his murderers ...

Do we not hear anything yet of the noise of the gravediggers who are burying God? Do we not smell anything yet of God's decomposition? Gods, too, decompose. God is dead. God remains dead. And we have killed him …' It has been further related that on that same day the madman entered divers churches and there sang a *requiem aeternam deo*. Led out and quieted, he is said to have retorted each time: 'What are these churches now if they are not the tombs and sepulchres of God?' [23]

Nietzsche added a further comment: 'God is dead, but considering the state the species Man is in, there will perhaps be caves, for ages yet, in which his shadow will be shown.' He certainly inherited the tradition of the Enlightenment when it came to his strenuous efforts to rid human beings of their dependence upon 'illusions', but for him it was the 'illusion' that God exists, which was the chief obstacle to human progress. Yet in his attempts to eliminate the ultimate 'illusion' of a divine Creator, Nietzsche succeeded only in carrying atheism to its logical and destructive conclusion. Human beings, he insisted, are alone in a bleak universe that is doomed to extinction. It may be that his passionate service to the cause of human reason divorced from divine creativity helped him towards the state of insanity in which he ended his life in the year 1900, for if taken seriously—as he himself took it seriously—atheism confronts us with an abyss from which there is no escape. The Madman in Nietzsche's parable, far from trying to convince his hearers in the market-place that 'God is dead!', may well have been trying to show them from his own experience that the denial of God's sovereignty leads not to enlightenment and liberty but to the darkness of insanity.

Enlightenment

The eighteenth-century Enlightenment in Europe encouraged attempts to distinguish between *knowledge* acquired by empirical methods through the exercise of *reason* (and thus, indisputably, *reasonable*), and *faith* that is mediated and acquired through divine revelation (and thus, strictly speaking, *unreasonable*). This misleading distinction still has its advocates among secularists, but for thoughtful religious believers, faith and reason are not so easily separated. The prologue to the Gospel of St John speaks of Jesus as the Word of God, as the incarnation of the principle of cosmic order and reason in the form of the divine *logos*, and as true source of light and enlightenment (*John* 1.1–14.). In all the major religions of the world the source of ultimate reality is self-evidently (so it is affirmed) not only the principle of reason, but the ground of all our human reasoning. The prayer of Muslims, 'O my Lord, advance me in knowledge!' is not merely the plea of those who seek knowledge for its own sake, but of believers who recognise that the knowledge they seek cannot be other than knowledge of the God, who knows and reveals all.[24] *True knowledge*, from whatever source of human inquiry it comes, is—as Muslims habitually affirm—'knowledge of God' (in Arabic, *'ilm*). And as such, the human being in possession of such knowledge is *'âqil*, that is to say (in Arabic) one who has 'understanding', one who is 'rational' and 'discerning'. Hindus, Buddhists, Jews, Christians, Muslims, follow different paths. The metaphor of the *Path*, or the *Way*, recurs in each of these religious traditions, within which differences of belief and emphasis have led to internal division and conflict. Hinduism accommodates a multiplicity of sects. Buddhists interpret the teaching of the Buddha in different ways. Jews do not attempt to conceal the differences between them. For centuries, Christians have failed to agree amongst themselves about the Gospel of Jesus. Islam is by no means a monolithic, unified system of belief. Despite the ecumenical initiatives of the past fifty years or so controversy persists, and in some cases shows signs of growing. According to some observers, Britain 'is no longer a Christian country'. It appears that 'a tacit atheism' has gripped the country. The Archbishop of Canterbury is reported to have said as much at the beginning of the new millennium. Unbelievers and professing atheists have welcomed the public acknowledgement by such a prominent Christian of a fact they claim to have been obvious for years. It seems that for practical purposes large numbers of people believe that God is dead and that he has been dead for a long time. It is premature, not to say unreasonable, to account for the apparent rejection of theism by claiming that thoughtful people are increasingly convinced by the sweet reasonableness of atheism. On the contrary, there is evidence to support the view that large numbers of 'tacit atheists' choose to rely in one way or another on the solaces offered by materialism, hedonism, new age sects, astrology, and the various meditation techniques transposed from other cultures. Atheism offers bleak comfort to all but the irrepressibly self-confident. 'The telephone bell was ringing wildly, but without result, since there was no-one in the room but the corpse.'[25]

Light from the East

Spalding and Henderson were aware of these currents of opinion in the West. They knew well enough that the divisions among religious believers did little to commend religion to its cultured despisers. Despite this they believed that beneath all the outward differences there was a unity waiting to be discovered. By 1909, the year in which HN married Miss Nellie Cayford in Florence, many echoes of Nietzsche's notice of God's demise, were to be heard in Europe. The end of revealed and institutionalised religion was confidently predicted. Could the same be said about Eastern religions, about the paths of Hinduism and Buddhism, for example? Was it really the case that religion was dead, that God is dead, 'killed', as Nietzsche put it, by the human beings who had created him? Or had something important been overlooked? The religions of the East had certainly been largely overlooked in the West. HN believed that this could be rectified. He maintained that the West had much to learn about true religion and authentic spirituality from the East. At the same time he insisted that the West had a spiritual contribution to make to the East. For this contribution to be made, he held that any notions of the supremacy of one religious system must be abandoned. This presented a particular challenge to Christians in the West, whose religion was so often associated in Africa and Asia with an alien imperial and colonial power.

The meticulous investigations of scholars, European as well as Asian, into the history and the ancient religious texts of Hinduism and Buddhism brought to Western readers hitherto unsuspected light from the East. One of the leading nineteenth-century figures in this scholarly exploration was the German-born British philologist and orientalist, Friedrich Max-Müller (1823–1900). He studied Sanskrit during the course of his studies in Dessau, Leipzig, and Berlin. In Paris he began work on a critical edition of the collections of Hindu sacred hymns, travelling to England in 1848 in order to study manuscripts. A year later the East India Company commissioned him to edit the texts. They were published in six volumes, at the Company's expense, between 1849 and 1874, under the title *Rig Veda with Commentary*. In 1854 he was appointed Taylorian Professor of Modern Languages at Oxford, and in 1868 he became Professor of Comparative Philology. He did much to popularise the study of philology and mythology, advancing the theory that myths originate the metaphors used to describe natural phenomena. In addition to his translations of Eastern religious texts, Müller produced several popular introductory books on the subject of the study of religion. Among the former is the series of volumes *The Upanishads* (Clarendon Press, Oxford, 1879–84). Among the latter is a small book based on the lectures he gave at the University of Cambridge to candidates preparing for entry into the Indian Civil Service. The book was called *India: What Can It Teach Us?*[26] His greatest contribution to the comparative study of religion was the work he did until his death as editor of the *Sacred Books of the East*, a series in which translations of many hitherto unknown oriental non-Christian religious texts were made available to readers in the West. The fifty-one volumes, published between 1879 and 1910, remain as a monument to his ground-breaking industry.[27]

During the period in which Max-Müller was at work, others were making their own studies of societies in different parts of the world.[28] It came as no surprise to discover that human societies everywhere are rooted in, and sustained by, some form of religion. More surprising was the revelation of the antiquity and the diversity of the civilisations of the East. Hinduism, with its 5,000 years of history and continuing development, emerged as the oldest living faith in the world.[29] It was troubling in many cases for people in nineteenth-century Europe to learn that Africa—far from being the Dark Continent of popular belief—was a continent with a long, though largely unwritten, history of religious diversity and cultural achievement. The darkness that concealed Africa was that of European ignorance. Similarly, the news of the gospel of the Buddha was slow in reaching the West. When it did, together with more and more information about the ancient wisdom of India, it began to attract appreciative attention. In the case of a *savant* like Max-Müller, the appreciation was generous to the point of hyperbole.

> If I were to look over the whole world to find out the country most richly endowed with all the wealth, power, and beauty that nature can bestow—in some parts a very paradise on earth—I should point to India. If I were asked under what sky the human mind has most fully developed some of its choicest gifts, has most deeply pondered on the greatest problems of life, and has found solutions of some of them which well deserve the attention even of those who have studied Plato and Kant—I should point to India. And if I were to ask myself from what literature we, here in Europe, we who have been nurtured almost exclusively on the thoughts of Greeks and Romans, and of one Semitic race, the Jewish, may draw that corrective which is most wanted in order to make our inner life more perfect, more comprehensive, more universal, in fact more truly human, a life, not for this life only, but a transfigured and eternal life—again I should point to India.[30]

The light that came from the East had another salutary effect. It stimulated some in the West to look again into their own religious history and to gain fresh insights into their own scriptures. Could it be, for instance, that Christians in the West had overlooked rather than ignored the significance of references in their own sacred books to the provision made by God for the salvation of His human creatures? In the well-known passage of the fourth Gospel, in which Jesus develops his teaching about himself as the Good Shepherd, he is recorded as saying: 'I have other sheep that are not of this fold; I must bring them also, and they will heed my voice. So there shall be one flock, one shepherd' (*John* 10.16). In the prayer he made before leaving for the garden of Gethsemane, Jesus expressed his concern not just for the small group of his disciples, 'but for all those who believe in me through their word, that they may all be one, even as you, Father, are in me, and I in you, that they may also be in us, so that the world may believe that you have sent me' (*John* 17.20–1). For Christians, the high-priestly prayer of Jesus expresses a desire for the widest and most inclusive ecumenism.

For centuries Christians had presumed to have an unique lien on the redemptive work of Christ. Many had gone as far as to insist that 'outside the Church there is no salvation' (*extra ecclesiam non est salus*). Intra-religious disputes between members of different Christian communities, as well as inter-religious conflicts between Christians and adherents of other faiths had compromised the witness of those who claimed to follow Jesus of Nazareth. By the end of the nineteenth century, when evidence from other religions was becoming accessible to anyone with sufficient interest to examine it, no-one could deny that Jesus had an honoured—if different—place in the non-Christian religions of the Near and the Far East. His place in Judaism was about to be re-assessed, by Jews as well as Christians. He was born, and remained, a Jew. In an important and indisputable sense, he belonged to the Jewish community.[31] It was not only Jews and Christians, however, who claimed an affinity with Jesus of Nazareth. His teaching was not disregarded by Hindus or Buddhists, who acknowledged him as a spiritual master. In HN's opinion it was time for Christians to reconsider the questions put by Jesus to his closest disciples when they were at Caesarea-Philippi, '"Whom do men say that I am?" And they told him, "John the Baptist, others say, Elijah, and others say one of the prophets". And he asked them: "But whom do you say that I am?" Peter answered him, "You are the Christ"' (*Mark* 8.27–9). Spalding was never much concerned with theological niceties that sought to distinguish between the Jesus of history and the Christ of faith.

Alienation and Impercipience

A different kind of challenge to religious belief, not just to Christian belief, came from another quarter in the nineteenth century. For some fiery spirits the world had to be changed, but this could only come about—as they believed—by liberating the peoples of the world from the shackles of institutional religion. When revolution was in the air, no accommodation with religion could be tolerated. The concept of pluralism, whether religious or political, was considered to be a bourgeois fiction. In organised religion, especially in Christianity, Karl Marx claimed to see institutions of oppression, which enslaved the masses. Religion, he averred, was one of the principal instruments with which the privileged classes controlled the underprivileged. Its effects on the workers of the world were uniformly repressive. In the style of a Hebrew prophet or an evangelical preacher he challenged his contemporaries to free themselves from God, from the fetters of religious practice and from the illusory solace of religious belief. Criticisms of religious belief have been part of European life and thought since the beginning of the Christian era. At points of crisis in the history of Christianity as decisive as the Reformation in the sixteenth century, the struggle was not merely between the reformers and the traditionalists, but between those who held to any religious convictions and those who had none. It was not just a difference of opinion between those who insisted that *this* form of Christianity should prevail over *that*, but a fundamental disagreement about the validity of any form of religious belief.

In the nineteenth century it was the impact of industrialisation on the lives of ordinary people which gave sharpness to the social and economic critiques of thinkers like Marx. It was an age in which *Entfremdung* (alienation) was identified by them as a universal human sickness, the symptom of which was a dependence on the unseen (and, for Marx, the non-existent) spiritual forces conjured up by the disreputable lackeys of organised religion. Furthermore, in Europe at least, it was a time in which the Christian churches were criticised for having nothing to offer the socially and economically deprived, other than a promise that things would be different in a future life. This hope sustained many, despite the jibes about 'pie in the sky'. But there were others whose present condition gave sufficient reason for abandoning religion. As is often the case, the rejection of religion is the result of considerations that are pragmatic rather than metaphysical. Religion, it is claimed, 'does not work', or 'one can live well enough without it'. Once these conclusions are drawn, it matters little what efforts are made by religious believers to re-awaken interest in the benefits of a coherent religious view of life. As the benefits of scientific discovery and applied technology continue to be enjoyed by increasing numbers of people, confidence in man's own capacity to solve problems tends to increase. What further need can there be for ancient, pre-scientific, creeds? Secularism had always provided a theoretical alternative to religious belief. A thorough-going process of secularisation was now under way. Was Christianity to be considered as no more than one of the many ways that human beings have devised for themselves for probing into the mystery of existence? Are all religions no more than human constructs? The nineteenth century witnessed what today seems to have been an unseemly as well as an unnecessary conflict between those who saw in science a threat to established religion and those who saw in religion a negation of science.

Scientism and Relativism

Today, these simplistic notions, which helped to encourage the growth of an arid scientism on the one hand and an uncritical religious syncretism on the other, are being subjected to scrutiny by thoughtful religious believers and unbelievers alike. *Scientism*, as an ideology, reflects a naïve belief that human beings can solve the problems that face them, and understand the universe in which they find themselves, by adopting strictly 'scientific methods'— without further recourse to the obsolete and superstitious beliefs of institutional (and, specifically, theistic) religion. Needless to say, scientism is to be distinguished from science. The purpose of science is to discover generalisations that cover all the known facts.[32] The difficulty is that those with a predilection for the atheistic beliefs of scientism tend to take a narrow view of what constitutes a *fact*. This tendency excludes, *a priori*, the facts of religious experience. With the exclusion comes, unfortunately, a rejection of all that it means to be fully human. Nothing, it is asserted by the opponents of religious belief is too absurd to be accepted, once the decision to believe has been taken. Those who accept the first principle of scientism would appear to be in a good position to illustrate the validity of that peculiar statement. Scientism provides too narrow a focus for human experience, from which religion is not so easily dismissed. Scientism, nonetheless, (not science) presents itself as an alternative belief system—as the 'reasonable' alternative for reasoning individuals—to faith in God or the gods.

Our perceptions may well mislead us about the nature of 'reality'. Despite this uncertainty, it is confidently asserted—with the vigour of an unchallenge-able dogmatism—that 'truth' is relative, especially when it comes to religion. How can all the religions of the world be 'true'? How are we to evaluate such claims? How is one religion to be judged 'truer' than another? Is the attempt to make such value-judgements merely another example of a human predilection for the absurd? More sensible, perhaps, to remain silent or to take the line that all religions can, at best, be only relatively true. Comparisons are seldom so odious as they are when made about religion. Is it 'true' that we do not know, and can not know, the 'truth'? The word agnosticism is used almost exclusively today to express scepticism about revealed religion. Agnostics may include among their number those who are uncertain about the claims advanced for any institutionalised religion, but it may be truer to say that they are *convinced* about the irrelevance of such claims. To put it another way, their agnosticism is selective, in that their 'not-knowing' does not extend to social ideals, values, politics, business, or education. On these matters they are usually as certain as the most devout believers are about their religious convictions. In theory, agnosticism is not an absolute position, but when it comes to the world's religions, agnostics and atheists have much in common. For much of the Agnosticism of the age, the Gnosticism of theologians is undeniably responsible. 'They have inconsiderately overstrained the language of religion till its meaning breaks; and the coherent thinker easily picks up its ruins to show they can contain nothing.'[33]

The Irritant of Agnosticism

The Victorian Agnostics, of whom Thomas Huxley is probably the best known, sought to remind their contemporaries of the ineluctable limits of human knowledge.[34] In the opinion of G. K. Chesterton, 'Huxley preached a humility content to learn from Nature. But the new sceptic is so humble that he doubts if he can ever learn'.[35] The corpus of human knowledge is always increasing, but there are limits *to what we are able to know*. Some agnostics are scrupulous in their attitude to atheism, preferring neither to affirm nor deny the God of religion. At the same time God is dethroned *de facto*, set aside, when it is asserted that nothing is knowable about the ultimate origins and final purpose of the universe. Commenting on the way in which agnosticism soon began to assume a more dogmatic character, the English convert to Islam, Gai Eaton, wrote,

> Agnosticism raises a personal incapacity to the dignity of a universal law. It amounts to the dogmatic assertion that what 'I' do not know cannot be known, and it limits the very concept of what is knowable to the little area of observation open to the unsanctified and unillumi- nated human mentality. The agnostic attitude derives from a refusal to admit that anyone can be, or ever could have been, our superior in this, the most important realm of all; the true knowledge of what there is to be known. Religion is now seen exclusively in terms of faith rather than of supernatural knowledge. In egalitarian terms, faith is acceptable; you may believe in fairies if you wish to. But the claim to a direct and certain knowledge of realities beyond the mind's normal compass excludes those who do not possess it and savours of presumption. The idea that a saint among the saints may have *known* God—not merely *believed* in him—suggests 'unfairness' and implies the superiority of some men to others. It puts us in our place.[36]

The nineteenth century saw the sharpening of a sustained attack on Christian faith and practice, at least as far as Western Europe was concerned. During that high period of humanistic idealism, in which the statement that human beings were alone in an unfriendly universe was defiantly accepted by an influential minority of evangelical atheists, some less strident voices were to be heard. Among them was that of the poet and literary critic Matthew Arnold (1822–88). Middle-class Philistines were subjected to his fastidious scrutiny. More pungent criticisms of religious hypocrisy came from Ibsen, Tolstoi, Nietzsche, and later from Anatole France, George Bernard Shaw, H. G. Wells, G. K. Chesterton and Hilaire Belloc. Arnold's frequently quoted poem *Dover Beach* evokes a mood of melancholy reflection about a past that can never return. The age of religious faith seemed to have come to an end. Cathedrals, parish churches, and the remnants of religious faith lodged in consciousness, were regarded as the fossil remains in the life of a people. Yet Arnold does not exult because men and women are liberated from the fetters of an outworn creed.

And we are here as on a darkling plain
Swept with confused alarms of struggle and flight,
Where ignorant armies clash by night.[37]

An English poet, for whom agnosticism was clearly an irritant, is Thomas Hardy (1840–1928). One of his poems, written in 1898, has the significant title, *The Impercipient: (at A Cathedral Service)*.[38] The poem is more like a cry from the heart of a reluctant unbeliever. Hardy echoes the image of the distant sea in Arnold's poem, *Dover Beach*. That one thing that the poet wishes to see, the vision he would like to share with the religious believer, is (or so it appears) *withheld* from him. This is why he is obliged to count himself among the *Impercipient*, those who lack perception. Not to be able to see and know what others see in the religion they profess is the real irritant, rendered more disconcerting by the fact that those in whose company he finds himself have an experience which they are, it would seem, *unwilling* to explain or share. He sits in the cathedral, isolated during a service in which he cannot participate fully. We are not told why he was there. It may have been no more than the pressure of the social conventions at that time. The Victorians have been criticised, not always fairly, for their religious attitudes and beliefs. They have been charged with hypocrisy for their failure to deal adequately with social and economic inequality, whilst professing to follow the teachings of their professed religion. They, or at any rate many of their leaders, are accused of obscurantism, of persistence in defending the inerrancy of Scripture against the findings of historical and literary criticism, and of opposition to the discoveries of science. Towards the end of the nineteenth century the Catholic Church in particular stood accused of silencing the voice of theological liberalism in her struggle against Modernism.

Religion Without Revelation?

The Victorian Age is one which is often identified with the rise of a self-confident agnosticism and an increasingly hostile spirit of atheism, both of which helped to weaken belief in a revealed religion. The phrase 'revealed religion' is important because not all the Victorian agnostics denied the value of religion, or even of 'religious' or 'spiritual' belief. The task they proposed was that of choosing the *right* religion—by which was meant the religion of and for humanity, without reference to God—and then of propagating it. An interesting exposition of non-theistic religious belief was given by Julian Huxley (1887–1975) in his monograph, *Religion Without Revelation*.

> In that new religion, man must make up his mind to take upon himself
> his full burden, by acknowledging that he is the highest entity of which
> he has any knowledge, that his values are the only basis for any

categorical imperative, and that he must work out both his own salvation and destiny, and the standards on which they are based. To put off this burden on to the shoulders of an imaginary God is to shrink from full responsibility, and to hinder man from arriving at his full stature.

Nor is it true to-day that theology is irrelevant to spiritual and moral attitude. What I have just written is proof to the contrary. It is obvious that any religion which lays primary emphasis on salvation in the next world will be something of an obstacle towards getting the best out of this world as speedily as possible. It is equally obvious that any religion which stresses the need for propitiating an external Power will be diverted away from the more essential task of using and organising the spiritual forces that lie within each individual. 'The Kingdom of Heaven is within you' is a saying that has not been sufficiently taken into account in orthodox theology.[39]

After a moving analysis of the human predicament and of the means by which human existence might be improved by an adoption of the new religion for which he argues, Julian Huxley concluded his book with a personal testimony of faith.

I believe that the great sacrifice needed for religion is that of her old certitude, to be offered up on the altar of humility. And that demanded by organised science, and all the doers of good works and planners of the future to boot, is that of all narrowness and aggressiveness, to be offered on the altar of reverence and imaginative love. But today the sacrifice of organised religion is more necessary and more called for than that of science, and failure to make it will be not only more blameworthy but, from her own standpoint, more foolish ...

I have no doubt of the ultimate issue. The verdict of the trend of human history, in the fifteen thousand years since civilization dawned in the later Old Stone Age, is too clear to permit a doubt. But in what way it will come, and after how long, and what it will be like, the future religion of this world and of all humanity—that nobody can know ...

A religion which takes this as its central core and interprets it with wide vision, both of the possibilities open to man and of the limitations in which he is confined, will be a true religion, because it is coterminous with life; it will encourage the growth of life, and will itself grow with that growth. I believe in the religion of life.[40]

There is an inconsistency in this powerful final statement between the uncertainty of its author's predictions about the future of religion and the certitude of his personal faith. Despite expressing unexceptionably visionary sentiments for the future development of human existence and happiness, he says nothing about how the necessary changes in human nature are to be brought about by relying solely on human resources. The idealistic view of humanity taken by Huxley sounds naïvely mistaken today. Spalding and Henderson were in partnership to challenge it in so far as it sought to promote human progress by excluding belief in God. From the early 1920s until his death in 1953 Spalding was to devote his time and the relatively considerable financial resources to which he had access, to the re-exploration and the re-exposition of what he chose to call *The Divine Universe, or the Many and the One: A Study of Religions and Religion*.[41] His motives were unselfish, his approach timely, his actions generous, and his methods scholarly. He had become convinced that the widespread rejection of organised, institutionalised religion by so many of his contemporaries, though understandable in the light of tragic conflicts and personal misfortunes, was premature. About belief in God there was much more to be said. For him it was not the so-called conflict between religion and science in the nineteenth century, or the concomitant growth of agnosticism and atheism during the same period, or even the comfortably decadent self-confidence of the Edwardian era, which seemed to account most reasonably for the decline of belief in God, or at least for the widespread collapse of belief in a benign and loving deity. What appeared to Spalding to be the most likely cause of a decline in religious belief was the experience of war in the killing fields of the First World War.

Resurrection and Renaissance

For the rebirth of civilization—'resurrection' and 'renaissance' were among his favourite words—HN believed that it was necessary to look for enlightenment and spiritual renewal beyond a war-torn Europe. For many years people in Britain had been pleased to call India 'the jewel in the crown' of the Empire. For reasons unsuspected by those who took a lofty view of Western cultural superiority at that time, India was indeed a multi-faceted jewel, the true beauty of which was just beginning to be revealed to Western eyes. He was one of the Western observers for whom, as he grew older, the beauty of that jewel became increasingly apparent. The antiquity and continuing resilience of Indian religions and cultures awakened in him hospitable thoughts about what an American contemporary, the philosopher and psychologist William James, had called *The Varieties of Religious Experience: A Study in Human Nature*.[42] For Spalding the striking feature about human religious experience—as it presents itself in the lives of religious believers, their traditions and scriptures—was not the divergence of belief and practice, but the underlying unity of aspiration to which all religions bear witness. This was a vision shared by Henderson. Some critics considered that HN's knowledge of other religions and cultures was superficial, that his vision was naïve, and that his efforts were the work of an amateur—a dilettante with a peculiar agenda—but this was not the judgement of at least one reviewer of his *magnum opus*, who wrote,

> [Mr Spalding's] scholarship is good, as far as I can test it—that is, as regards Greece and India ... In his final summary Mr Spalding rises to real eloquence, the eloquence of noble thoughts and simplicity, for there is no trace of showing off, no self-consciousness, only the consciousness of a great theme and a real faith.[43]

The tension between academics engaged in the discrete but related fields of theological studies and comparative religious studies, shows little sign of being resolved. The situation is further complicated by the objections raised by specialists in the fields of Asian, Islamic, or African studies, who maintain that no-one can acquire an expert knowledge of more than one religion and its culture. Since those who are engaged in the study of world religions are expected to work in a wider field, the implication is that they can not pretend to be strictly scholars. In a note published in the October 1956 issue of *The Hibbert Journal*, Professor S. G. F. Brandon, then Professor of Comparative Religion in the University of Manchester, responded to the criticism in a way of which Spalding approved. If the criticism were to be generally accepted, it would mean

> that anyone who attempts a comparative study of religion is obliged to use, for the most part, material with which he has no first-hand acquaintance. And this in turn means that he inevitably lays himself open to the criticisms of the specialist, into whose field he has entered. Some scholars keenly feel the inherent weakness of this position and are tempted not to venture themselves thus, but to keep within such fields as they think that they have reasonably mastered. The temptation is indeed a strong one; but, if none were to resist it and tread the harder path, there would be an end to any synoptic view of mankind's religious faith and practice. Instead there would be only a series of highly-specialized and unrelated studies of specific religions.[44]

Despite this kind of criticism of 'the intruding amateur' and the 'ill-informed generalist', Spalding was convinced that the great religions of the world have an unique role to play in the less exalted spheres of education. In schools there are (or ought to be, as he believed) opportunities in the curriculum for teaching about these religious systems and the cultures that are associated with them. The promotion of an understanding of the unity that he claimed to see beneath the outward differences of name and form in different religions, led him to advocate a wider approach to religious and moral education in schools at a time when the need for such a broadening of the curriculum was not as generally recognised as it is today. On this particular point about education in schools, no less than in his advocacy of a wider exploration of the accumulated wisdom of sages East and West by thoughtful adults, he has claims to be considered in the broadest sense as a pioneer in the field of education.

Through the efforts of Spalding, Henderson, not to forget Mrs Spalding's contribution to the total effort and the support of many others, the work of the Spalding Trust was to become widely known and respected, not only in Britain but across the face of the globe. It was not by chance that the first practical steps in the venture were taken under the aegis of *The Spalding Educational Trusts* (plural). Eventually the financial resources were consolidated, and the work co-ordinated, in a single Trust, but there was always to be some criticism of the work of the Trust, on the grounds that its leaders were burdened with a quasi-evangelical agenda, which does not serve to promote a properly objective approach to the study of religious and cultural diversity in a pluralist world. Furthermore, critics were in the habit of observing somewhat peevishly that Spalding and Henderson, though intelligent men, were amateurs, generalists at best, with little right to engage in serious studies in the field of Eastern religions. The criticisms were unfair at the time and they are unfair today.

Notes and References

1. H. N. Spalding, 1952, *In Praise of Life* (IPL), Basil Blackwell, Oxford, p. 90. Other sonnets in the same volume, which focus on the figure of Christ, include: *The Christ-Apollo, He Rose Again, Marx or Christ, Christos Woskresse* (sic, see below, p. 53), *Christ's Followers*, and *Thy Kingdom Come*.
2. From a letter sent to me by the Chairman of the Trust, Anne C. Spalding.
3. See the Bibliography.
4. SFP; in the margin of the Air Letter HN added in his own handwriting, 'Thanks, 23.3.'47. KEEP, Lines by Bill Henderson to H.N., Christmas, 1946'.
5. KDDH (ed.), 1952, *An Administrator's Anthology, Douglas Newbold*, McCorquodale & Co. (Sudan) Ltd, Khartoum.
6. Henderson, NUSGR 29, Summer 1972, p. 8.
7. In 1970 it was decided to take steps to re-absorb the Movement Trust, which was formed to administer the affairs of the Union for the Study of the Great Religions, into the parent Trust which originally endowed it, and which had financed its projects. From that date the Union was to function as before, with its branches, book-lists, and news letters, but after the amalgamation there was to be one set of Trustees and one set of accounts instead of two (NUSGR 27, Summer 1970, p. 1). The history of the two trusts was outlined in a lecture delivered at Younghusband House in London, in December 1969. The lecture was printed in *World Faiths*, the journal of the World Congress of Faiths, Spring number (79), 1970.

8. Sir Douglas Veale Registrar of Oxford University from 1930 to 1958, was one of H. N. Spalding's closest associates, and a chosen Trustee.

9. SFP. The letter, written in the Osborne Hotel, Torquay, Devon, is dated 11 November 1953.

10. That is, to the Spalding family house at number 9 South Parks Road, Oxford.

11. 'The Movement' was the Union for the Study of the Great Religions.

12. K. D. D. Henderson in NUSGR, number 8, June 1957, p. 1.

13. H. N. Spalding CEW, 1939, Preface, p. xi.

14. In the United Kingdom, that is to say, a private, independent school.

15. The words of Maurice Platnauer, a Fellow of the College, in *The Brazen Nose, a College Magazine*, vol. xiii, no. 2, 1962, p. 101.

16. From KJ's obituary in *The Times*, 24 January 1962.

17. *The Brazen Nose, a College Magazine*, vol. xiii, no. 2, 1962, p. 102.

18. Dr, J. M. K. Spalding, son of the founder. provides another comment on KJ: 'K. J. Spalding (17.3.1879–20.1.1962) was considered by his mother, Ellen Rebe, to be the brilliant member of the family and H.N. seemed to agree. Their sisters, Selma and Eva, on the other hand, referred to 'the myth of Ken' and seemed to think that he had advantages in their youth which might just as well have come their way ... In 1922 he published *Desire and Reason*, a substantial volume of which I have a copy. Chairs were quite scarce in those days and he deserves congratulations on his appointment, but perhaps his tenure was a modest success for he moved to a Senior Research Fellowship at BNC funded by my parents. He lived in or near High Wycombe until his wife, Amy Katherine née Baynes died on 15.3.1932. Thereafter he lived in BNC until he retired, and then with his sister Selma at Woodcote, Churt, Surrey. When I knew him he was very agreeable but quiet and did not radiate energy. During the second war he learned to make tea. Even after that he preferred to walk from the bottom of South Parks Road [Oxford] to Brasenose so that the porter could dial a telephone number for him rather than learn to dial it himself. The only publication I know of from his time in Oxford is a slim volume *Talks on Philosophy*, of which I have a copy. He was disappointed that it did not get critical acclaim, indeed hardly any reviews. Norman H. Baynes, brother of KJ's wife, commented that if you do not keep your name before the public by a steady flow of publications, lack of notice is likely to be the result. NHB had a personal Chair at London University in Byzantine history at a time when hardly anyone was working on it.' (In a note from JMKS to the author, dated 28 April 2001).

19. Sarvepalli Radhakrishnan called Tagore 'the greatest figure of the Indian renaissance'.

20. Majuba Hill is in the Drakensberg Range in East Natal, South Africa. It is the place where, on 27 February 1888, a British force of 500 men was routed by Boer troops under the command of P. J. Joubert.

21. W. Somerset Maugham, 1952, *A Choice of Kipling's Prose*, Macmillan & Co. Ltd, London, p. vii.

22. *John* 14.6.

23. F. W. Nietzsche, 1882, *Die Fröhliche Wissenschaft* (*The Gay Science*), quoted in R. J. Hollingdale, 1977ff, *A Nietzsche Reader*, Penguin Classics, pp. 202–3.

24. The Holy *Qur'ân, sûrah* 20.114.

25. Charles Williams, 1982 (first published in 1930), *War in Heaven*, Wm B. Eerdmans Publishing Company, Grand Rapids, Michigan, p. 7.

26. The American edition used by the present author was published in 1883 by Funk & Wagnall, New York.

27. Müller's other works include *Lectures on the Science of Language* (1861–64) and *My Indian Friends* (1898).

28. See, for example, Sir James Frazer, 1894, *The Golden Bough: A Study in Magic and Religion*, Macmillan, London.

29. cf. K. M. Sen, 1961, *Hinduism: The World's Oldest Faith*, Penguin Books.

30. F. Max-Müller, 1883, *India: What Can It Teach Us?*, p. 24.

31. See Geza Vermes, 1983, *Jesus the Jew*. SCM Press, London; 2001, *The Changing Faces of Jesus*, Penguin Books.

32. 'The very soul of science consists in theoretical generalization leading to the formation of quantitative laws and systems of laws.' Stanley L. Jaki, 1974, *Science and Creation: From Eternal Cycles to an Oscillating Universe*, Scottish Academic Press, p. 14.

33. James Martineau, 1888, *A Study of Religion: Its Sources and Contents*, Clarendon Press, Oxford, vol. 1, p. xi.

34. The word 'agnosticism' seems to have been coined by Thomas Huxley, in an informal conversation during the course of an evening with friends in 1869.

35. G. K. Chesterton, (1908), *Orthodoxy*, Collins Fontana edition, 1963, pp. 31–2.

36. Gai Eaton, 1977, *King of the Castle: Choice and Responsibility in the Modern World*, The Bodley Head, pp. 144–5.

37. Matthew Arnold, *Dover Beach* (1867), lines 35–7.

38. Hardy's poem is a perceptive comment on the failure of Christians (in this instance) to explain to those who have no such belief what it means to be a religious believer.

> That with this bright believing band
> I have no claims to be,
> That faiths by which my comrades stand
> Seem fantasies to me,
> And mirage-mists their Shining Land,
> Is a strange destiny.
>
> Why thus my soul should be consigned
> To infelicity,
> Why always I must feel as blind
> To sights my brethren see,
> Why joys they've found I cannot find,
> Abides a mystery.
>
> Since heart of mine knows not that ease
> Which they know; since it be
> That He who breathes All's
> Well to these
> Breathes no All's Well to me,
> My lack might move their sympathies
> And Christian charity!
>
> I am like a gazer who should mark
> An inland company
> Standing upfingered, with,
> 'Hark! Hark!
> The glorious distant sea!'
> And feel, 'Alas, 'tis but yon dark
> And wind-swept pine to me!'

Yet I would bear my shortcomings
With meet tranquillity,
But for the charge that blessed things
I'd liefer not have be.
O, doth a bird deprived of wings
Go earth-bound willfully!

Enough. As yet disquiet clings
About us. Rest shall we.

39. Julian Huxley, 1941, *Religion Without Revelation*, Thinker's Library, no. 83, Watts & Co., London, pp. vi–vii.
40. Julian Huxley (1941), pp. 112–13.
41. This was the title of the book by Spalding, published posthumously by Basil Blackwell in 1958.
42. Published in New York in 1902, the year in which Spalding, having recently left New College, Oxford after reading Greats, began to broaden his intellectual horizons, not least by looking to the civilizations of the East.
43. W. H. D. Rouse, in his review of H. N. Spalding's *Civilization in East and West: An Introduction to the Study of Human Progress*, Oxford University Press, 1939. The review appeared in *The Manchester Guardian* on 12 January 1940.
44. The paragraph is quoted by K. D. D. Henderson in the appendix to NUSGR, number 7, November 1956. Professor Brandon held the Chair at Manchester from 1951 to 1971.

CHAPTER TWO

'The Renaissance of the Future'

A Universal *Malaise* and a Cure

The partnership between H. N. Spalding and K. D. D. Henderson was based upon a shared conviction about the value of religion in helping to heal the ills of the world. They believed that religion was an integral, indeed a *necessary*, element in the prescription of any cure for the disunity that afflicts humanity. It was not a popular belief to hold in their day, when the conviction was growing that religion was one of its principal causes of human conflict. Despite the often articulate and rationalistic expression of anti-religious sentiment in the society of their time, neither Spalding nor Henderson was convinced that the time had come, or ever would come, to abandon religious belief. On the contrary, they held that this was a time for a serious re-examination of the claims of religion. In their view it was precisely because the world was divided by different religions and cultures that such careful investigation was required. Experience persuaded them that atheism as advocated in Marxist-Leninist theory, for example, could never provide the means for discovering practicable answers to the human predicament. In this they were not alone in pointing to the consequences of unbelief that were the results of Stalinism in the Soviet empire and Hitlerism in Europe. The call for religion to be rejected as inimical to human progress was one that Spalding and Henderson challenged, not least for empirical reasons. Ignorance, not knowledge, of what the great religions teach seemed to them to account in large measure for the premature rejection of religious belief among many of their contemporaries. The task, therefore, was to counter this ignorance by focusing attention on the common ground to be found in the religious experience of mankind, without overlooking or discounting the profound differences of belief that can lead to disunity and conflict. This was the task that Spalding believed would prepare the way for what he called 'the Renaissance of the Future'. His thoughts on the subject of this 'renaissance' are expressed in the seventh and final part of his book, *Civilization in East and West*, under the significant chapter-heading, 'The Coming of the Kingdom'.[1]

In practical terms the task of promoting knowledge of this healing unity centred on Spalding's plans for the Union for the Study of the Great Religions ('the Union'). The Union was founded in Oxford in 1950/1951 by Sir Sarvepalli Radhakrishnan, Canon Charles E. Raven, and H. N. Spalding. Radhakrishnan was the first scholar to be elected to the Spalding Chair of Eastern Religions and Ethics. In later life he was to become Vice-President and finally President of India. He and Spalding soon established a firm personal friendship that was to continue until the latter's death. Radhakrishnan was appointed to the Oxford Chair in 1936 after Spalding had made the necessary funds available to the University. HN's intention was to provide the resources for distinguished Asian scholars to come to Oxford in order to share their knowledge and experience of the religions of the East with members of the wider, as well as the academic, community. Charles Raven retired from the Regius Professorship of Divinity in Cambridge in 1950, having already served as Master of Christ's College and Vice-Chancellor of the University. Spalding, who had read Classics at New College, Oxford from 1898 to 1902, was the motivator, the idealistic visionary, whose peculiar gift it was to encourage these men and many others to share his vision of a future renaissance based upon a recovery of religious conviction and spiritual insight.

'Not a Learned Man'

Oxford draws scholars and visitors from all over the world. Between the two World Wars many of them were invited, or otherwise drawn, to the Spalding house at 'Shotover Cleve' or later and more accessibly, at number 9 South Parks Road. In both these houses visitors found generous hospitality, congenial company, and wide-ranging conversation. It was the cut and thrust of conversation that encouraged Spalding to write his books. Of his *Civilization in East and West*, he wrote: 'The book is the child of talks rather than of books'. A voracious reader, though dependent for his knowledge of the spiritual classics of the East on English translations, he pursued his studies with a disciplined determination. He did not find writing books easy, observing that it was 'the loving patience of a wife' that enabled him to complete them. His religio-philosophical works, not to mention his poetry, kept him at work long after his other commitments for the day had been met. In some ways it was fortunate that he was an insomniac. When others were sleeping he was all too often wakeful. Yet during these hours of sleeplessness he would continue to write. His capacity for sustained effort, even in the closing years of his life when he was weakened by illness, was remarkable. He was modest about what he produced. Of himself he wrote,

He does not claim to be a philosopher; rather he is a small boy peering

through the palings into the delectable pleasance of philosophy. He is
not a learned man; but the scraps of information he has acquired are
of infinite value to him, and may perhaps be valuable to others. The
book, though conservative, challenges convention. He knows that much
of the material he handles can be interpreted in different ways; but
unfortunately he can lay no claim to infallibility for the interpretations
he has too summarily presented. His fallibility will no doubt be amply
recognised by the critics (if the book is lucky enough to have any);
what is remarkable is that the author himself is aware of it.

A religion is often vague or self-contradictory, and it is tempting to
state its doctrine too sharply and precisely. The same religion may give
different accounts of such matters as the stage of contemplation of the
Divine Mind; yet one account only may be here represented. When
the meaning of such words as *Citta, Vijnan, Nous, Logos,* or as *Rita*
and *Dharma* varies or is open to doubt, to compare them is difficult
and dangerous. Comparison is no easy task, and it is to be feared that
this book will, unwittingly and unwillingly, illustrate not only its path,
but its pitfalls. Still, progress proceeds by trial and error. In the writing
of this book there have been many trials; no doubt in the result there
are many errors.[2]

Spalding concluded the Prologue to *The Divine Universe* with a moving
invocation, which illustrates how committed he was to a belief in the unity
of creation. His words express both a conviction and an expectation: 'May
God and man forgive [the book's] errors, and prosper the Truth it reports.
And may better and wiser minds follow who will re-write it with deeper
insight into the Divine Universe. For that way lies the Renaissance of the
future.'[3] On a stylistic note, Spalding wrote his key concepts with initial
capitals. His most important assumption, one that he seldom made explicit
because he took it for granted that no reasonable person would ever wish to
deny it, was that the universe is contingent. It is strictly dependent upon the
Creator, the *Self-Existent Being,* the *Organising Principle,* the *Absolute.* He
would readily have agreed with Isidore Epstein.

Even an infinite universe is only of 'possible existence', and as such
requires as its ground a necessary existent being. As a being of merely
possible existence, the world is no longer a natural necessity of cause
and effect but a product of the Will of God. The highest attribute of
the Will of God is Love, and creation is a contingent means whereby
God diffuses his Love to give existence to all beings.'[4]

Neither Spalding nor Henderson explicitly quoted the New Testament
text that was later to serve as a watchword for Christians who, whilst firmly

H. N. Spalding (standing, centre) 'entertains Sidney Sussex at tea' at Henley, a
photograph taken and captioned by W. T. S. Stallybrass on 30 June 1914.

committed to the faith they profess, are open to dialogue with those of other
faiths and of none: 'But in your hearts set apart Christ as Lord. Always be
prepared to give an answer to everyone who asks you to give the reason for
the hope you have. But do this with gentleness and respect, keeping a clear
conscience.'[5] Spalding approached the central theme of his spiritual quest
with gentleness and respect. The tributes that flowed in to the members of
his family after his death in 1953 provide evidence of the high regard in which
he was held. He was a generous man, giving freely of his time and resources
to those who came to him for advice and help. Nor was his philanthropy
limited to those who asked for assistance. During his years as a member of
the Senior Common Room at Brasenose College, he made several anonymous
gifts to help needy students.

> Many generations of the readers of these pages will remember in a
> more personal way his keen interest in and generosity to many under-
> graduate activities—in particular to the boat Club, which enjoyed
> through many years between the wars the hospitality of 'H.N.' and his
> wife at their house in Henley at Regatta-time. The greater part of his
> generosity was, however, unobtrusive and unseen—to College Societies,
> to the College Servants' Clubs, and above all to many individual under-
> graduates in need of help. Many Brasenose men, with many others,
> will also remember with affection Sunday afternoons in the Spaldings'

H. N. Spalding at Henley regatta, a photograph taken by W. T. S. Stallybrass on
1 July 1914.

house when 'H.N.' would exercise his rare talent for stimulating and maintaining intelligent and interesting conversation between undergraduates of diverse tastes and often of different nationalities or races. Many a shy guest must have been surprised at his own conversational ability. Perhaps the secret of 'H.N.'s' success in this lay in the youthful interest, which he retained to the end of his life, in almost all the things of the mind.[6]

'An old friend who understood HN's ideals perfectly'

The Spalding Trusts (*sic*) were founded in 1923 and 1928. There are two distinct Trust Deeds, but both were drafted for similar purposes. Today it is more convenient to speak of the Spalding Trust, singular, if only to avoid having to answer the question, 'What's the difference?' The answer would seem to be that there is none.[7] The Trust was founded to promote a better understanding between men and women from different religions and cultures, by encouraging the study of the religious principles on which these cultures are based. To help to promote this the Trust began to make grants to individuals, places of learning, libraries, other groups, and institutions. concerned with the study of the great religions of the world. The Union for the Study of the Great Religions (USGR) was founded in 1950/1951 and incorporated by a trust deed in 1953 after HN's death. The object of the USGR was defined in the original Statement of Aims as being to promote ethical, philosophic, and religious education and culture through the study of the great civilizations of East and West. In this way it was hoped to foster better international understanding between the peoples of the world and to enrich their spiritual life. The founders believed that just as European civilization achieved unity in diversity on the basis of Judaism, Hellenism, and Christianity, so a world culture could be built up and a world renaissance made possible, if educational institutions throughout the world were re-inspired by a common study of the spirit of man as reflected in his approach to God.

When her husband died in 1953, Mrs Nellie Spalding did not want to run the Trust herself. Someone who could undertake the task needed to be found. She was re-assured when K. D. D. Henderson agreed to act as Secretary to the Trustees. It was she who described him as 'and old friend who understood HN's ideals perfectly'. Henderson was an only child. His father was a general practitioner in the East End of London, who lived above his surgery during the week and only returned home occasionally. The boy saw little enough of his father. He saw him less when he was sent to school at Glenalmond in Perthshire, in order (as his father put it) that he might learn at least something of his Scottish inheritance. Henderson's churchmanship was that of a low-church Anglican. In retirement he was a critic of what he considered to be the banalities of the liturgical experiments and theological speculations of the established Church. For theologians who (as he put it) 'throw out the baby with the bath-water', he coined the adjective *cenobalian*, the etymology of which he helpfully traced to *cenos*, 'empty' and *balaneion*, 'a bath'.[8] His frustration extended to synodical government in the Church of England and what appeared to him to be futile attempts to catch the skirts of the spirit of the age as it hurried past on a frantic search for renewal. He was frustrated by the apparent refusal of the leaders of the Church to admit that, by permitting the replacement of the sonorous and still intelligible language of Cranmer with the uninspiring verbalism of a series of newly-devised alternative services, a gradual decline in church-going was inevitable. He put his frustration into words.

> We who have called upon our God as Thee,
> Like lovers their Beloved; who have prayed
> And praised in words the Holy Spirit blessed
> With a perpetual fragrance, still unstaled
> By countless repetitions; who have felt
> Past congregations throng the silent pews
> From twenty thousand Sundays, we must go.
> Leaving the zealot busy in his stall
> On some new Series, almost up-to-date;
> The studious pedant careful to point out
> The Gadarene was really Gergasene
> And Simeon was granted a discharge;
> The sons of Eli, tendering the Cup
> To maenads worshipping their Unknown Gods.
>
> Let us seek out some lost redundant church,
> Unsuitable for hall or house or barn,
> And worship there, perhaps his ghost to meet
> Who once at Bemerton did sit and eat.[9]

In his later years Henderson was often tempted to abandon church attendance, feeling acutely the loss of the elegance, the beauty, and the spiritual power of the 1662 Prayer Book. In his regard for the felicity of Cranmer's language he found an ally in the Catholic, Robert Speaight, the English actor and author who was one of his contemporaries at Oxford.

> Let us try out our experiments with liturgical language very carefully in private before we set them up in competition with Cranmer. If Cranmer were still in Purgatory—though I'm sure he has long since been promoted to a better place—the worst of his pains would surely be the knowledge of how atrociously the Roman Catholics of today

have translated the prayers which he once translated so sublimely. He might even imagine that this was their way of getting their own back. But let him have no such fears. I can assure you that many of us who are of the Roman obedience would ask for nothing better, now that we worship in our own language, than to use wherever possible the language that the genius of the Church of England has bequeathed to its posterity. We should grow much closer together in our thoughts and in our feelings if we gave expression to them in identical words.[10]

In his adult years HN chose to be a member of the Church of England, though he was not a regular church-goer. As a child in London he had been brought up in a Presbyterian household. His lack of enthusiasm for worship in church did not signify a lack of interest in Christianity, however. On the contrary he was deeply attached to the personality and the teaching of Jesus Christ, as given in the Gospels and preserved in 'the Church of Christ' which, in HN's view, consists not of priests and prelates, but of 'the sons of man'.[11] Several of his poems show this lasting influence on him of the person of Christ. 'Every generation must try to construct a more perfect portrait of Jesus as more material becomes available and powers of comprehension develop.' [12] Spalding's Christology veered towards unitarianism at times, but Henderson's was decidedly trinitarian. On several occasions the present writer heard Henderson expressing his disappointment that the Christian churches (as he thought) were neglecting to place sufficient emphasis on the work of the Holy Spirit in the story of mankind's redemption and salvation.

Is Religion Necessary?

To this question Henderson, agreeing with Spalding, responded with an emphatic *Yes*. In his answer to this question, Henderson noted that

[half a century ago Spalding] was to watch the spread of two rival materialist ideologies like a veneer of acid across the world, eating corrosively into the various indigenous cultures and putting nothing back in their place. He saw the weakening resistance of European civilization with its roots in Jerusalem, Athens and Rome, and he foresaw the collapse of the other great world cultures unless they could be induced to make common cause. He suggested as one method of bolstering resistance the introduction into the education of the future rulers of a common factor akin to what used in Europe to be called the liberal arts. This factor he thought to find in the study of man's spiritual needs and of the various ways in which they had been satisfied at sundry times and in divers places. He recognised no threat to the integrity of the various faiths because he knew from experience that familiarity with another's religion heightens understanding and appreciation of one's own.

This attitude is, of course, consonant with the strictly historical approach to the study of world religions which opened the door to the claim of humanism for inclusion as a social phenomenon. But Spalding's own underlying dream was the possibility of a world renaissance brought to birth by what we now call dialogue, the cross-fertilisation of powerful intellects bedded in spiritual understanding.[13]

Both Spalding and Henderson instinctively reacted against attempts to make comparisons on the basis of what were, in effect, western reifications of highly complicated systems of religious belief and practice. 'Hinduism' and 'Buddhism', for example, could well be *described*—a favourite word in some Western circles—from their extensive literature, iconography, and architecture. The translation and elucidation of the sacred books of Eastern religions could provide the student with important new tools for investigating exotic cultures, but both men held that the Western predilection for taxonomy, for the analysis and classification of *objects*, was insufficient for 'the study of religions and religion'. They found the reductionism of the age dispiriting. A strictly phenomenological approach to religion and religions struck them as interesting but needlessly narrow. They believed that religion and religions are not the objects to be described from a distance *de haut en bas*, so to speak, but living options, which call for personal engagement of the most demanding nature. The American scholar, Huston Smith, echoing William James' distinction between religion as a dull habit and religion as an acute fever, observed that

> wherever religion comes to life it displays a startling quality; it takes over. All else, while not silenced, becomes subdued and thrown without contest into a supporting role. Religion alive confronts the individual with the most momentous option this world can present. It calls the soul to the highest adventure it can undertake, a proposed journey across the jungles, peaks, and deserts of the human spirit. The call is to confront reality, to master the self. Those who dare to hear and follow this secret call soon learn the dangers and difficulties of its lonely journey.[14]

This was a point of view that Spalding and Henderson shared. It expresses humility in the presence of mysteries that may be prematurely dismissed as absurd. The task was one of trying 'to understand faith as those who hold faith understand it, in its infinite complexity and continual movement'.[15] There was another possible pitfall for the 'objective' observer of religion, a hazard to which the Canadian scholar, W. Cantwell Smith, drew attention.

The concept of 'a religion' reflects what he took to be a characteristically Western attitude—that of categorizing and differentiating religious systems—which then appear to be more distinct from each other than they are.[16] The point was picked up by John Hick.

> The notion of religions as mutually exclusive entities with their own characteristics and histories, although it now tends to operate as a habitual category of our thinking, may well be another example of the illicit reification, the turning of good adjectives into bad substantives, to which the Western mind is prone and against which contemporary philosophy has armed us. In this case a powerful but false conceptuality has helped to create phenomena answering to it, namely, the religions of the world seeing themselves and each other as rival ideological communities.[17]

A measure of humility and *personal* engagement is required of the student who approaches the faiths of others. It was inconceivable to Spalding and Henderson that anyone could remain for long a detached observer of sacred mysteries, and remain personally unchallenged by the claims and evidences of *faith*. Two quotations will serve to express their approach to religious belief and to faith. The first is the familiar verse from the Bible, quoted here in the words of the King James version that both men preferred: 'It is a fearful thing to fall into the hands of the living God' (*Hebrews* 10.31). The nineteenth-century philosopher, Søren Kierkegaard, knew what it was to take God seriously. At the prospect of the existential *dread* that was the consequence of too close a personal engagement with the claims made on him by the Christian God, he was tempted to prefer a studious detachment. Yet disengagement was impossible. Once drawn to the source of enlightenment, the individual is consumed by its overpowering proximity. Neither Spalding nor Henderson ever spoke in such dramatic terms, but each was aware that one of the ways of not taking the Divine Vision seriously is to stress the importance of religion 'for *other* people—people of the past, people of other cultures, people whose ego strength needs bolstering'.[18] The second quotation, from an essay by the Jewish philosopher Martin Buber, points to the *risk* involved in an exploration of religious faith.

> A time of genuine religious conversations is beginning—not those so-called but fictitious conversations where none regarded and addressed his partner in reality—but genuine dialogues, speech from certainty to certainty, from one open-hearted person to another open-hearted person. Only then will genuine common life appear, not that of an identical content of faith which is alleged to be found in all religions, but that of the situation, of anguish and of expectation.[19]

Learning through Experience

Spalding was an assiduous advocate of an inclusive, rather than a syncretistic, approach to religious belief and experience. The word 'experience' is significant. His study 'of religions and of religion', to quote the phrase he liked to use, was not simply the private pursuit of an intellectual interest. It was directed (as he saw it) towards a higher purpose. Religion *mattered* to him. He was personally involved in the quest for spiritual truth. Religion might be in decline, but it was not dead; it might be in retreat in parts of Europe, but this was not true of many other parts of the world. He grew up in Victorian and Edwardian England, in which rapid and astonishing developments in science and technology had a profound, even disturbing, influence on religious belief and practice. The faith of English Christians like Spalding, whose childhood, adolescence, and early manhood, had been spent in a society influenced by imperial splendour and the comfortable certainties of an established religion, was to be questioned by the historical-critical study of the Scriptures, textual criticism, the evolutionary theories of Charles Darwin and Alfred Wallace, and the progress of the natural sciences. The impressively unified triumphs of science and technology present an interesting comparison with the disunity that had arisen out of religious diversity. The methods of scientific inquiry are universally discernible, assimilable, and applicable. The achievements and the benefits of science and technology can be seen, if not yet enjoyed, by all. The results of scientific investigation can be checked, confirmed or refuted. Experiments can be repeated. In such circumstances science itself begins to assume a quasi-religious function. By contrast, religious 'knowledge', in so far as it is to be distinguished from the 'knowledge' that accrues from scientific inquiry, is held by some observers to be illusory.

Both Spalding and Henderson were possessed of a religious faith that was capable of being enriched, rather than subverted or displaced, by claims that there were other paths, discrete and coherent, by which human beings may attain a knowledge of ultimate reality. In Spalding's case this appreciation of religious and cultural diversity was to come progressively through his study of other civilizations, notably, those of India and China. In Henderson's case, his awareness of the pluralism of religious truth was strengthened by his experiences as a political officer and finally as a Governor in the predominantly Islamic regions of the Sudan. He sought to discourage Christian missionaries from working in the Islamic communities in his administrative areas, chiefly because he considered that attempts to convert Muslims from Islam in such regions were likely to threaten social stability. Muslims, after all, were not unbelievers, awaiting the arrival of divine revelation. He was not the first European colonial administrator to take this view. For pragmatic administrative reasons in the early years of the twentieth century, in what was to become known as Nigeria, the British High Commissioner, Lord Lugard, with his predilection for Indirect Rule in colonial territories, sought to preserve local social and religious stability by discouraging Christians from presenting themselves as missionaries in the northern Islamic parts of the areas he administered.

On one occasion in Khartoum, Henderson was taken to one side by a Sudanese friend, who suggested that he should have a quiet word with an English official working in the city, a man who was apparently irritating local people by commending the Christian faith too openly, almost as if he were a Christian missionary in a heathen land. Henderson found an opportunity to say as much to the man, reminding him that Muslims were not without their own approach to God.[20] This lesson in humility, when faced with the religious traditions and experiences of others, was one that Henderson believed it necessary for others to learn as he had learned it. This was one of the experiences that shaped his own religious development and led him in time to co-operate with Spalding in calling for a more sensitive understanding of religious belief and practice. One of the ways in which this might be done was to press for a recognition of religious and cultural diversity in education, first in the universities and then, by extension, in schools. This work required the co-operation of like-minded people in different parts of the world. In the Union for the Study of the Great Religions, the task of organising regional inter-faith activities and conferences was delegated to Area Committees and co-ordinated by the local Area Secretary.[21] These regional groups were active and successful for a time, although they all failed to operate with the enthusiasm and efficiency for which the General Secretary, Henderson, repeatedly pressed. As he grew older and less capable of travelling the world as he had once done it became clear that the work of the Union was coming to an end.

Uncertainty, Doubt, and Devout Scepticism

Ralph Waldo Emerson (1803–82) entertained an idea that was to enjoy wide, if uncritical, acceptance in the Western world as the nineteenth and twentieth centuries proceeded. In consequence, doubt (by which he meant religious doubt and the disposition to go on doubting) was, paradoxically, to assume a neo-credal status for many believers and unbelievers alike in the years that followed. Uncertainty and doubt were to be welcomed by some as hallmarks of a 'mature' belief, whether religious or secular. Emerson declared his hand when he wrote of the modern men and women like himself, 'in whose doubt is more than in all your creeds'. In the nineteenth century he was not alone in his rather contemptuous dismissal of the religious beliefs of others as groundless and irrational metaphysical speculations. There was nothing new in his rejection of revealed religion. In England, two hundred years earlier, William Law was confronted by the indifference, rather than the hostility, of many of his contemporaries to the claims of the Christian religion. He was born in King's Cliffe, Northamptonshire in 1686 and died in 1761. From an explicitly Christian point of view he sought to engage his readers in a thoughtful consideration of the claims of the Gospel of Jesus. The result was his *A Serious Call to a Devout and Holy Life* published in 1728. It was to become a spiritual classic. Its influence on the indifferent, the sceptical, and the unbelieving, is unclear, but it certainly encouraged the faithful. In the eighteenth and nineteenth centuries Christians as different in temperament and conviction as Dr Samuel Johnson (1709–84), John Wesley (1703–91), and John Henry Newman (1801–90), were to find inspiration in it.

From a very different perspective, and in his own way, H. N. Spalding, set out to engage his contemporaries in a serious call to consider (or to re-consider) the importance of the religious dimension in human experience. Unlike Law, Spalding was not an apologist for any one or other of the great religions of the world. As his friend Sarvepalli Radhakrishnan observed, HN was a deeply religious man, whose religion 'was not confined to a code of conduct and respect for outward forms. These latter were experienced as opening the door to the truths of spirit. Man is not a finished creation. He is an experiment of which he can be partly the creator. Religion is essentially the art and theory of the re-making of man. It assumes man's ability to change himself.' [22] For many of their contemporaries, the agnosticism of gifted individuals such as Thomas Huxley, Matthew Arnold, and Thomas Hardy, helped to shake the foundations of the authority claimed for organised religion. For others, especially those who survived its horrors, the First World War provided the clinching reason for abandoning a religious faith that had once seemed reasonable and well-founded. In consequence, the voice of atheism grew more self-confident and strident as religious faith was exposed to the corrosive effects of scepticism and uncertainty.

In the nineteenth century the poet Matthew Arnold had recorded his sense of loss as he reflected on the decline of a religious faith that was steadily losing its influence on him and many of his contemporaries. His familiar image of 'the Sea of Faith', slowly ebbing to the sounds of a 'melancholy, long withdrawing roar', expresses his sense of regret that the authority of traditional religious structures must inevitably be abandoned in favour of a liberating, yet disconcerting, reliance on critical thought.[23] Arnold expressed the growing unease and uncertainty about the cultural life of England. In his Introduction to a compilation of the works of Arnold, Martin Corner writes,

> Much about nineteenth-century England, its complacency and narrow self-satisfaction, grated on him, and Arnold, permeated with the high-

culture of Europe, saw it as his role to be England's intellectual conscience and better self. He was able, in a manner more personal and more universal than Tennyson or Browning, to register the characteristic pressure of cultivated consciousness in his age; the liberating inevitability of critical thought alongside the pain of withdrawal from traditional structures, and the need, exciting as well as alarming, to establish new ones. Arnold grew up in a liberal religious setting, where critical reflection on faith was accepted, and he did not experience, in any sudden or acute form, the classic Victorian 'loss of faith'. But no poet conveyed more acutely the existential dilemma of the contemporary reflective mind: the need, and at the same time the difficulty, of finding some new basis for an authentic life.[24]

Spalding, no romantic visionary, did not question the inevitability of the changes that were coming, but he took a more positive line than Arnold with regard to the future of religion. He noted the decline of Christianity in the developed Western world and the concomitant decline of the culture built upon it, but he was more optimistic than Arnold. The tide that ebbs flows again. The incoming tide flows back to refresh and re-invigorate the land it recovers. The dismissal of religious belief is premature, however refined the terms in which it is expressed. Spalding sought to find a way of expressing this in a way that might commend itself to the uncertain, the sceptical, and the merely curious. He might well have associated the phrase 'round earth's shore', in Arnold's poem, *Dover Beach*, not with a retreating sea of faith but with the promise of its irresistible return, surging in with revitalising power from distant parts of the world. In the first instance Spalding's purpose was to help to re-instate the religious hypothesis, at a time when the reasonableness of religion (the established Christian religion, in particular) was being questioned as never before by many voices in the Western world.

HN was convinced that 'the knowledge of our buried life', words from another of Arnold's poems,[25] could be revealed, *dis-covered*, through study of what the great religions teach, if only men and women would have the courage to look. His own Christian beliefs were not of an evangelistic or proselytising kind, however, so they were unshaken by the kind of theological controversy or philosophical scepticism that helped to disturb convictions about the truth of orthodox Christian doctrine. Indeed, he believed that challenges to the uniqueness of Christianity, above all to its superiority in the universe of faiths, might serve to further the task to which he was personally committed. This task was to draw attention to 'the Divine Vision', to which all the religions of mankind bear witness in different but complementary ways. The notion that one or other of the great religions could claim to be the true religion for all did not seem to him to be reasonable.

From his perspective, it followed that if human beings the world over neglect this vision they will continue to suffer from a spiritual malaise. That there was a health-threatening imbalance in human affairs was clear enough to him in the wake of a savage world war. Spalding's diagnosis of the human condition may have been naïvely expressed, but he was consistent in prescribing the cure he thought necessary. The cure, he argued, was not to be found in any one religion, not even in Christianity. If religious faith was to be renewed in order to meet the spiritual needs of a world that grew smaller and more complex by the day, it could only be done by discovering the essential *unity* that lies behind the multiplicity of name and forms in all the great religions of the world.

Henderson shared that belief. After a visit to the newly established Harvard Center for the Study of World Religions in 1961, he wrote,

> On May 4th Robert Slater[26] drove me up to Madison, New Hampshire. Here we spent two nights in a granite house looking north-west across wooded hills and valleys to a dark range topped by the snow-clad slopes of Mount Washington, seemingly as high and remote as Kanchenjunga. This is the home of Ernest Hocking.[27] During the visit we talked, among other things, of Schweitzer and his 'focal point of good'; also of the Arab concept of *baraka*, a quality which some men possess in such measure that it influences even those whose contact with it is casual, and without which 'though I have all knowledge, I am nothing'. This grace adorned the house we were visiting and one can count oneself fortunate, after seven years' association with Richard Livingstone,[28] to find it again so soon ... Some of us exist for long periods and suddenly come to life for brief unforgettable intervals. Such was our stay in New Hampshire.
>
> It came to mind a fortnight later at the bedside in London of a Muslim friend, who also possessed *baraka* in a marked degree and that combination of goodness and gentleness without weakness which enables a man to overstep the barriers of race and creed and which, in a fellow-countryman of his thirty years ago, first brought home to me that no religion can claim a monopoly of revelation or salvation. The goodness of some men certainly lives after them.[29]

Henderson was deeply impressed by W. E. Hocking's 'lucid, easily intelligible wisdom', in which the doubts and uncertainties associated with religious belief were positively rather than negatively explored. In May 1961 Henderson thanked the elderly philosopher for the inspiration he had received during that visit to Madison. Unable to express himself adequately in prose, he chose to write in verse. Like Spalding he had no illusions about the quality of his poetic effusions.[30] The following poem survives—with an unconscious plagiarism from G. K. Chesterton, as Henderson himself said—chiefly because it elicited a response from Hocking.

> High places know no boundaries, You may stand
> On Kosciusko or in Kalimpong
> And watch blue threads of shadow spread along
> The shadeless snow, regardless of the land
> Stretched out below. Wise men who understand
> And seek high places overtop the throng
> Of races, faiths, and years. They belong
> To levels where all boundaries are spanned.
> So there in Madison the world looked small
> And dear; dear, too, the eddying sons of man,
> Who know not what they do, yet one and all
> Play their small part in furthering the Plan.
>
> So now, like swimmers freshly breathed, do we
> Lower our heads to battle with the sea.

Hocking responded,

> As—seen from Tiger Hill—the sun's first ray
> Swathes Kanchenjunga's bulk in radiant light,
> So—through the poet, in whose eyes the sight
> Shines with a glory not its own, we rise
> To the high Source of all transforming day,
> To the life-fire within the skies.   [W.] E. H.

The Great Religions

Both Spalding and Henderson were convinced that men and women the world over suffer from a sickness caused by spiritual deprivation. They were equally convinced that there is a cure for this universal human malaise, and that the treatment of the illness is to be found by turning to the accumulated wisdom of the great religions, 'studied in their ethical, philosophic, devotional and mystical aspects'. For Spalding, 'the Great Religions' were,

> Hinduism, its child Buddhism, its brother Zarathustrianism; Confucianism and mystical Taoism; Judaism and Greek thought, and their offspring Christianity and Islam. These nine have been the chief source of the great literature, the great art and the great music of the world. And when they are examined and compared, a marvellous truth stands revealed: while they differ widely on minor and sometimes on major points, they agree or harmonize (vary without contradiction) on broad

principles: on man's approach to God and on the Divine Nature Itself, whether regarded as the Godhead as He is in Himself, or as God as He is in relation to His creatures. As the same light of the one sun shines through the many different stained-glass windows, so the same truth of the one God shines through the various colours of different civilizations and different minds.[31]

The list of the great religions and cultures of East and West lengthened to include representatives from the Far East, China, Japan, India. It extended to include the religions of ancient Greece, Palestine, Slav, Latin and Nordic Europe, North and South America. These sources of wisdom and spiritual insight were to be studied in their independence, integrity, and fruitful diversity. A demanding programme, to be sure, and one for which three lines of approach were suggested. The first was through the study of the religions themselves. The second was through the fostering of mutual understanding between men and women of faith. The third was through the co-operation of religious leaders in making common cause against materialism. The immediate aim was to further the study of the great religions in universities, where the students should obtain an outline knowledge of the great cultures as a whole and a more detailed knowledge of one of them. The studies of a student

> would be cultural rather than philological and sound translations will have to be provided where they are not already available.[32] Use should also be made of the appeal to eye and ear of art, architecture and music in specimen, picture and record. The importance of studying the arts as a means to the understanding of a religion was stressed by the founders. The recommendations of the *Ramakrishnan University Education Committee for India*, which have been accepted by the Indian Government, and have commended themselves to high educational authorities elsewhere, are that all university students should study, in their first year, the lives of the great religious leaders; in the second, selections from the scriptures of the world; and in their third, the central problems of the philosophy of religion. This scheme also provides a guide for the ordinary person who wishes to study religions as part of his general education.[33]

Holy Russia

To the list of 'great religions' Spalding added the religion of 'Holy Russia'. The Orthodox traditions, especially those of Holy Mother Russia, caught and held his attention, inspiring him to reflect upon the experience to which the mystics of all religions bear common witness. Even so, he detected a fundamental difference between civilizations which are anthropocentric and those which are essentially theocentric.

> Hinduism with Buddhism and Orthodoxy [are] at the opposite pole from China and the Nordics, as the other world is at the opposite pole from this. The Chinese and Nordic ideal, being social, did not admit of anything in the nature of a flight from ordinary human experience: as Confucius said, 'absorption in the study of the supernatural is most harmful'. In India and Russia, however, precisely such a flight from experience did take place; and with it came a certain neglect of experience and interest in the world of things and men. If the Chinese and the Nordics are the Marthas among the nations, India and Russia are the Marys; not busy and practical, but on the whole meditative and mystic.[34]

Spalding described Russia as 'this vast world of resurrection'. He thought of Russia as a huge land-mass of mountain and steppe in which even the dullest observer could not fail to be awakened by the sudden Easter-burst of spring after the long darkness and the bitter cold of winter. For HN the resurrection of all living things to a new life of light, love and rejoicing, was Nature's exemplary response to the Divine Will. Prompted by the sight of such recurring wonders, an Orthodox Christian is helped to glimpse the Unseen in the midst of what is seen. In the Orthodox liturgy the worshipper is led into the very presence of the Unseen.[35] Spalding believed that Holy Russia was itself an icon, a window into Heaven, through which streamed the glory of the Divine Vision. At the time when he was writing about these things, Russia was gripped by a political system that actively sought to destroy religion. After the Bolshevik revolution of 1917, Christians were among the first to suffer persecution. The body of Christ was once more suffering crucifixion, but after the crucifixion would come the resurrection. One of Spalding's sonnets is called *Christos Woskresse* (*sic*). The title comes from the greeting exchanged by Russian Orthodox believers on Easter Day: *Christos voskrese! Voistinu voskrese!*, that is, 'Christ is Risen! He is risen Indeed!' The poem shows that, unlike some of his more gullible contemporaries who should have known what was actually going on in the Soviet Union because they had been there, ostensibly to see for themselves, Spalding was aware of the tragedy that was unfolding in that country.

Christ is Risen!
Look ye at Holy Russia crucified:
Behold the nails, the thorns, the dying breath;
Hark to the cry of anguish; and beneath,
The passing scoffers, daring to deride.

Wisdom she hath forgot, the Christ denied;
God hath forsaken her, she perisheth;
Great darkness glooms about the cross of death;
She hath put on the mortal, and hath died.
See, from the tomb the stone is roll'd away;
The dark is empty of the dead, and rife
The dawn with Paschal light and Paschal bird:
Lo! Russia risen to Eternal Life,
Ringing the bells of Resurrection Day,
And in her heart the Everlasting Word.[36]

Seventy years later the Communist system collapsed in the Soviet Union. It remains to be seen whether or not Spalding's words were prophetic, but there are clear signs of a revival of religion in that part of the world. He believed, but could not have known for certain, that in the darkest days of Communist oppression in the USSR there were individuals who strove, often at great personal cost, to preserve the Divine Vision in Holy Russia. The writer of the short prayer that follows experienced persecution, imprisonment, 'internal exile', and ultimately exile from his own country. He was to become famous for novels like *In the First Circle, Cancer Ward,* and for his meticulous documentation of life and death in the Soviet *Gulag Archipelago.* Aleksandr Isayevich Solzhenitsyn speaks of the responsibility that human beings bear for reflecting the radiance of God, however inadequately, a conviction that HN would clearly have shared.

Prayer
How easy it is for me to live with you, O Lord!
How easy it is for me to believe in you!
Whenever my mind is uncertain, or I am consumed by perplexity,
Or when clever people fail to see further than today,
Not aware of what they must do tomorrow—
You send down to me from heaven the clear certainty
That you exist and that you are taking care of me
So that not all the favourable paths for me are closed.

On the crest of human fame, I grow accustomed
With astonishment to a journey
That one is never capable of devising for oneself;
An astonishing journey through hopelessness up to this point,
Whence I am able to send to humanity
Reflections of your radiance.
Yet you will give me the time that is necessary
For me to continue to reflect that radiance.

But as to how much time I have—that you know
And determine—as with everything else.[37]

Spalding's respect—one might say, his reverence—for Orthodoxy was expressed practically in 1948. In that year he provided the funds for a University Lectureship at Oxford, to be held by Dr Nicolas Zernov. Dr Zernov's book, *Eastern Christendom: A Study of the Origin and Development of the Eastern Orthodox Church*,[38] is dedicated 'to the memory of H. N. Spalding, 1877–1953 and of his wife Nellie Spalding, 1876–1957, whose vision and generosity endowed the study of Eastern Christianity in the University of Oxford'.[39] Four decades earlier, on the outbreak of the First World War in August 1914, Spalding wrote a sonnet with the title *Holy Russia*.[40] Like most of his other poems it was not published until 1952, because of the 'idleness' that the author claimed to have been one of his virtues. Spalding's respect for the Orthodox Tradition of Holy Russia was never to waver, but the horrors of the First World War, the barbarity of the Bolshevik revolution, and the totalitarian dictatorships of atheistic Communism in the Soviet Union and Communist China, changed his understanding of the relationship between Church and State, the meaning of patriotism, and the source of Light from the East. Another of his sonnets illustrates this.

> *Bolshevik Russia*:
> Massacre seized me; mad, I swung the knife
> And stab'd my bosom—I the murderer
> And I the murder'd! Godless self-slaughter,
> Russian and Russian, soul and soul at strife!
> Henceforth is the whole earth with horror rife:
> Look, young and old, with starving eyes, wander
> Thro' cornless Volga's crowded sepulchre,
> Then drink the river in despair of life.
> Yet have I deeper drunk, yea, deadlier know.
> Where love was, hate is; whom I saved before
> Now smite I. Still of Hell remains the worst:
> Ah, fires of anguish! bottomless pit of woe!
> God loved I, now I see His Face no more,
> Call me not human; I am the Accurst.[41]

The brutality of Adolf Hitler's Third Reich was still to come, but by then Spalding had already turned further East, to the ancient traditions of India and China, for confirmation of his belief that the religious insight and the wisdom for which human beings seek (or can be encouraged to seek) is universal, though differently expressed. This common wisdom—Eastern and Western—points towards unity, justice, and peace. This is the wisdom that promises *renaissance*. This is the knowledge that leads to *resurrection*. As he was to comment later, when his poems were published,

> The energies of mankind are at present directed to avoiding a Third World War. But necessary as this is, it is not enough; they must also be devoted to preparing for the first World-wide Renaissance, the true alternative to another war. It is a Renaissance centring upon God, to which East and West will alike contribute.[42]

Light from Many Sources

The notion of a universal religion, in which tolerance is the principal article of faith and education the means by which it is to be inculcated, is by no means new. It assumes importance as the extent of religious and cultural diversity becomes more apparent, and potentially more threatening. How are the rights, the needs, the aspirations, of different cultural and religious communities to be recognised (not to say, reconciled) without damaging social stability? How are the convictions of believers, unbelievers, agnostics, and atheists, to be accommodated in a society that may be described with the best intentions, but prematurely, as 'pluralist' and 'multi-cultural'? Secularism, inside as well as outside the different religious traditions, has fostered indifference to the claims of institutionalised religion. It is not that religion has been decisively rejected because of the sophisticated disinclination on the part of modern men and women to accept outdated metaphysics. The rejection of organised religion is often the consequence of an unreflective pragmatism nourished by ignorance. It is widely believed that in order to live a 'reasonable' and a 'reasonably successful' life it is not necessary to consider the claims and counter-claims of any religion. Henderson's hold on institutional religion loosened when he began to feel that traditional religious systems were too specifically prescriptive and constricting. Dauntingly, they presented the seeker of truth with what Dr Carmen Blacker called, 'a number of metaphysical propositions in which to believe and a set of moral principles with which to conform'.[43]

Light, and the enlightenment it brings, is to be welcomed from whatever source it comes. Spalding and Henderson acknowledged that many lamps light the path to truth. The religions of India, China, and Japan promise deliverance from darkness to light. Hinduism promises deliverance from ignorance of the real to knowledge of the real, furnishing the seeker after truth with a strategic and a progressive plan of salvation. Siddharta Gautama, the *Buddha*, with his gospel of liberation from the suffering and the *dis*-ease of existence, is the exemplary 'enlightened one'—as his title reveals. In Judaism, Christianity, and Islam, light illuminates the path to wholeness, well-being, and salvation. Each of these religions, in its distinctive and particular way, satisfies a universal human need. Does any one religion take precedence over the others? *Can* any one religion contain the truth for everyone and for all time? It was one thing for Spalding and Henderson to assert—at a time when it was less common to do so than it is today—that there are many different ways in which spiritual insight and wisdom is to be attained. This they did, *ex animo*, but neither man was ever to be a campaigner for a new universal system of beliefs (whether reformed but 'secular', or reformed and 'religious') based upon the abandonment of doctrinal particularity. This point is worth making if only to refute the charge laid against both men (but especially against HN by Professor R. C. Zaehner during the course of his inaugural lecture in Oxford) that their interest in world religions concealed an attempt to use the study of comparative religion in order to promote a universal syncretism. This, quite simply, was not true of either Spalding or Henderson.[44]

In each case of an experiment with religious truth the test is both empirical and pragmatic. The approach to the claims of a religion is heuristic. What is there to know and learn? What is there to discover and experience? Is a commitment to belief *reasonable or absurd?* In a more utilitarian vein, and in plain language, *Does religion deliver what it promises to the believer?* The great religious teachers, among whom are Siddharta Gautama, the *Buddha* and Jesus, the *Christ*, issue the invitation, 'Come and see', to the would-be seeker after truth. The claims of religion are thus to be tested only in the crucible of personal experience. The *Gâyatrî Mantra*, the prayer to the Sun, is the most sacred of Vedic *mantras*, repeated three times each day by an orthodox initiated Brahmin, in the early morning when the sun rises, at midday when the sun is at its zenith, and at sunset. In this prayer it is the light of the Sun which provides an appropriate metaphor for the blaze of enlightenment which may come, only faintly at first, when vision is clouded by sin, doubt, and uncertainty. At such times the believer may be compared to one who patiently waits for illumination, knowing that the dim light to be seen is the promise not the fulfilment. That which is just discernible on the horizon before dawn will give way ultimately to the effulgence of the risen sun. So the daily prayer is for light, for liberation, for salvation, for a knowledge of the Truth. It was Mohandas Karamchand Gandhi—*Mahatma Gandhi*—who declared that 'Truth is God'. What we seek in our search for Truth is, according to this view, nothing less than that for which in our present state of ignorance we can only call *God*.

> *Om:* Let us meditate on
> The radiance of the divine
> May it inspire and illuminate our intellects. *Om.* [45]

The theme of the revelatory power of light is picked up in *al-Qur'ân*. The Holy Book of Islam is itself the light that is manifest, a revelation sent down by God. The 'convincing proof' of its illuminating truth is given not so much in prepositional statements about doctrine—though these are important enough—but in the personal example of the Prophet Muhammad's response in every particular to the divine call he received.

> O Mankind! Verily
> There hath come to you
> A convincing proof
> From your Lord:
> For We [i.e. God] have sent unto you
> A light (that is) manifest.   (4.174) [46]

The twenty-fourth *sûrah* of the *Qur'ân* carries the title *al-Nûr*, 'the Light'. It contains the 'Verse of Light'.

> God is the Light
> Of the heavens and the earth.
> The parable of His Light
> Is as if there were a Niche
> And within it a Lamp:
> The Lamp enclosed in Glass:
> The glass as it were
> A brilliant star:
> Lit from a blessed Tree,
> An Olive, neither of the East
> Nor of the West,
> Whose Oil is well-nigh
> Luminous,
> Though fire scarce touched it:
> Light upon Light!
> God doth guide
> Whom He will
> To His Light:
> God doth set forth Parables
> For men: and God
> Doth know all things.   (verse 35)

Then come the lines,

> (Lit is such a light)
> In houses, which God
> Hath permitted to be raised

To honour; for the celebration
In them of His name:
In them He is glorified
In the mornings and
In the evenings, (again and again),
By men whom neither
Traffic nor merchandise
Can divert from the Remembrance
Of God, nor from regular Prayer,
Nor from the practice
Of regular Charity ...   (verses 36–7) [47]

Opportunity and Responsibility in Education

Could a new universal religion be founded upon human solidarity in the face of cosmic indifference? The prospect of a godless chaos rather than a divinely ordered cosmos offers a bleak view of human existence in a universe from which even the possibility of supernatural intervention is excluded. Spalding and Henderson would have none of that. The denial of the Divine Vision was to be vigorously challenged. The notion that it is the denial of God that is the beginning of wisdom was a poisoned inversion of the truth, which Spalding established the Trust and the Union to counter. At the same time he was fully aware of the fact that two separate groups were brought into a formidable anti-theistic alliance by the secularist tendency. On the one hand were the dogmatic atheists, with their own counter-gospel to propagate. On the other hand were those whose practical atheism had never been subjected to critical scrutiny and whose lives appeared to them to stand in no need of spiritual inquiry, except at infrequent moments of personal stress. These are the ones who are indifferent rather than hostile to the claims of religion. Both Spalding and Henderson took a great interest in educational theory and practice. What is the role of education in a pluralist, multi-ethnic, multi-faith, multi-cultural society? If 'God' exists, and if all men and women belong to the same family of created beings, can disagreements about revelation be allowed to obstruct human progress? Can it be that 'God' should wilfully confuse the most important issue of all by dividing those who 'He' has created to be obedient to 'His' will? Such questions often exercised the minds of both men. Much of what they had to say by way of answers focused on education and especially on religious and moral education in schools. Without the adequate preparation of teachers, however, the inclusion of teaching about world religions in the school curriculum is questionable. This was one of the concerns of the Anglican scholar, Canon Spencer Leeson, whose teaching career took him to the headship of Winchester College, one of England's leading public schools. In 1944 he gave the Bampton Lectures in Oxford. In one of the notes to the published lectures he wrote:

> It is hardly fair to confront a child with his mind as yet undeveloped with Christianity, Islam, Buddhism and Confucianism, laying them side by side as it were on the table, and inviting him to choose for himself. He is not ready to appreciate either the differences or the common elements, and if told that he must exercise a choice between alternative ideas about God and man, would either feel bewildered or would cease to listen. Those who have had practical experience of dealing with children of that age would not be likely to commend this proposal. As every teacher knows, if any impression is to be made upon children, he must be definite, clear and, above all, concrete. Moreover it is doubtful whether a teacher with any strong convictions of his own could maintain an objective attitude towards these alternatives. He would be required by implication to believe, or at least suggest, that all of them were equally true; this would be impossible unless he was indifferent to them all, and a teacher with an outlook of that sort might well be unwilling to give any religious teaching.
>
> Again, to discover common elements among competing creeds long study of them is necessary, and if possible practical experience of their working in the countries where they command assent. I do not envy a teacher who believes in the value of religious training being compelled by State regulation to extract these common elements at second-hand from books of reference, and then present them to a class of 13-year-olds, implying that they are all of them equally valuable and that they must make their own choice. Children of that age have a right to look to their teacher for guidance; and he, if he has any faith at all, will be eager to give it. If he has no faith, he should not be called upon to teach religion.
>
> There is everything to be said for the conscientious study of comparative religion at a later stage, and it does in fact form part of many sixth form courses ... But no religious teacher worth the name would encourage his pupils to regard other faiths with intolerance or contempt. If he is a Christian, he must believe that his faith is the truth of God; but he must equally certainly hold that wherever there is honest thinking and right action, there the Holy Spirit is working.[48]

With much of this Spalding would have agreed in principle. A broader approach to religious education in schools was a matter of importance to him. But who was to take up the challenge? Who was to widen the curriculum? Who was to question the established practice, so familiar to members of his own generation and not unknown in his later years, of equating terms such as Religious Instruction, Divinity, Scripture, with a presentation in schools of the beliefs and practices of Christianity? Was this an appropriate task for State schools? Did not such attempts amount to indoctrination? Leeson had given his Bampton lectures in Oxford in 1944, the year in which the forward-looking Education Act, associated with the name R. A. Butler, appeared on the statute book. Butler was Minister of Education from 1941 to 1945 in the National Coalition government, which served Britain during the Second World War. The Act re-organised secondary school education and introduced the 11-plus examination for selection to the grammar schools. It also set important guide-lines for the provision of religious education in County and Voluntary schools. These parts of the Act were to become so important, so widely discussed, and ultimately so fiercely challenged, that is useful to quote them.

Section 25

(1) Subject to the provisions of this section, the school day in every county school and in every voluntary school shall begin with collective worship on the part of all pupils in attendance at the school, and the arrangements made therefore shall provide for a single act of worship attended by all such pupils unless, in the opinion of the local education authority or, in the case of a voluntary school, of the managers or governors thereof, the school premises are such as to make it impracticable to assemble them for that purpose.

(2) Subject to the provisions of this section, religious instruction shall he given in every county school and in every voluntary school.

(3) It shall not be required, as a condition of any pupil attending any county school or any voluntary school, that he shall attend or abstain from attending any Sunday school or any place of religious worship.

(4) If the parent of any pupil in attendance at any county school or any voluntary school requests that he be wholly or partly excused from attendance at religious worship in the school, or from attendance at religious instruction in the school, or from attendance at both religious worship and religious instruction in the school, then, until the request is withdrawn, the pupil shall be excused from such attendance accordingly ...

Section 26

Subject as hereinafter provided, the collective worship required by subsection (1) of the last foregoing section shall not, in any county school, be distinctive of any particular religious denomination, and the religious instruction given to any pupils in attendance at a county school in conformity with the requirements of subsection (2) of the said section shall be given in accordance with an agreed syllabus adopted for the school or for those pupils and shall not include any catechism or formulary which is distinctive of any particular religious denomination.

The importance of religious education was thus recognised, and the position of the 'subject' in the curriculum ensured. Within a short period of time, however, the unique status of religious education as the only school subject to be made compulsory began to be questioned. An approach to religious education, which focused almost exclusively on Christianity, became more controversial after the end of the Second World War, when immigration to this country increased the numbers of adherents of other faiths. The situation was further complicated by the rising secularism in a country that was now being described as 'post-Christian'. If religious education was to survive it would have to be re-designed in order to meet the needs of a pluralist society. The changes were not long in coming. In the 1960s moves to broaden the content of religious education in schools and to redefine its aims and objectives were being made. Perhaps the most far-reaching of the changes now being advocated was that which called for the inclusion of *teaching about* religions other than Christianity.

The phrase 'teaching about' is important because it reflects a growing insistence that State schools are not places in which religion ought to be *taught*. Religious beliefs and practices may legitimately be *described* but not *taught* in a confessional way that may be appropriate in a synagogue, a church, a mosque, or a rationalist ethical society. A more important place in the school curriculum for a descriptive, phenomenological, approach to the great religions (not excluding Christianity) was thus envisaged and designed. This was a development for which Spalding had argued, but he did not live to see the formal introduction of world religions as an integral element of 'the new religious education'. Among the most prominent advocates of this change were the members of the *Shap Working Party on World Religions in Education*, led by Professor Ninian Smart of the University of Lancaster and Professor Geoffrey Parrinder of King's College, London. 'Shap', as it is popularly known, combined theory with practice (as it continues to do), offering teachers and educational administrators practical help in the planning of syllabuses and the preparation of materials about different religions, suitable for use in schools.

Henderson welcomed the new developments and for several years was a member of the Shap Working Party, so called because the early group of enthusiasts first met for discussion at the Shap Wells Hotel, in a remote part of Westmorland (now in Cumbria), near the village of Shap. His enthusiasm waned somewhat with the onset of age, when he noted that the emphasis of the innovators did not appear to be the same as he and Spalding had expected. He felt, probably mistakenly, that in what was becoming known as the New Religious Education, the approach to world religions was too studiously descriptive. There appeared to be little room for encouraging an awareness of the Divine Vision that is our common spiritual heritage, and no place for encouraging the search for Truth. He thought that the approach to religious studies (and, hence, 'to the teaching of religion in schools', as he still preferred to call it) was becoming too reductionist, too self-consciously 'neutral', and sadly, too superficial. He no doubt misunderstood what the innovators were attempting to do, but he feared that religion and religions might be trivialised in the process. He also feared that, by simply presenting facts about different religions to immature minds in a way that could hardly be other than selective, the unfortunate result might be an induction into agnosticism—unintended, perhaps—about the worth, not to speak of the truth, of *any* religion. The irony of an approach to religious education, which might well result in the rejection of a personal commitment to any form of religious belief, was not lost on him. Although he made his personal reservations known, however, he commended the Shap initiative in such a way that the Spalding Trustees were able to support it for several years with an annual grant. HN can not be said to have appreciated the problem of *preparing* teachers to deal effectively with religious education in schools. In Henderson's time the problem was becoming acute, and he did understand what was needed. In his twilight years, however, he was obliged to concede that the educational renaissance for which he and Spalding had laboured in their different ways was not about to occur. In education there were other priorities of a less than spiritual kind. To the claims of religion and religions there was growing indifference and apathy rather than real curiosity and sustained interest. The comparative study of world religions seemed to him to be increasingly remote from the needs of most people. Despite the efforts of enthusiastic teachers to ensure that this did not happen, he felt that the 'subject' was not being taught in a sufficiently imaginative way. Furthermore, there seemed to be little evidence to show that religious belief and moral action were being significantly improved by the teaching of a subject that still had to fight for survival in the curriculum. Old age and infirmity did not extinguish his idealism, although towards the end he was clearly tired of life. The gleam in his eyes and the sound of his laughter still evoked the love and enthusiasm of family and friends. His death in 1988 marked the end of the partnership in the service of Spalding's ideal, but it did not mark the end of the work with which both men had been so intimately involved.

Notes and References

1. CEW, pp. 293ff.
2. H. N. Spalding, 1958, *The Divine Universe or the Many and the One: A Study of Religions and Religion*, Basil Blackwell, Oxford, Prologue, pp. 10–11. The book was published posthumously.
3. HNS, TDU, *op. cit.*, p. 11.
4. Isidore Epstein, 1959, *Judaism: A Historical Presentation*, Penguin Books, p. 217.
5. *1 Peter* 3.15. For the word translated here as 'reason', the Greek text has ἀπολογία, 'a reasoned (and reasoning) defence'.
6. Obituary notice of HN in *The Brazen Nose, A College Magazine*, Oxford, 1954, pp. 342–3.
7. The point is one of historical interest. See Appendix 1, Directions to Trustees.
8. Letter to Dr Carmen Blacker, 26 October 1967, HFP file F2/6.
9. NUSGR, number 32, Summer 1975, p. 14. The reference in the last line is to the English poet and Anglican priest, George Herbert (1593–1633), who spent his last years serving the parish of Bemerton in Wiltshire, not far from Henderson's house in Steeple Langford. Herbert's poem 'Love' (III) ends with the lines: 'You must sit down', says Love, 'and taste my meat'/So I did sit and eat.
10. This extract from Robert Speaight's article 'Liturgy and Language' appeared in NUSGR number 30, Summer, 1973, p. 5.
11. See above, page 10, for the lines of Spalding's sonnet that contains the words quoted here.
12. A comment of Spalding, recalled by Henderson, NUSGR, number 26, Summer 1969, p. 6.
13. K. D. D. Henderson, 1976, 'Is Religion Necessary?', *Occasional Papers 1976–1986*, edited by Edward Hulmes, Farmington, Oxford, p. 11.
14. Huston Smith, 1958, *The Religions of Man*, Mentor Books, The New American Library, New York, p. 20. The last sentence in this quotation is from the *Katha Upanishad*, 1, iii, 14.
15. Kathleen Bliss, 1969, *The Future of Religion*, The New Thinker's Library, C. A. Watts & Co. Ltd, London, p. 2.
16. See W. Cantwell Smith, 1964, *The Meaning and End of Religion*, New York.
17. John Hick, 'Towards a Global Theology', in *Theology*, September 1970.
18. Huston Smith, *op. cit.*, 1958, p. 19.
19. Martin Buber, 1961, *Between Man and Man*, translated by R. Gregor Smith, Collins Fontana Books, p. 24.
20. The incident in Henderson's life, which convinced him that missionary efforts to convert Muslims to Christianity were not always well-advised, was recalled by his son David during K.D.D.H.'s funeral service in All Saints' Church, Steeple Langford, Wiltshire, on Wednesday, 30 March 1988. See below, page 168.
21. See Appendix 2.
22. Sir Sarvepalli Radhakrishnan, 1958, in his foreword to Spalding's TDU, *op. cit.*, p. vii.
23. See page 28.
24. Martin Corner, 1995, in his Introduction to *The Works of Matthew Arnold*, Wordsworth Poetry Library, p. v.
25. Matthew Arnold, *The Buried Life*, lines 45–54, first published in 1852.
26. Professor Robert Slater of Harvard University.
27. Professor W. E. Hocking of Harvard University.
28. Sir Richard Livingstone died a few months before on 26 December 1960. He served as

Chairman of the Union for the Study of the Great Religions from 1953. In tribute, Henderson wrote, 'What strikes us is the power of a liberal education to make England's greatest and most distinguished classicist work for the extension of the western classical tradition, [and] to embrace the cultural heritage of India and China'. NUSGR, number 14, February 1961, p. 1.

29. NUSGR, number 15, October 1961, p. 7.

30. Spalding wrote many poems, mostly sonnets, for which he claimed no special merit. They were not, as he put it, 'for the fashion of these times'. As for criticism, he added in Greek, 'the author doesn't care!

31. H. N. Spalding, TDU, pp. 1–2.

32. The Trust encouraged the work of providing such translations by supporting the commissioning and publication of *Ethical and Religious Classics*, published by George Allen & Unwin.

33. From a leaflet about the USGR drafted in June 1954, by the General Secretary, KDDH, pp. 1–2.

34. HNS, 1939, CEW, p. 190.

35. *Ibid*, pp. 232–54.

36. HNS, IPL (1952), p. 88. In a letter (dated 28 April 2001) to the present author by JMKS, Spalding's son, there is the following note: 'HN wrote and published anonymously *Russia in Resurrection*. I do not have a copy, but it was published while we lived at Shotover Cleve, probably about 1926–30. It had no index because it was published in a hurry for some reason which I forget'. In this case JMKS was probably correct to attribute the omission of an index to the need for hasty publication, but this can not be said of his father's other published works. None of Spalding's major publications contains an index. In his review of *Civilization in East and West* G. Stanley Whitby suggested a different reason for the omission: 'An index is desirable, although with such a wealth of scholarship to be catalogued one can forgive a compiler for shrinking from the task'. The review of CEW was published in the American journal *Ethics*. HN typed the review (undated) from a handwritten transcript sent from Oriel College, Oxford, on 15 March 1941 by Jim Kincade. HN pasted his typescript into a copy of CEW that is now in my possession. On the last page of the same copy of the book HN wrote the three words 'Add an Index'. He never did.

37. The Russian text of this 'Prayer' (*Molitva*), written in 1962 by Aleksandr Isayevich Solzhenitsyn, was sent to me, typed on an old fashioned machine, from his home in exile in Vermont in 1981. Here I have included my English version of the Russian text.

38. Published by Weidenfeld & Nicolson in 1961.

39. The lectureship was originally called *The Spalding Lectureship in Eastern Orthodox Culture*. It was subsequently renamed *The Spalding Lectureship in Eastern Orthodox Studies*, after it was felt that the word *Culture* in the original wording was too ambiguous.

40. HNS, IPL, p. 7.

41. HNS, IPL, p. 31.

42. HNS, IPL, pp. viii–ix.

43. Dr Blacker's comment was made in her Charles Strong Memorial Lecture in Melbourne, Australia, in July 1968.

44. The charge against Spalding, the founder of the Chair to which Zaehner had just been elected, was made in the new Professor's inaugural lecture, 'Foolishness to the Greeks', to an audience which included HN and his wife. Zaehner also used the occasion to make the same criticism of his predecessor, Sarvepalli Radhakrishnan. The ensuing hostility between HN and Zaehner, which arose not only as a result of Spalding's

objection to Zaehner's election but out of the latter's declaration of intent to change the emphasis of the work of the Chair, is considered in chapter four, pp. 114ff.

45. *Rig Veda*, 3.62.10.

46. The English versions of the Arabic original are those of A Yusuf Ali, in *The Holy Qur'an: Text, Translation and Commentary*, Dar al Arabia, Beirut, Lebanon, 1968.

47. *Ibid.*

48. Spencer Leeson, 1947, *Christian Education*, being eight lectures delivered before the University of Oxford, in the year 1944, on the foundation of The Rev. John Bampton, Canon of Salisbury, Longmans, Green & Co., London, p. 24.

CHAPTER THREE

'A Practical Dreamer
and a Poet'

In February 1954 K. D. D. Henderson, received an Airletter from Dr Nicolas
Zernov, requesting some biographical information about H. N. Spalding.
The letter also asked for a photograph of HN who, together with his wife,
had recently made a donation to the Catholicate College, Pathanamthitta,
Travancore, in South India. The gift was to be used to help finance the
development of the College library, which needed furniture as well as books.
Zernov was working at the College in a temporary capacity, on leave from
his lectureship at Oxford. He and his wife were about to return home. His
Indian hosts wanted the details quickly. HN, who died in the previous
September, was to be honoured in a ceremony during which a memorial
plaque was to be unveiled in the College library. The inscription on the
memorial plaque reads:

IN MEMORY OF

H.N. SPALDING, PHILOSOPHER,

POET AND BELIEVER,

WHO SOUGHT MAN'S WAY OF RETURN

TO GOD IN EAST AND WEST.

TO HIS INTEREST AND BENEFACTION

THE FOUNDATION OF THIS

LIBRARY IS DUE

A few days later, on 11 February, Henderson sent the following reply: 'Spalding,
Henry Norman, M.A. (Oxon.), Hon. D.C.L., Durham, F.R.S.L.; born at
Blackheath 15th August 1877. Educated in Switzerland and France, at Eastbourne College, New College, Oxford; Barrister-at-Law, Lincoln's Inn. Publications:- *From Youth to Age*, verse, 1930; *Poem of Praise*, 1950; *Civilization in
East and West*, 1939.' To this terse summary Henderson added, 'Would you like
a fuller biography by his brother?' [1] The grateful College authorities appeared
to be satisfied with what they already had. No further details were requested
and no photograph was sent. Zernov and his wife returned to Oxford. [2]

The account of H. N. Spalding's life and career given in this chapter is based on two primary sources. The first consists of the personal memories and the family records of his son, Dr John Spalding. On several occasions he agreed to talk to me about his father. These conversations were recorded by agreement and subsequently transcribed. In addition Dr Spalding sent me a document, extending to several closely typed pages, in which he supplied important biographical details of HN and his family, adding notes by way of comment and explanation. The second source is the written record of the thoughts, ideas, plans, and aspirations, left by HN himself. His written work, unpublished as well as published, reveals a great deal about his remarkable life. He conducted a voluminous correspondence with friends and acquaintances in many parts of the world. Few of these letters survive except those to be found in the papers of others who were caught up in the pursuit of some of the causes he espoused. His determination to get something done made him an importunate correspondent at times, whenever he felt that persistent advocacy was required. As often as not his letters were written in his own hand. At other times he needed secretarial help with the work he undertook from the house at number 9 South Parks Road.

Despite his public profile, his scholarly researches and the generous benefactions made jointly by him and his wife, comparatively little is known about his life, especially about his childhood. He was reluctant to talk about himself and diffident about his accomplishments. He was a private person who, whilst ready to engage in conversation and debate with others about the practical and theoretical issues that interested him most, seemed unwilling to share his thoughts and feelings even with the members of his own family. This is not to suggest that his relationships with those closest to him lacked warmth. It is to acknowledge that he lived at a time when it was less common than it is today for parents—fathers in particular—to spend much time with their children or to express their thoughts and emotions without inhibition. For parents who could afford it, the supervision of children passed in any case to others, in the home as well as at school.

Members of the Spalding family regard themselves as belonging (if only at some remove) to a minor Scottish clan. At one time they may have been connected with Spalding, a small English town in Lincolnshire. In 1318 a Spalding commanded the English garrison of Berwick-on-Tweed on the border between the two countries. He betrayed it to the Scots and afterwards found it wise to live north of the border. Ashintully Castle, little more than a country house 22 miles north of Perth, became his home. It is regularly visited by Spaldings from all over the world. By all accounts the Spaldings of those days were a rough lot even by the standards of the day, but they were good soldiers and sold their fighting skills abroad. One branch of the family went to Sweden. The records of the Swedish House of Lords

(*Riddarhus*) show that Spaldings were in Sweden for two generations before 1624. They prospered because their arms are still to be seen in the Riddarhus in Stockholm. Other members of the family went to North America, but there is no evidence to suggest that they went as soldiers, either to assist those who were fighting for their independence from British rule, or in the service of the forces trying to prevent their defection in the name of the King. Whatever the case may be, HN laid no claim to an American connection.[3]

Henry Norman Spalding was born at Lennox House in Blackheath, in south-east London, on 15 August, 1877, the eldest of the four children borne by Henry Benjamin's second wife, Ellen Rebe Spalding. There are no clear details about his early life. He spoke little about his childhood or his father, but he was devoted to his mother throughout her life.[4] His brother, Kenneth Jay Spalding, was born two years later on 17 March 1879. His sister Selma Nellie was born on 27 November 1880. Eva Ruth followed on 20 December 1882. HN was brought up by his parents as a Protestant Christian in the Presbyterian Church. In later life he was nominally a member of the Church of England, but he was rarely to be seen in a church, except on special occasions such as weddings or funerals. His father, Henry Benjamin Spalding, an elder in the Presbyterian Church, was born on 11 December, 1817 and died on 1 January 1908. Henry Benjamin had nine children by his first wife, Ann Seger (née King). She was born on 10 April 1816 and died on 11 July, 1874. His second wife was Ellen Rebe (pronounced Reebee), *née* Jay, who was born on 26 January, 1848 and died on 6 March 1938. She was 30 years younger than her husband. She and Henry Benjamin were married in Lewisham Congregational church on 7 September 1876. They lived successively at Hartham Cottage, 31 Campden Road Villas, and 3 Montague Place, all in Kentish Town, London. They moved to Lennox House, Manor Way, Blackheath, and then to Sunny Bank, Milnthorpe in Eastbourne. He is buried in Ocklynge Cemetery, Eastbourne. As a widow, Ellen Rebe lived with her daughter Selma, who had married Sir Thomas Lennard, the shoe manufacturer. They lived together for a time in a house overlooking the entrance to Dartmouth harbour and then at Medland Manor near Cheriton Bishop on Dartmoor. Ellen Rebe is buried in Cheriton Bishop churchyard.

Spalding and Hodge

The Spalding family's assets were invested originally in the firm of *Spalding and Hodge*, which had been founded by HN's grandfather in 1797. The founder of *Spalding and Hodge* had ten children, of whom HN's father, the afore-mentioned Henry Benjamin Spalding, was the youngest. Some of his descendants have been known to describe him as a man who ran a paper shop in London. The understatement is tongue in cheek and rather English.

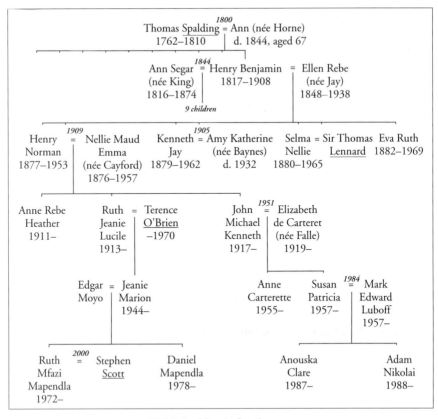

H. N. Spalding's family tree.

It is true, but misleading. It is true that Henry Benjamin did start his business in a modest way, quite probably by opening a newspaper shop, or its equivalent in those days, but he soon saw a niche in the market for making and selling paper, which he exploited successfully. The 'papers' that began to be sold were produced principally for the publication of books. The works of Thackeray were originally published on paper provided by the firm, and works of Dickens were also among the notable titles to be printed on S & H paper. Established in the closing years of the eighteenth century, the partnership of *Spalding and Hodge* supplied paper for discerning customers from premises in The Strand, London. The business prospered. In due course it was removed to Drury Lane. The business did not remain successful, however. For want of careful supervision and management the business went into decline. It was unfortunate, perhaps, that HN's father was not more closely involved in the day-to-day running of the company. That was left to a relative, who possessed less business acumen than the family would have cared to see in him. The result was that the finances of *Spalding and Hodge* fell to an alarming level.

School and University

At this time HN, already living with his family in Eastbourne, was a boy at Eastbourne College, but as funds ran low, he and the other members of his family were obliged to move to Switzerland where living, strange as it may seem today, was cheaper than at home. He managed to learn a useful amount of French whilst there, but spoke the language with a marked English accent. The brief note from Henderson to Zernov quoted at the beginning of this chapter might be taken to suggest that Spalding's education 'in Switzerland and France' was grander that it was in fact. HN's days on the continent were spent there of necessity rather than by choice. The family soon returned to Eastbourne. HN resumed his education at Eastbourne College. He stayed there without leaving much of a mark, either academically or in sport. It seems that he enjoyed his time at school without being enthusiastic about it. In 1898 he went up to New College, Oxford, to read *Greats*, in Oxford's demanding and prestigious school of the Classics. In later life he frequently observed that his studies at Oxford opened up a completely new world to him. In the Classics he found a lasting source of inspiration. Philosophy, ancient and modern, fascinated him and furnished him with a life-long source of intellectual delight. The subjects also helped to refine his capacity for careful reasoning. It seems, however, that when it came to science he had a blind spot. His son, who followed a distinguished career in medicine, states that HN had no interest in science, and that his father's inability, or unwillingness, to appreciate the value of scientific inquiry became something of a barrier between them.

Work in London

On leaving Oxford in 1901, HN went to work at the Admiralty in London. His responsibilities, modest enough at the time, seem to have been chiefly on the financial side. He did not find the work of a junior Civil Servant especially congenial, but he applied himself and was chosen to be private secretary to Sir Gordon Miller, Accountant-General of the Navy. When he subsequently became clerk to the Naval Income Tax Commissioners, his main achievement was to simplify some of the complicated Income Tax regulations. He resigned from the Admiralty in 1909, the year of his marriage. The British Navy was rather grander than the Admiralty that served it in those days. HN's son, Dr John Spalding, still has an umbrella used by his father during that period. It bears the inscription '*Spalding, Admiralty*'. That was apparently sufficient to ensure that if lost and found the umbrella could be safely returned to its rightful owner. It is more likely that the brief inscription is evidence of the relatively small size of the Admiralty than of

the seniority of the umbrella's owner. In 1906 HN was called to the Bar but
he never practised. There were two General Elections in 1910. The first
campaign lasted from 14 January to 9 February. The second campaign lasted
from 2–19 December. In the former he fought the East Grinstead constituency
as the Liberal candidate, but failed to win the seat. His decision to involve
himself in political affairs under the banner of the Liberal Party scandalised
some of his neighbours. He and his wife were ostracised by some of their
former friends and acquaintances, who could not see why a man of his talents
and distinction should identify himself with the Liberals and challenge the
Conservatives. Two reasons may be given for his failure to be elected. The
first is that he chose to contest a safe seat held by a Conservative. The second
reason has more to do with HN's personality and temperament than with
his political acumen. He was too open and straightforward for the intrigues
of political life.

Some time later he was persuaded to stand for Parliament again, this time
at Reading. He was chosen to fight the seat in succession to the sitting Liberal
member for the constituency, Sir Rufus Isaacs, who had been appointed Lord
Chief Justice in 1913. Isaacs was later to be Viceroy of India and 1st Marquess
of Reading.[5] At this point there is confusion about what happened to HN's
candidacy. Members of the Spalding family believe that he stood for Parliament again and was defeated for a second time. The chronology of events
places this in some doubt, however. Sir Rufus Isaacs did not become Lord
Chief Justice until 1913, but there were no further Parliamentary elections
until 1918. HN's obituary in *The Times* (17 September 1953) reads in part:

> [HN] was invited to stand in the Liberal interest in succession to Sir
> Rufus Isaacs when he became Lord Chief Justice, but his candidature
> never became effective because of the outbreak of war, which took
> Spalding back to the Admiralty and then to the Ministry of Munitions,
> where he was deputy director of the welfare department.

The Reading constituency was chosen quite probably because Mrs Spalding
owned two small houses, 'The Holt' and 'Meads', on the river above Marsh
Lock at Henley. The houses were given to her by her father. They were
usually let, but 'The Holt' had an annual break when it was lent to the crew
of Brasenose College for Henley week. One year the BNC crew failed to
qualify, so the house was lent to the crew from Magdalen College, Oxford.
As a token of their appreciation, the members of the Magdalen crew gave
HN some decanters, which are still in Dr John Spalding's possession.

The world of ideas was to occupy him henceforward. Before leaving
Reading, however, he was to give lectures for the Workers' Educational
Association.[6] When his daughter Ruth was born in 1913 the members of his
audience presented her with a silver spoon inscribed with the subject of HN's

lectures, 'From Wages and Hours'. He returned to the Civil Service in 1915, serving once more in the Admiralty and then in the Ministry of Munitions under Lloyd George, who was appointed Minister of Munitions in the same year. As Deputy Director of the Welfare Department HN helped Seebohm Rowntree to organise a welfare service for women working in the nation's munitions factories.

The Spaldings were living at 109 St George's Square, Westminster, an easy walk up the Thames from the Houses of Parliament. They also had a home at Tivoli (now the Hotel Buena Vista) in Lyme Regis, a delightful small town on the south coast of Dorset. It was the First World War, however, which put an end to his political ambitions. He had twice tried to enlist in the Army but was turned down on both occasions because of poor eyesight. Professor A. J. Arberry, who met Spalding for the first time in 1928 at Parson's Pleasure in Oxford, wrote: 'After the end of the first war [Spalding] returned to live in Oxford, and began that long series of munificent benefactions to good causes with which his name will always be associated.' [7] Financial security had made it possible for HN and his wife to devote themselves more and more to charitable causes.

Marriage

Spalding met his future wife, Nellie Maud Emma Cayford, in Eastbourne. She was born in the year before him, on 16 January, 1876. In her youth she lived with her family in Hampstead and attended Hampstead High School. Her younger brother, Alfred, was said to be 'backward' following a fall from a horse, although his disability may date from before that accident. He was more probably a spastic child. He died in 1930. Her mother, Emma Cayford (née Puddefoot), was seriously disabled for several years before she died on 14 November 1904. Nellie Maud Emma was obliged to leave school at the age of 14, probably in 1890, in order to run the family home, which from about that time was at Huntsland, Crawley Down, near East Grinstead in West Sussex, some 30 miles away from Eastbourne. Her father, Ebenezer Cayford, travelled to work in the city of London by train on the Brighton line from Crawley. Among the responsibilities she undertook was that of accompanying her father on some of his overseas business trips. She escorted him several times to Hamburg and once to Tenerife. As a result of these dislocations she would have described her education as inadequate. Her son John says that when he was small he did not notice this, but he does remember that his mother was a little overwhelmed at the time by HN's 'intellectual friends'. Like many others of her generation, especially women, she educated herself, overcame her diffidence, and in her case also acquired what her son calls a knowledge of biology and medicine superior to that of her husband.

From the family home at Huntsland she made frequent visits to Eastbourne, where she met HN. After that first meeting it was not long before they decided to be married.

Her financial resources were eventually to come from the investments made by her father in the various shipping companies with which he had been involved. These companies conducted a lucrative trade with South America, chiefly with the Argentine. They also developed commercial interests further afield. One such development was linked to the phosphate trade in the Pacific. The couple were keen to marry as soon as possible, but Miss Cayford's father, Ebenezer, refused to give his consent, considering that HN lacked experience, had not had time to prove himself, and lacked the ability to manage the inheritance that he would share when married. The father was concerned about what might happen to the settlement he intended to make on his daughter. As he lay dying after a prostatectomy, he told her 'I expect you will marry that young man'. Whatever his motives or intentions, the death-bed conversion was taken to be a real, if reluctant, approval of the union. The couple did not want to delay the wedding. HN was 32 years old. Nellie Maud Emma was 33. They decided to marry abroad. As a matter of course she took with her as chaperone a lady friend whom she had known since childhood. It would have been insensitive to have arranged a big wedding so soon after the death of the bride's father, so the marriage took place quietly and without publicity in Florence on 21 October 1909. The honeymoon was spent in Italy.

After their marriage the couple lived in the bride's family home, Huntsland, a medium sized, comfortable looking, house set in rural surroundings and with a pleasant garden. It was from here that he fought unsuccessfully his campaign for a seat in the House of Commons for the Liberal Party in the General Election of 1910. From Huntsland he and his wife moved to a flat in London close to Grosvenor Square. HN described it as 'snooty'. The house at 109 St George's Square, London W1 was purchased in 1913. HN lived at this address whilst working in London during the First World War. For most of the time his young family was sent to live in Lyme Regis 'to get away from the bombs' that were dropped infrequently by the few comparatively small German Zeppelins. To complete the sequence of family moves, mention should be made of Tivoli (now the hotel Buena Vista) in Lyme Regis, Dorset; Shotover Cleve, The Ridings, Headington, Oxford; and 9 South Parks Road. Dr John Spalding states that the house in South Parks Road was 'destroyed' after his mother's death in 1938, 'to make a University laboratory'.

The new Mrs Spalding's father, Ebenezer Cayford, had not always enjoyed affluence. He was born in Somerset, not far from Frome, where his family were farmers. In his youth there was much uncertainty about the future of farming after a decline in the agricultural industry in this country. As a result he decided to seek his fortune in London. To begin with he, too, started to sell papers. He sold them on the street. He then applied for a job in a shipping firm. He failed to get the post, which was offered to another youth, J. T. Arundel. For some reason Ebenezer omitted to give his home address to the company, but he happened to see a further advertisement in which he was asked to get in touch with the company again. This he did, joining Arundel in a career that was to take him to the boardroom. Near the end of his life Arundel was one of Dr John Spalding's two god-fathers.

Shipping and Trade

The shipping companies with which Ebenezer was associated were the Houlder Line, Houlder Bros., and Furness Withy.[8] Diligent and ready to learn, he began to make progress. His promotion to the boardroom was steady. The companies in which he had interests were engaged in trade with the Argentine. Among the goods imported to this country were large tonnages of beef. These commercial interests extended into the Pacific region. There was an office in Sydney, Australia, run by Mr Arundel. The companies also traded in coconuts imported from a number of islands in the Pacific. A lucrative business opportunity came in an unexpected way after a piece of rock was picked up on an island in the Pacific. The rock was brought to the office in Sydney and used as a door-stop in one of the rooms until a sharp-eyed employee, a young chemist by training, spotted its potential, had it analysed, and then revealed that it contained phosphate. This led to the discovery of large amounts of phosphate in the mineral deposits on Nauru and Ocean Islands. In various forms the chemical is used as a fertiliser. Ebenezer's shares in the companies that started to exploit these deposits began to rise in value. He died a comparatively wealthy man, leaving his daughter in a relatively sound financial position, although it was not immediately clear how large his estate was. His director's fees ceased on his death. His daughter and a few female companions went away to a cottage in Scotland while his affairs were sorted out. Investigations confirmed that she was going to be comfortably well off, but the money she inherited still had to be managed responsibly. It was HN who assumed this responsibility. He made the financial decisions, but always regarded himself as a trustee of his wife's money, and never committed himself to any substantial project without her prior agreement. The investments were prudently made. Mrs Spalding retained her shares in a phosphate company and in Houlder Bros. The returns on capital proved to be satisfactory. His father-in-law need not have doubted either his business acumen or his financial probity.

Family and Friends

The Spalding's first child was still-born at Huntsland, Crawley Down. The doctor involved in the delivery is reported to have wept because he had not managed the birth adequately. The three other children were born in London, at St George's Square, under the care of an obstetrician. The eldest, Anne Rebe Heather was born on 18 November 1911. Ruth Jeanie Lucile was born on 30 November 1913. John Michael Kenneth—the future Chairman of the Spalding Trust—was born on 18 September 1917. The three young children were taught reading, writing and arithmetic by their Norland nurse, Lydia Dawson. She also taught them swimming and took them on country walks. Anne also went to a Mr Harding, a retired teacher, for more tuition, including Latin. John remembers life in St George's Square—bowling hoops in the Square's gardens, hearing the tugs hooting on the river Thames in fog, and throwing Sunday's sausage skins to the seagulls—but most of the time was spent by the family at Lyme Regis.

Anne became an artist. She trained at the Ruskin School of Drawing, now the Ruskin School of Art. It was then in the west wing of the Ashmolean Museum in Oxford, which now houses the museum shop. The School of Art is now in the High Street, between the entrance to Merton Street and the Examination Schools. She was taught by Barnett Freedman, who became a life-long friend. Albert Rutherstone and Gilbert Spencer were among her teachers. Her friends included Richard Naish, later to become head of the Ruskin School. He and his wife Martha went to live in Lewknor and encouraged Anne to live there too. Anne painted mainly in oils, sometimes in water-colours. She also made woodcuts and lithographs, at first in a studio in St Giles, Oxford and then in flats in Notting Hill and in Kent before she bought her house in Lewknor. She did not marry. Ruth took a degree in politics, philosophy and economics (PPE) at Somerville College, Oxford. Already keen on amateur dramatics, she became an actress and a producer of plays. She also enjoyed success as an author under her maiden name. She wrote *The Improbable Puritan: A Life of Bulstrode Whitlocke 1605–1675*, which was published by Faber & Faber in 1975. This biography was awarded a Whitbread Prize in the same year. She also edited *The Diary of Bulstrode Whitlocke 1605–1675*, published by Oxford University Press for the British Academy in 1991. John, as recounted in the Preface, became a distinguished neurologist in Oxford.

Whilst still living in London, Mrs Spalding invited to tea a Russian refugee, Madame Narishkin, who lived nearby. Madame Narishkin declined to remove her coat, even though the weather was warm. The coat was worn to conceal the fact that her wardrobe was otherwise somewhat inadequate. The Spaldings discreetly offered financial assistance. The friendship between the Spaldings and the Narishkins was to last. The Spaldings began to help other Russian refugee families as well. For HN such encounters helped to stimulate a developing interest in Russian culture, art, and religion. In 1923 the London house was sold. The family then lived entirely at Lyme Regis, where the children were very happy, and (as John put it) 'were taught the rudiments by a wise and loving nanny'. This was the year in which the financial independence enjoyed by the Spaldings enabled them to establish the first Spalding Trust. This was followed in 1928 by the creation of a second Trust with similar aims to the first.[9] The chief effect of the second foundation was to add to the funds that were available to the 1923 Trust. Both Trusts were described as Education Trusts, but the resources could be used without restriction for any charitable purpose. Apart from gifts to the University of Oxford, the Spaldings befriended and assisted many others. During the First World War these included refugees from Belgium. Indigent relatives of Mrs Spalding were also helped from time to time.

A Critical Influence

In 1914 HN was in his middle thirties. Though spared from military service on medical grounds, he was profoundly affected by the grievous losses suffered by so many of his contemporaries in the armed conflict of the First World War. During World War I he read the casualty lists that were published daily, recording the deaths of thousands of men not much younger than himself. They included friends, former colleagues and associates. The suffering inflicted by human beings on others in that conflict was a critical influence— perhaps the most crucial influence—on his development. It is difficult for anyone born after the end of World War II to imagine the scale of the horror of such conflict. A single example, one of far too many that could be cited, conveys something of the destruction of human life at that time. On the first day of the Battle of the Somme, 1 July 1916, British casualties rose to 60,000. Over the four months of the battle on French soil, the British lost 410,000 men, the German losses amounted to 500,000, and the French lost 190,000. HN could only note what was happening from afar. As the war dragged on and the casualty lists lengthened, he began to wear a black tie in honour of those who had fallen. He continued to wear this symbol of mourning each day for the rest of his life.

In July 2001 a service of commemoration was held at Lutyen's memorial to the Missing at Thiepval, a village close to the then German lines, on the 85th anniversary of that first day of the Battle of the Somme. The names on the memorial appear 'like footnotes on the sky', in the phrase of Sebastian Faulks, who attended the service.[10] The names were certainly that and more to HN, who was prevented by poor eyesight from serving in the Army. The conflict increased his desire to do everything he could to promote world peace. During and after the war he was a keen supporter of the League of Nations Union, serving on the League's Executive Committee in London.[11] The Second World War merely confirmed what he already knew about human frailty. He remained an optimist about the future, although he did not believe that human progress is inevitable. Progress, in his view, depended upon the recognition and the acceptance of truths that were in danger of being forgotten, or at least temporarily overlooked. These truths, so he believed, lie waiting to be discovered (or re-discovered), if men and women can only be persuaded to locate their source. In his literary works he points consistently to that source of truth and spiritual insight. His thesis was that truth—universally applicable—is to be found, not necessarily in institutional religion, but in the accumulated wisdom of the world's great religious teachers.

Oxford, Brasenose College, and 'Shotover Cleve'

In 1925, when Anne Spalding, HN's eldest daughter, was 14 years old, she and her sister Ruth needed the kind of education that it was felt Lyme Regis could no longer provide. HN and his wife did not want them to go to boarding school, so the decision was made to move. They decided on Oxford and made plans to build a house there. They chose a site some three miles from Carfax in the centre of Oxford, on elevated ground on Shotover Hill. Oxford was chosen as the place to live for three main reasons. The first requirement was for good schools for the children. Oxford had those. The second reason was that HN had happy memories of his time as an undergraduate at New College. To be within easy distance of the academic community in Oxford was most desirable. The third reason for choosing Oxford was that his great friend 'Sonners' was a Fellow of Brasenose College. 'Sonners' was the nickname of William Teulon Swan Stallybrass (1883–1948), who had changed his surname from Sonnenschein during World War I. He was not a German, but anti-German prejudice in those days was quickly aroused at the sight and sound of a Teutonic-looking surname. So far from being German, Stallybrass is reputed to have tried to learn the German language several times but never with much success. HN, his wife Nellie, and Stallybrass, were the original Trustees of the 1923 and 1928 Spalding Educational Trusts.

Stallybrass later became Principal of Brasenose College and Vice-Chancellor of Oxford University, remaining throughout a good friend of the Spaldings. In 1919 HN became a member of the Senior Common Room at Brasenose and often dined in College after moving to Oxford. The friendship was increased when K. J. Spalding, HN's younger brother was elected to a Senior Research Fellowship in Philosophy at the College. Stallybrass helped to arrange

'Shotover Cleve', the Spaldings' new house, built in 1925 at Oxford.
The photograph was taken by W. T. S. Stallybrass in 1929.

for KJ's appointment at Brasenose College in 1928. Whilst still a bachelor in London, HN had been a member of the *Thames Hare and Hounds Running Club*.[12] So was Stallybrass. Both men worked at the Ministry of Munitions during the First World War. 'Sonners' was awarded an O.B.E. for his work during that period. Neither at that time nor in the years that followed were Spalding's achievements recognised by the award of a civic honour. It was when 'Sonners' was working in the Ministry that he decided to follow his father and adopt the surname of his paternal grandmother as his own. The name 'Sonnenschein' was too problematic to live with at a time when Britain was at war with Germany. The lifelong friendship between Spalding and Stallybrass had begun some years earlier, however. A recently discovered collection of photographs taken by Stallybrass includes pictures of HN and members of his family that were taken a few months before the outbreak of World War I. Some of them appear in this book.[13]

'Sonners' died tragically in 1948. He had been in London for a meeting of the University Grants Committee. After the meeting he dined at the Middle Temple and then left for Paddington station to catch the midnight train to Oxford. He was travelling alone. Somewhere near Iver in Buckinghamshire he fell from the train to his death. No-one witnessed the accident. His body was found on the track in the early hours of 28 October. Various theories were advanced to account for the accident. The most likely seems to be that being visually impaired, he mistook an external door of his compartment for the door to the corridor of the train, A cataract operation during the Second World War cost him the sight of one eye and left him with partial vision in the other. He had almost lost his life in the same way once before, but friends were with him on that occasion to save him. Despite his handicap he was able to administer the affairs of Brasenose College with exemplary efficiency.[14] HN, who counted him among his closest friends, felt the loss acutely.

Plans for the new family home near Oxford were drawn up in 1925. 'Shotover Cleve' was a substantial country house. After the Second World War it was large enough to be divided into five parts in order to accommodate family, friends and undergraduate students.[15] The skills of the carpenter, Mr Bing, proved to be invaluable at that time. The meaning of the name HN chose for the house is uncertain. It has been noted that of its three elements the first and the second may be translated 'steep', whilst the third may be a variant of 'cliff'. There were indeed slopes in plenty around the house. The architect was O. P. Milne, Dr John Spalding's second god-father. Disagreements between the client and the architect led to a permanent breach of friendship. Transport from Shotover Cleve to central Oxford was a little difficult. Neither HN nor his wife Nellie were drivers. The walk from the house to the nearest bus stop was almost a mile, and the bus-service was infrequent. Mrs Spalding needed to be able to visit the shops; HN had an increasing number of engagements in Oxford; many of which were of uncertain length; Anne and Ruth wanted to visit their school friends. The solution was a chauffeur-driven car, driven by the handyman, whose services the family already retained. The arrangement worked reasonably well until it became clear that the car was often needed by different members of the family at the same time. The decision was made to keep Shotover Cleve, but to move to a more convenient place nearer to the centre of Oxford. If necessary, Shotover Cleve could be let to tenants. One of the tenants in the 1930s was Kenneth Clark, later Lord Clark, who was then Keeper of Fine Arts at the Ashmolean Museum in Oxford. Later, he moved to the National Gallery in London. In his autobiography he is not enthusiastic about Shotover Cleve, but he did make some improvements during his tenancy.

Over the years many refugees were to visit Shotover Cleve. HN was involved in what was called Russian Eurasianism, the purpose of which was to enable aristocrats still in the Soviet Union to escape to the West. Colonel Malevsky-Malevitch was also involved, staying at the house for several months. Another Russian, who returned to the USSR to help in the planned escapes, disappeared. It was never established whether he had been captured or whether he had been planted by the Soviets as an agent. From the intelligence sources now becoming accessible since the collapse of the USSR, it appears that the man was an agent and that the efforts of the would-be helpers in the West were well known to the Soviet authorities. Spalding himself felt a little betrayed by the episode, so much so that his feelings for Shotover Cleve were never quite the same. Despite this, increasing contact with Russian refugees stimulated Spalding's interest in Russian culture and religion. His interest in Eastern Orthodoxy led him to wonder about other religions in the East, of which he then had little knowledge.

There is a long drive to Shotover Cleve, off which the Spaldings built a smaller but still substantial family house for the Narishkins that was at first known as 'Domic'. There was speculation about the choice of the name. The Russian diminutive *domik* means 'cabin'. The Narishkins were grateful to have been granted asylum in Britain but they had been accustomed to a grander lifestyle in pre-revolutionary St Petersburg. A Narishkin ancestor was the mother of Peter the Great. The *muzei-domik Petra I* ('the Cabin of Peter the Great', now a museum) stands on the Petrovskaya embankment in the northern part of the Russian city. Built in three days for Peter by his soldier-carpenters in 1703, the two-roomed cabin is a reminder of his simple life-style during the six years he lived there whilst supervising construction work in St Petersburg. The Narishkins may have had this in mind when they called their new dwelling 'Domic'. They had two sons. The elder was called Vadim. He was of the same age as John Spalding. Their daughter, Moira, was a little younger. The second son was Theodore, known in the family as 'B' (for Baby). These children were among the young Spaldings' playmates. With the help of HN and his wife, the Narishkins then moved from the house built for them at Shotover to a house in Old Headington, Oxford. The 'Cabin' was eventually re-named *The Orchard*. Captain Narishkin used his knowledge of art—almost universal among Russian aristocratic *émigrés*—to make or put together *objets d'art* for sale in Oxford. He dealt in small pictures and decorative boxes, selling them on to local shops. This brought in a modest income. Profitable deals were few and far between. His wife was an enthusiastic hostess but not a provident housekeeper. Their guests included Prince and Princess Galitzine (who had a shop on Hay Hill, Berkeley Square in London, a venture supported by the Spaldings), the Arapoffs, the harmonica virtuoso Larry Adler, and others, some of whom stayed or visited the Spaldings at Shotover Cleve next door.

Number 9 South Parks Road and Parson's Pleasure

In 1930 the Spalding family moved to number 9 South Parks Road, a house situated no more than a mile from the city centre The house stood on the site that now extends to accommodate part of the University of Oxford's Science Area. John Spalding recalls his disappointment when the family moved away from Shotover Cleve. At the time when the matter was being discussed he was a boarder at Summerfields Preparatory school in Summer-town near Oxford. He remembers being aware that he would miss the space and freedom of living in the country. It was a feeling that stayed with him when he went subsequently to Eton. The house in South Parks Road was the nearest but one to Parson's Pleasure, the headquarters of a curious Oxford institution with which HN was closely associated. Parson's Pleasure was the male nude bathing place on the river Cherwell, to which HN loved to resort for the company of congenial spirits.[16] 'The spectacle of a dozen [nude] young men, playing in a circle under the trees, gave one a charming idea of what an Athenian gymnasium must have looked like.'[17] HN had enjoyed the place as an undergraduate when at New College. As an Oxford resident he liked it no less and used it more. He particularly admired the view of the meadows, seen across the river Cherwell. At certain times of the year the meadow was a sea of green and yellow, covered in buttercups. Parson's Pleasure itself was a grassy area, surrounded by trees and protected from prying eyes by an opaque fence. Used no longer for the purposes of male nude bathing, it is now part of the University Parks, where a seat was placed with a plate dedicating it to the memory of HN. When the decision to make this gesture was taken, the Curator of the University Parks wrote to Dr John Spalding, asking which of the two spellings, Parson's Pleasure and Parsons' Pleasure (both spellings were in use), he preferred. How had the name arisen? Was there a Mr Parson who had once enjoyed the spot? No record of such an individual was ever found. Or did the plural form suggest that gentlemen in Holy Orders were especially fond of the place? No clear and authoritative answer about the origins of the name emerged.

The photograph of Parson's Pleasure on page 83 was taken in the mid-1930s. Behind the diving board there is a punt coming upstream from the rollers. It would have been dragged up the rollers from the lower Cherwell, because Parson's Pleasure was at the higher level needed to power the long-closed water-mill. The walk between the mill stream and the lower Cherwell was aptly named 'Mesopotamia'. A punt would have to be pulled up the rollers and taken through Parson's Pleasure by its male occupants. An attendant supervised the use of the rollers. It was his responsibility to ensure that those taking the boats downstream realised that although most of the rollers were over concrete, the lower ones had nothing beneath them but water. This fact was concealed by the shape of the punt from uninitiated boaters, who sometimes fell in as they continued to walk their boats through. If, excep-tionally, there were only ladies in a boat, the attendant would take the craft through the restricted area for them. At least one lady from St Hugh's College complained that the attendant demanded payment for his services. Just downstream from Parson's Pleasure a ladies' bathing place was built in the 1930s. It was known as Dames' Delight. At first, ladies appeared without

Bathers at Parson's Pleasure, Oxford, photographed in the mid-1930s.

costumes but the custom died out. The site was not well used and it fell into disrepair during the Second World War.

HN would often take a manuscript to Parson's Pleasure and work on it. He was extremely fond of the place. It was said that he spent every possible moment there. In the Summer he followed convention, appearing in the nude. In Winter he continued to work there, but prudently kept his clothes on. At Parson's Pleasure he met many men, often encouraging visitors to join in games designed to improve physique by means of strenuous exercises. These included games with a heavy medicine ball. Swimming, diving, and football were also popular among the denizens of this unique part of Oxford. On one occasion in the city a stranger asked HN's daughter Anne, 'Are you related to the King of Parson's Pleasure?' HN's love of that part of the city led to another of his benefactions to the University. It was in 1943 that he and his wife arranged for the purchase of 18¾ acres in 'Mesopotamia', opposite Parson's Pleasure, from Magdalen College and donated them to the University, to be kept as a permanent nature reserve in memory of Dr L. H. Dudley Buxton, a University official who was known to HN as a particular admirer of the place.

The house at number 9 South Parks Road became a centre of concentrated activity, Visitors came and went. HN always had a scheme on hand—sometimes more than one—to 'improve' the University of Oxford. Many of them came to nothing but his efforts did not go unappreciated. The Creweian Oration at the Oxford *Encaenia*, in which it is the custom for the University to thank benefactors and donors, often mentioned HN and his wife. In 1935 Spalding began to sound out opinion in Oxford about a new proposal that was forming in his mind. His idea was to establish a new Chair in the University and to finance it personally for a trial period at least. A year later the Spalding Chair in Eastern Religions and Ethics was established. Sarvepalli Radhakrishnan, eventually to become Vice-President and President of India, was invited to occupy it. In 1949 Congregation at Oxford approved a form of statute making the Chair permanent. 'Deep gratitude to the benefactors, Mr and Mrs H. N. Spalding, whose new gift of £42,000 has made this possible' was recorded.

He had a clear understanding about the kind of person who ought to be appointed to hold the Chair, and the kind of work that the occupant should undertake. In time the benefactor's prescriptive approach led to disagreements between him, the University, and one subsequent holder of the Professorship in particular. His dissatisfaction with what he considered to be a betrayal of trust led to his direction that 'no further benefactions are to be made to or in the University of Oxford until these abuses and their cause have been remedied'. This strained relationship was considered to be responsible, in part, for Spalding's death in 1953.[18] But there were successes before the war. These included K. J. Spalding's Senior Research Fellowship in Philosophy at Brasenose College, and Nicolas Zernov's Spalding Lectureship in Eastern Orthodox Culture.[19] He also established an Advisership in Eastern Art. HN never went to India, His friendship with Radhakrishnan brought him into contact with other Indians, with their thinking and their political aspirations, but he never went to India to see something of the sub-continent for himself. Some of his friends reckoned that he should have gone, and that if he had visited the sub-continent the experience might have altered what they took to be his somewhat selective and romantic opinions about Indian religion and culture.

Juvenal's aphorism *orandum est ut sit mens sana in corpore sano* comes to mind not only with regard to HN's own efforts to keep a healthy mind in a healthy body by means of regular physical exercise, but also with reference to his concern for the physical condition of undergraduates. A series of photographs taken by W. T. S. Stallybrass from 1909 onwards contains several showing HN and like-minded male companions swimming, reclining, or posing, in the sea, in a river, on the beach or in a meadow. The nude figures appear indistinctly on most of the prints, which are now almost 100 years old, but in some of them HN appears in sharply defined classical sculptural poses. The women and children who, needless to say, are never seen near the nude males, are shown, *au contraire*, in voluminous Edwardian dresses and hats.[20] During a lengthy stay in the United States from 1939 to 1945, which will be considered later, he was impressed by the sporting facilities made available to university students over there. He reflected on the lack of comparable facilities in Oxford, and determined to do something to change the situation. He was particularly impressed in America by the swimming pools. Oxford appeared to favour the idea, but whenever HN suggested a possible site for the building of a similar facility the University declared it to be unsuitable. No reasons were given at the time, although it became clear later that the University already had plans for the development of at least one suggested site, that of the Law library, for a different purpose.

HN's interest in outdoor pursuits encouraged him to support the Oxford University Exploration Society with an annual gift. The only restriction on his munificence was placed by a clause in the Trust deeds debarring Trustees from supporting 'training or research in economics, natural science, craftsmanship, or historical source, as provision has already to a large extent been made for these by others'. Throughout his time in Oxford Spalding kept in touch with undergraduates, and in particular with Rhodes scholars, who came from America, the British Commonwealth, and Germany. Writing in 1953, shortly after Spalding's death, someone identified only by his initials wrote:

> May I add to what you have already written of Mr H. N. Spalding that his generosity will be remembered by undergraduates of more than one Oxford college, and that his desire for the meeting of east and west was combined with a deep and wise concern for the fostering of Anglo-American friendship. Few generations of American Rhodes scholars have left Oxford since 1919 without taking with them memories of his stimulating talk and companionship. In later years H. N. had lived for a time in the United States and got to know several of the university communities of eastern America, and this helped him as he grew older to continue to establish friendships with new American students in Oxford.
>
> In this he was indefatigable and his sympathy with American life was trans-continental ... His superb memory, resilient mind, and buoyant hopefulness, made him always 'a good mixer', but there was much more to it than that. A little thing but worth recording is that he helped some of us to fulfil our vision of Oxford. In the overcrowded, sober, post-war years H. N. was our satisfying, visible link with Edwardian England. Of this I think he was probably unaware; just as, he was unaware that with all his cosmopolitan knowledge of our country, it was his generous, confidant Englishness which left the last impression.[21]

Spalding Benefactions

In 1937 HN established at Brasenose College two Senior Research Fellowships in Indian Studies One, in Indian folk music, was held by Dr Baké. The other, in Indian Humanism, was held by Dr Chakravarty. Neither of these foundations was to 'bear full fruit', as a consequence of the outbreak of the Second World War. HN was one of the founders of the Museum of Eastern Art in Oxford. In 1946 and 1947 the Spaldings contributed money to enable the University to purchase and send books, periodicals, and academic journals, to universities in Europe and Asia devastated by the war. In 1951 he and his wife gave to the recently founded National University of Australia in Canberra a silver stave. It is probable that Oxford University's Registrar, Sir Douglas Veale, Chairman of the Spalding Trust from 1950 to 1953, was influential in arranging for this particular gift to be made. In 1955 an ebony and silver mace was presented to University College Ibadan, Western Nigeria, by Mrs Spalding in memory of her husband. The Registrar of the College described it as 'a magnificent piece of work and a fitting symbol; for this young and growing institution'. The mace was designed by Ben Enwonwu and executed by him and Leslie Durbin.[22]

The University of Durham was to benefit on several occasions. In 1949 the Spaldings made it possible for Durham to purchase the Alnwick collection of Egyptian and Mesopotamian antiquities from the Duke of Northumberland. Professor T. W. Thacker, a Spalding Trustee from 1953 until his death in 1984, was closely associated with developments in the departments of Oriental and Middle Eastern Studies at Durham. He built up the School of Oriental Studies at Durham, from its modest beginnings in a house on South Road into an internationally respected academic department. He accomplished this through tireless efforts to promote the School's interests. In the process, he tended to neglect his own career, but he did not consider that this involved any personal sacrifice, because the whole of his working life was devoted to this one satisfying objective. It was he who represented the Union for the Study of the Great Religions in 1954–55, visiting American universities for discussions and negotiations that led to the foundation of the Center for the Study of World Religions at Harvard.

In 1952 HN and his wife enabled the University of Durham to acquire some 6,000 books concerned with the study of China.[23] Two Spalding lectureships in Oriental Studies were established at Durham, one in Indian Studies, the other in Chinese Studies.[24] The latter survives. In 1988 the Trust made an annual grant for three years in support of the Spalding Professorial Fellowship in Comparative Theology held by the present writer. The Gulbenkian Museum of Oriental Art and Archaeology was opened officially by the Earl of Scarbrough on 28 May 1960. It was built at Elvet Hill Durham by the Gulbenkian Trust to house the collections lent or presented by A. E. K. Hull, Malcolm Macdonald, Sir Victor Sassoon, Mrs E. Hedley, Mr and Mrs Loke of Singapore, and Sir Charles Hardinge's collection of jade and other stone carvings. The Alnwick collection, mentioned above, acquired by the University with the help of the Spaldings, was also housed in the Museum. The Selboe-Indic Collection was purchased from Norway with money donated by Mrs Spalding in 1954, and presented to Durham University. It consisted of 1,200 volumes, in Sanskrit and other Indian languages. The collection was made by Professor Swami Sri Ananda Acharya of Calcutta, an Indian monk and author. After his retirement he settled in Alvdal in Norway. His books passed to the Selboe family. In 1957 the Spalding Trust received an anonymous donation of $50,000 from an American benefactor for the purchase of books to fill the gaps in the Oriental library at Elvet Hill in Durham, and for the general work of the University's School of Oriental Studies.

In 1951 HN was awarded the honorary degree of Doctor of Civil Law by the University of Durham, an honour that delighted him. The Spalding Room in Elvet Hill House, Durham, was opened on 13 October 1955. It still serves as a staff common room in the Department of East Asian Studies. Sir James Duff, Warden of the University of Durham at the time, hoped that Mrs Spalding would be able to attend the ceremony in the newly acquired premises of the School of Oriental Studies. She was unable to accept his invitation so he wrote to her son, Dr John Spalding'

> [Your Mother] was going to name the principal room of the School 'The Spalding Room' in memory of your Father's great interest in, and benefactions to, the School. I hear today from Professor Thacker, with great regret, that your Mother does not feel able to come to Durham for that occasion. Would you be willing to come and name the Spalding Room instead of her? We should greatly appreciate it if you could.[25]

Dr Spalding accepted the invitation, attended the ceremony, and gave an address from which the following extracts are taken:

> Later in [my father's] life he began to know something of the religion, philosophy and art of the Oriental civilizations, and though he would never have pretended that he was an expert in any Oriental field, it became his aim and hope that students in the future would be able to have a revelation of a new and wonderful world provided not merely from the limited field of Athens in the fifth century [BC], but from the thousands of years and millions of square miles covered by the great Oriental civilisations. This hope had been formed in my father's mind more than 20 years ago, and subsequent political events, disagreeable as for the most part they were, introduced many young men to the

East. Moreover, they aroused a greatly increased interest in the East among western populations in general, and indeed made a knowledge of the East a matter of expediency.

Holding these views, my father could only look with delight on the enterprising spirit in which this University set about the task of enlarging the school of Oriental studies, and he counted himself fortunate to be able to help in an undertaking so much after his own heart. He was delighted, too, at the speed with which it grew and at the way in which its reputation became so great among students of the East in so many countries. He was sorry that Durham's enterprise was not always equalled elsewhere, but would now be glad to know that some other Universities are belatedly beginning to follow Durham's lead in this respect ...

When already very ill, he was cheered to know that this University was undertaking this great work. He was *very* grateful for the Honorary degree of Doctor of Civil Law which you conferred on him in recognition of the work he tried to do for the better understanding of the Eastern point of view in art and religion. He thoroughly enjoyed his visit here for the conferment of the degree, and especially the Public Orator's speech on that occasion, particularly the joke about the Wild Life of Oxford.[26] He often spoke afterwards both of the beauties of your University precincts and of the great friendliness shown to him on that occasion.

My father delighted in friendly talk and the interchange of ideas. He liked people—nearly all people—so much, and enjoyed exchanging ideas with all sorts and conditions, of all ages, nationalities, and occupations. He liked to do this perhaps best of all at his favourite bathing place, Parson's Pleasure, but there are seasons when this location is not practicable. He would be delighted at the kind tribute of naming after him this room, whose function is the interchange of ideas both in a formal and a casual setting, and it is therefore with very much pleasure that I name this room the Spalding Room.[27]

Mrs Spalding did send a personal message that contained the following lines:

It would have greatly pleased my husband that this room is to be used for the interchange of ideas and for friendly talk (assisted by cups of coffee) ... He worked hard but he enjoyed relaxation and play too. I want to thank the members of Durham University for the great joy they brought to him in his old age and when he was already very ill ... [And of the conferral of the honorary degree of DCL in 1951] he often spoke of the very impressive service in the Cathedral after the ceremony.[28]

The War Years in the United States

In the Spring of 1939 Spalding and his wife went to the United States. They went at the invitation of friends, some of whom had been Rhodes scholars at Oxford. The idea was that the Spaldings would visit academic communities in the north-east of the country, and that HN would give some lectures and talks. He was able to do this, although a hectically peripatetic lifestyle in the hot and humid months of a Summer in the north-eastern part of America did little to improve his health. There was much talk about a war with Hitler's Germany, but it still seemed safe to make the journey. They were still there on the outbreak of war and were unable to return to England because space on ships and aircraft was reserved for the transport of people whose services were considered to be more essential for the war effort. During their absence their daughter Anne ran the family home at 9 South Parks Road in Oxford. In the first years of the war anyone who had spare accommodation was obliged to take evacuees from parts of the country threatened by enemy air attacks. The Spaldings were more fortunate than most in that they were able to choose who came to stay in their house. Among those who did come were Charles Williams (one of the 'Inklings', amongst whose company C. S. Lewis and J. R. R. Tolkien were numbered) and Gerard Hopkins, nephew of the poet Gerard Manley Hopkins. Williams and Hopkins were both employed by the Oxford University Press, which had been evacuated to Oxford from Amen House in London. Another frequent visitor was the economist Barbara Ward. Others who came included refugees from Europe with their families, who stayed for longer or shorter periods. The house was also a base from which Ruth Spalding ran her touring company, *The Pilgrim Players*. The company took religious plays—many written by Charles Williams—to different parts of the country during World War II. At least one member of the company was to be found living in the house. The rest came when a play was being rehearsed. All this activity left little room for Anne to concentrate for long on her painting in oils. She concentrated on lithography, an art form of which her teacher Barnett Freedman had been a notable exponent.[29]

When they left for the United States the Spaldings had taken substantial sums of money with them but their extended stay quickly exhausted the supply. Restrictions on the transfer of money from the United Kingdom left them with little on which to live. Mail went by sea, and much of it was lost through enemy action. In this potentially embarrassing situation they were to meet much kindness from American friends. There may have been another reason for the visit to the United States, however. Canon Anson Phelps Stokes, who became a close friend of the Spaldings at the time, stated that HN had gone to the USA for 'certain medical treatment', but did not add any explanation.[30] The need for it is strongly disputed by HN's son, however, who states, 'HN did not go to the USA in 1939 to receive medical treatment. He was healthy before he went and did not fall sick until some years after his return'.[31] Phelps Stokes was probably wrong, but he knew that HN was ill whilst in the United States. The illness is confirmed in a letter HN wrote to Sarvepalli Radhakrishnan, dated 15 September 1939 and written from a temporary address on west 119th Street, New York. Spalding wrote, 'I have been ill, but am out of danger (as the silly phrase is)'.

I have a copy of HN's *Civilization in East and West*, in which HN, as was his custom, made copious annotations in the margins in his miniscule angular hand-writing. On the flyleaf he has written: *Lake Cottage, Lenox, Mass. 4th April 1941*. Whether by coincidence or design the Spaldings chose to live in the small town of Lenox.[32] HN had been born in Lennox House, in Blackheath. The prospect of living in an American town with the same sounding name as the house in which he started his life may well have appealed to him. Stokes records that the Spaldings rented a house in Lenox, a small town situated in western Massachusetts, a few miles south of Pittsfield on route 7, not far from the border with New York State, and set among the Berkshire Hills.

> [The Spaldings] lived for a short time in New York, Princeton and Cambridge, but Berkshire County, and especially the Brook Farm on Stockbridge Bowl, where they rented a house, was their home for most of the time. No distinguished visitors from England, from Matthew Arnold on have been greater lovers of the region. Many of us have received at Christmastime poems from Mr Spalding, extolling Berkshire County with its rural beauty and charm. He interested himself in many of our institutions, perhaps particularly in the Lenox Library, the Pleasant Valley Bird Sanctuary, and the music festivals.[33]

Canon Phelps Stokes added that the Spaldings were very generous to the cause of relief in China during the war, and that they made it financially possible for instruction in Christianity to be given at Santiniketan, ninety miles north-west of Calcutta, in an institution founded by the philosopher/poet Rabindranath Tagore in 1901 as a communal school near Bolpur. The school sought to blend Eastern and Western approaches to education, and thus to work towards 'the union of these two hemispheres of spirit'.[34] It developed into the Visva-Bharati University. On the face of it this was an approach likely to commend itself to Spalding.[35] Whilst in New York the Spaldings met up with Colonel Malevsky-Malevitch once again. He had married an American lady and they had a shop in New York. Their stock-in-trade was antique furniture.

The Spaldings returned to England at the end of the war in Europe in

1945, but before the victory against Japan was won. Their return inspired Spalding to write a number of patriotic verses. They are modest enough by the highest poetic standards, but should be read in context. They are included among the Christmas verses in a section called *Interlude*, written with 'a spice of mild fun' as he put it. He was always realistic about his versification, conceding that 'it is evident that such poems are entirely not *for the fashion of these times*, alike in manner and in matter. But the author doesn't care, οὐ φροντίσ Ἱπποκλείδη! The following example illustrates his affection for both countries:

> *England-America, Christmas 1945*
> Now we are home in England,
>   The self-same skies above,
> We see two lands together,
>   And either land we love,
> The land of rolling rivers,
>   And forests flaming far,
> The land of plough and pasture,
>   Where quiet brooks are.
>
> By Magdalen Tower in Oxford
>   The Tower of Princeton stands,
> And Charles and Cherwell mingle,
>   Quad, campus couple hands,
> And Berkshire Downs are green,
>   Here Williams and here Oxford
> No ocean lies between.
>
> Here are the friends we longed for,
>   And other friends are here
> From Lenox, Boston, Washington,
>   The dear among the dear.
> Where are the critic nations
>   When love is in the heart?
> Whom friendship holds together
>   Can frontiers hold apart?
>
> Now peace is in our England,
>   And peace is round the world,
> From Pole to Pole, from soul to soul,
>   The battle-flags are furl'd.
> And now the nations gather,
>   Where every child would be.

In longing expectation
  Around the Christmas Tree.

O peal, ye bells, in England,
  Across New England peal,
Ye Christmas bells, ye Christmas bells,
  Bring all the peoples heal!
Ye have a message to us
  Of joy to still our pain:
'Christ is born, Christ is born,
  Christ is born again!' [36]

Last Illness and Death

The nature of HN's final illness was not diagnosed for some years. In 1948 he underwent a prostate operation. He was to suffer progressive physical weakness although his mind remained clear.[37] Even when he was very ill he continued to attend to his correspondence. He was certainly very unwell at the time when the election to the Spalding Chair was being conducted in 1952. He was aggrieved rather than disappointed by the choice made by the electors on that occasion. His illness may have contributed to the outrage he clearly felt at the way the electors appeared to have ignored his wishes, but there were good reasons for his dissatisfaction with their decision. An account of what took place is given in the next chapter. His life was, in any case, coming to an end. He died of leukaemia on 6 September 1953. His funeral service, before cremation, was held in St Cross church, Holywell, Oxford. He had never been an apologist for the kind of circumscribed religious orthodoxy which he believed could too easily become exclusive. He was rather an advocate of an inclusive spirituality that was sensitive to the wide range of mankind's religious experience. He was not interested in promoting some kind of universal religious syncretism. He took religious doubt and uncertainty seriously, whilst addressing a serious call, to himself as much as to others, to consider carefully what he held to be the essential unity behind the diversity of mankind's spiritual aspirations and experiences.

Among the numerous tributes paid to his memory was one that was spoken during a quiet memorial service in a remote corner of the United States. Copake Falls is a small American town in New York State, some 40 miles south-east of the State capital, Albany, and 10 miles east of the Hudson River on route 22. HN and his wife came to know it well. When they were in the United States from 1939 to 1945 they lived not far away, in Lenox, across the Massachusetts border. On Sunday, 27 September 1953, a memorial service for Henry Norman Spalding was held there, in the church of St John in the

Wilderness, just three weeks to the day after he died in Oxford at the age of 76. It was conducted by Canon Anson Phelps Stokes, a personal friend. The words spoken on that day illustrate the regard and affection in which HN was held:

Our Father in Heaven, We come before Thee as a small group of friends of Thy departed servant, Henry Norman, to join in thanksgiving, meditation, and prayers as we call to mind his gracious personality, Christian ideals, and public services.

Realizing that our friend's whole life was a witness to his deep faith in Thee and his desire to serve Thee, it seems fitting at this time that we also should recognize Thee as the God and Father of mankind, from whom all gifts and blessings come, and without whom our lives have no higher meaning.

For our friend's love of Nature and his awareness of the Divine Hand in all creation, we thank Thee;

For his true patriotism and his yearning to see his Nation and our Nation leading the cause of world justice and peace, we thank Thee;

For his generous friendship and his inspiration in our own lives, we thank Thee;

For his devotion to the ideal of world unity, based on the things of the Spirit, and for all that he did through his various societies, and through his *Civilization in East and West*,[38] and his volumes of verse, to advance true religion and spiritual culture, we thank Thee;

For the many family benefactions in which he shared, including academic endowments in Comparative Religions [sic], the provision of educational privileges to working men, the support of the Red Cross in China, England and elsewhere, the fostering of the study of Nature and God, we thank Thee;

For a character that approached that of his Divine Master for purity, gentleness, and the desire to serve mankind, we thank Thee;

For the yearning of a mystic for the Divine Presence revealed in the founders and Saints of all the great religions of the world, and for the longing for Thy Holiness, Wisdom, and Love, which give life its highest meaning, we thank Thee;

For the loving care and encouragement of his devoted wife, family, and household, we thank Thee;

And to our thanks we add our prayers: For the soul of the faithful departed, that he may ever grow in the knowledge of God, and in the service of others;

For the bereaved family, that they may be given comfort and strength in their loneliness, and assurance of the great reunion;

For the many spiritual and humanitarian movements to which he gave himself without stint, especially the societies he helped found for the deeper understanding of all religions, East and West;

For the closer co-operation between all nations, and especially Great Britain and the United States, and between all religions, especially between Western Christianity, the Eastern Orthodox Church, and the ancient faith[s] of India;

And finally, we pray that we and all other friends of our dear and departed friend may be true to the spiritual ideals which dominated his life. These our thanksgivings and prayers we ask with deep gratitude and humble faith in the name of Jesus Christ our Lord.[39]

'A Dome of Many-Coloured Glass'

In a letter of condolence, written from Madingley Hall, Cambridge, to Mrs Nellie Spalding on hearing of the death of her husband, Canon Charles E. Raven wrote: 'I can as yet hardly realise it; for though I knew how precarious his health was, he had such amazing vitality & such powers of recuperation that I never questioned his length of days'. In his generous and moving letter Raven went on to adapt rather than quote part of a poem by Shelley. The adaptation was understandable, given that the poet's atheism rendered him incapable of contemplating the possibility of a future life such as Spalding himself entertained. Raven's letter to Mrs Spalding continued, 'But you are brave & have suffered & will know that when this *dome of many-coloured glass* is splintered, the white radiance of eternity remains the more clear and real.'[40] Canon Raven, sometime Vice-Chancellor of the University of Cambridge and Fellow and Master of Christ's College, Cambridge, was one of the small group who founded the *Union for the Study of the Great Religions* (USGR) in 1950/51.[41]

The metaphor used by Canon Raven may sound a little fanciful today, but at the time it expressed the spiritual sensitivity and the aesthetic sensibility of the men who, in their various ways worked together, if only a short period, in order to promote an appreciation of the rich diversity as well as the essential unity of human religious experience. The image is a reminder of the fragile nature of mankind's grasp of ultimate reality this side of eternity. They had little interest in devising a new, syncretistic, religion. Each man respected the particularity, the distinctiveness and the coherence of the culture in which he had been nurtured, but each understood that in religious terms what he now 'saw' from his particular perspective could only be a partial vision. Though partial, that vision was nonetheless illuminating, refracting the still greater light that streamed in through 'a dome of many-coloured glass'.

Tributes to HN

Of all the tributes paid to HN, few are more moving than that written by one of his secretaries, Mrs Daphne Young. She took up her duties with him after the 1939–45 war. She first met him on 15 February 1947. Fifty-five years later I was privileged to receive a small package of letters written by HN to Mrs Young. It was sent to me by her husband, Dr Stuart Young, now living in retirement in South Africa. The letters and notes, charming, gracious and often humourous, let her know precisely what HN wanted done. Nor was he slow to express his thanks for what had been done, as for example when he thanked her for typing his poems, which he referred to as 'your poems, Daphne'. What was the Secretary to do when HN was away from home or otherwise engaged? Where were the things he needed her to find? He was never less than helpful, leaving instructions like this: 'face the window in my room … furthest top drawer … to the left … two heaps of papers … set of papers addressed to delegates of the Press … list of books in the Chinese section … under the set … foolscap yellow sheet headed …' And then there were congratulatory messages to be sent to the parents of new-born children. How were they to be phrased? Invitations were to be sent out for all sorts of social occasions. Who, when and by whom were he and Mrs Spalding to be driven to whose wedding and thence to the subsequent reception or garden party? All these letters revealed HN's genuine concern for others. His innocent delight at the prospect of meeting friends and associates is shown, for instance, in one of his letters to Daphne, which included a message for her husband. 'It would be fun to play ball at PP [Parson's Pleasure] on Thursday'. Another letter told Daphne that Canon Charles Raven and his daughter may be moving in to Shotover Cleve 'until John and Elizabeth Spalding go there'. Instructions were given about what was to be done with the keys, but 'the burning issue' was the Canon's turn of duty with the boiler, 'We cannot expect a former Vice-Chancellor to turn stoker'. Among the papers sent to me by Stuart Young was a personal tribute to HN, hand-written by Mrs Young, just for herself, shortly before she gave up her work with HN in order to look after her home and her children. It was then put away among family papers. I have her husband's permission to quote it here.

> This has been the most instructive and wonderful secretarial post I have yet had. When I first arrived, I knew nothing whatsoever about Indian civilisation—philosophy, art etc.—Far Eastern, and very little about Western philosophy. Mr Spalding opened new worlds for me, and I do not think I shall ever be able to thank him enough for doing so. To me it was an honour to be able to re-type his book of verse called 'In Praise of Life'; it is a truly beautiful work; the verses to me are

filled with a mystical quality, a true love of nature and of people. And some of the verses have a quality of fun and laughter. One can truly say that never for a moment was I bored. The days passed too quickly and I could not learn enough. I loved every minute of it.

Then the most important [...] of all was Mr Spalding who was an ideal man for whom to work, kind, gentle and above all a man interested in people. Working for him showed me only too clearly how much people mattered, and how important it is in this life to do all for other people, and not want anything in return—a truly noble spirit.

With a great sense of sadness and loss do I leave this post. Oxford for me revolves round this circle; the simpleness of the truly academic man, the wonderful sense of humour, which makes life so pleasant, the kindness and the true way of life—not artificial and hard, but gentle and kind. However it may have given me something that will help both Stuart and me in our future life. I feel sure that it has given us a greater sense of responsibility that we ourselves do not matter, but what we can do to find a better way of life. Perhaps through helping people in less fortunate circumstances than ourselves—who knows? [42]

In the first of his thirty-nine News Letters, written in February 1954 for members, associates, and friends of the Union for the Study of the Great Religions, the newly appointed General Secretary, K. D. D. Henderson, wrote the following tribute to HN's memory:

I suppose there is no recipient of this letter who did not feel a sense of personal loss at the news of H. N. Spalding's death last September and a fear lest the Movement which he had fostered for so long and which finally found expression in this Union should lose its purpose or its vitality for lack of his living inspiration. Even those who had never met him in person have felt the force of that inspiration in his writing, and it would be impertinent to attempt here to sum up an achievement whose reality is apparent to every man who knew him or his works.

His faith and his purpose, his philosophy and his poetry, his interest in humanity and in the individual, his conviction that with goodwill, good understanding and belief in a divine purpose even the desperate troubles of the present time can be brought to an end, all these are familiar enough. What is perhaps less fully appreciated is the prodigious activity of his fertile mind. All through his last illness he continued to write and re-write memoranda, essays, poems, books and letters centring round his main theme of world renaissance based on man's return to God. Much of his expressed thought will remain in manuscript. (One book, 'The Divine Universe', will, it is hoped, be published). [43] Much is scattered through his correspondence. Reading through it one finds oneself checking dates in bewilderment only to find that a project which would have absorbed the waking hours of any normal man was in fact proceeding simultaneously with another of equal moment. At the time he might be studying university finance in America, or botanical projects on the Cherwell, or the best layout for a library or museum or swimming pool, or Indian sculpture and archaeology, or Chinese art. There was no limit to his interests but they all come back in the end to the one central theme.[44]

One of HN's closest friends, Sarvepalli Radhakrishnan, paid this tribute some years after Spalding's death.

The world over, men and women are uprooted from their traditions and are spiritually impoverished. We are much more aware of the scientific and technological, political and economic forces which bear upon the world's future than of the underlying spiritual backgrounds and ideals which influence peoples and shape their common destiny. For H.N. the understanding of the spiritual nature of man and the forms in which it finds expression is the supreme concern of all human thinking ...

   H.N.'s respect for the spirit in man made him respectful to the beliefs of others, ready always to seek for the deeper reasons underlying those beliefs which differed from his own. He was unhappy when some forms of religion became totalitarian in their demands on their adherents. The mark of uncertainty which a Socrates had about his own knowledge is a sign of true humility of spirit. Some religious teachers insist on a monopoly of wisdom, which makes them disinclined to acknowledge that there may be something of truth and value in what other religious teachers profess. The late Professor A. N. Whitehead observes: 'What I am objecting to is the absurd trust in the adequacy of our knowledge. The self-confidence of learned people is the comic tragedy of civilisation'. If religion is to regain the organic power in human society which it once possessed, rivalries of religions should give place to co-operation among religions. H.N.'s personal integrity, broad humanism and deep sense of the Divine gave him a great influence among the young men and women of Oxford. His death left an empty place difficult to fill in the affection of those who came into personal contact with him. To many he was a saint without the garb of asceticism, moving in a world of truth, purity and wisdom. His home was a hermitage.[45]

HN's friends and associates found him to be a congenial companion, although there must have been times when his persistent advocacy of the causes he favoured exasperated even his friends. His single-mindedness in pursuing his aims cannot have made him an easy person with whom to live at times, but he was fortunate in that his wife and children supported him, tolerating his enthusiasms with remarkable patience.

> The philosophy, the hopes, and the man were one. For in all three there was a broad humanity. His kindness, like his seeking for truth, and his hopes, did not know horizons. He was one of the most modest, and most unselfish, of men and often seemed to those who knew him to have the mark upon him, in his personal relationships, of the saintliness, in all its variety, which he so consistently and so diffidently studied.[46]

This is a fulsome and perceptive tribute, but it was Henderson, perhaps, who succeeded in finding the single phrase that will serve as HN's epitaph, describing him affectionately as a 'practical dreamer and a poet'.

Notes and References

1. STP, Pathanamthitta and Eastern Orthodox Christianity File.
2. The Spaldings found Zernov to be a man in many ways like the other Russians they knew, always pressing ahead with his plans and hopeful that something would come of them. Unlike some of his compatriots, however, he seemed to have the knack of making his plans financially viable. For an appreciation of Dr Zernov's life see Kallistos Ware, 'Nicolas Zernov (1898–1980)', in *Sobornost, incorporating Eastern Churches Review*, volume 3, number 1, 1981, pp. 11–38.
3. The Swedish House of Lords provided HN information about the branch of the Spalding family that lived in Sweden. The text was translated from the Swedish by Dr Elizabeth Spalding's cousin who lives in Sweden.
4. Spalding's book, CEW, is dedicated to his mother. The inscription reads: 'In remembrance of Ellen Rebe Spalding, and of ninety years of courage, faith, love, and gaiety'. His mother left him the sum of £3,000. He added it to the 1928 Spalding Trust settlement, stating that the money should be used by way of a memorial to her 'for the purpose of forming a collection of works of Eastern Art for some educational purpose endowing a scholarship or scholarships or for such other purpose falling within the charitable trusts of the within Settlement'. His mother's interests were decidedly domestic rather than educational so he thought of nothing suitable as a memorial. He added that his wife and KJ should administer the fund in the event of his death. The small sum invested became the Ellen Rebe Spalding Fund. It still exists. The interest is used from time to time at the discretion of the Spalding Trustees and with the assistance of the Oxfordshire Social Services to help women in need of help. Policy for the disbursement of all Spalding Trust funds is under review.
5. For an account of his life see Marquess of Reading, *Rufus Isaacs, First Marquess of Reading, by His Son*, in two volumes, volume 1, 1860–1914 (published in 1943), volume 2, 1914–1935 (published in 1945).
6. The Workers' Educational Association (WEA) was founded in 1903. It received its first grant in 1907. The original aim was to provide a 'highway' of educational opportunity

for the large numbers of working people hitherto excluded from the advantages brought by a liberal education. From the outset it was identified with left-leaning ideals of equal opportunity. The provision of courses for trades unionists became a priority. Over the years the Association's links with the extra-mural courses offered by universities have steadily developed. It continues to provide for the thousands of students enrolled for its many courses.

7. A. J. Arberry in his obituary of H. N. Spalding, in *Forum*, published by the World Congress of Faiths, no. 19, December 1953, p. 17.

8. JMKS has a copy of a book with the title *One Hundred Years of Houlder Bros.*, published in 1951 by The Mendip Press, Bath and London. The book covers the period 1849 to 1950.

9. See page 41.

10. In his Diary entry in *The Spectator*, 7 July, 2001, p. 9.

11. A memorandum dating from 1916, prepared by HN for the members of the Committee is lodged in the Special Collections (ref. 2/2) of the London School of Economics.

12. HN was keen on the 'paper-chases' organised by the Hare and Hounds club, in which a member would go ahead running round the countryside and throwing out pieces of paper to give an idea of his course at any parting of the ways. The pack would try to follow. These diversions are not popular today, for understandable reasons. Dr John Spalding recalls what may have been the last one to be held on Shotover, in about 1930.

13. See footnote 20 below.

14. The weakness of his eyesight, notwithstanding, Stallybrass was always an enthusiastic amateur photographer.

15. A photograph of Shotover Cleve appears on page 79. A framed copy of some verses, presented to Dr Elizabeth Spalding on her 80th birthday on 16 October 1999, hangs in the drawing room of the Spalding house in Old Headington. The verses, written by her son-in-law, Mark Luboff, with the title 'An Ode to Elizabeth', include the following lines:

> Their home was to be at Shotover
> In the 'City of Dreaming Spires'.
> A magnificent Spanish type villa
> Full of tenants, *au pairs*, and coal fires.

16. See illustration on page 83.

17. The words of an unnamed correspondent in a brief additional obituary notice of HN, in *The Times*, 17 September 1953.

18. Individual members of the University were not to be penalised in this way, provided that the Trustees were convinced that work in support of Spalding's ideas was being undertaken.

19. Subsequently renamed *The Spalding Lectureship in Eastern Orthodox Studies*. From 1948 to 1966, the lectureship was funded by the Spalding Trust. On Dr Zernov's retirement in that year, Timothy Ware (now Bishop Kallistos Ware) was appointed to the lectureship. In gratitude for the help provided by the Trust, the name Spalding was retained in the title of the lectureship, although the University assumed responsibility for financing the lectureship thereafter. The word 'Culture' in the title of the lectureship was considered to be ambiguous, so the title was changed. In the first instance, Dr Zernov's post was a University lectureship. He had no official College link, although he did have dining rights at Keble College, where he became an active member. Later he was elected to a Fellowship at St Cross College. In 1970, after the University encouraged Colleges to

have closer links with University lecturers, the new lecturer became a Fellow of Pembroke College by special election. I am grateful to Bishop Kallistos for this information.

20. This collection of 6,500 photographs and nitrate negatives has only recently been discovered by Mrs Elizabeth Boardman, Archivist of Brasenose College, where Stallybrass worked as Fellow, Vice-Principal and Principal until his unfortunate death in 1948. Each photograph is meticulously recorded by the photographer in a series of handbooks which show the date that picture was taken, the type of film used, the time of day, the state of the light, the aperture, the shutter speed, and a brief description of the subject. Mrs Boardman's article about the hitherto unpublished collection appears with the title 'The Splendid Pictorial Record of Stallybrass and His Faithful Camera' in *The Brazen Nose*, A College magazine, vol 34, January 2000, pp. 26–34. One of the several memoirs and appreciations of Stallybrass which in *The Brazen Nose*, vol ix May 1949, pp. 9–27, was contributed by HN (pp. 20–1). It was reprinted from *The Times* of 1 November 1948. It mentions Stallybrass's interest and help in Indian and other Eastern studies.

21. 'E.D.', in *The Times*, 9 September 1953.

22. NUSGR, number 4, April 1955, p. 8.

23. By the year 1991 the Chinese section in the library at Durham University contained some 50,000 volumes, apart from numerous periodicals. It incorporated the collections of scholars such as W. Percival Yetts and Arthur Waley, which included many rare items.

24. The University of Durham assumed full financial responsibility for these lectureships from October 1957.

25. Letter to JMKS from Sir James Duff, STP, 16 September 1955.

26. The publication of Durham University Gazettes was suspended during the Second World War and not revived until 1953. There is no record of the speech made by the Public Orator, the Revd, Professor Stanley Lawrence Greenslade, to which Dr Spalding refers in the passage quoted.

27. SFP, 13 October 1955.

28. *Ibid.*

29. In a note to the author JMKS writes: '[Anne] has long been a member of the Oxford Arts Society and her pictures have regularly been in its shows. She had a one-woman show in London just before or just after the war and another of her earlier work some ten years ago. Many of her fellow painters were struggling financially and whenever she sold a painting she felt that she was robbing them. I think this meant that she did not press for sales as she otherwise might have done.' Letter dated 3 August 2001.

30. Anson Phelps Stokes, 'A Wartime Visitor', in *The Berkshire Eagle*, 26 September 1953.

31. In a letter to me from JMKS, 18 August 2001.

32. The Spaldings were often on the move, even within the narrow confines of Lenox. Some of HN's letters are headed Brook Lodge, Richmond Road, Lenox, Mass. USA. One, dated 26 August 1941, is addressed to Radhakrishnan in India. The typed copy in the Spalding Papers is annotated by HN in his own handwriting, 'from 14 October, Hotel Continental'.

33. Phelps Stokes, *loc. cit.*, *The Berkshire Eagle*, 26 September 1953.

34. cf. Jawaharlal Nehru, 1936, *An Autobiography; with Musings on Recent Events in India*, John Lane, The Bodley Head, pp. 483–4, on Nehru's choice of Santiniketan for the education of his daughter Indira.

35. In May 1930 Tagore delivered the Hibbert lectures in Oxford. The lectures were expanded and published a year later with the title *The Religion of Man*. There is little evidence that Spalding was much influenced by Tagore's evolutionary approach to economics, social structures, national and international politics, public health, education, and religion.

36. H. N. Spalding, IPL, 1952, pp. 46–7.
37. The photograph of HN that appears at the beginning of this book has an interesting history, recalled by Dr John Spalding in a letter to the present writer. 'The well known photograph of HN was like him until his final illness but was taken in April 1936 in the sitting room at Bell Cliff, Lyme Regis. Bell Cliff was a delightful but unusual house on the sea front which my parents acquired unintentionally and was often let and often, especially out of season, used as a holiday home. Anne and Ruth [Spalding, daughters of HN] had at least one reading party there when Ruth was at Somerville [College, Oxford]. How does one acquire a house unintentionally? It is a long story but the children were delighted at the chance to get back to Lyme Regis.'
38. The reference is to CEW, Spalding's major work, published in 1939.
39. The text quoted here survives in flimsy form, hastily typewritten on two sheets of paper, and preserved in STP.
40. SFP, letter, dated 10 September 1953. Shelley's lines from stanza 52 of his poem *Adonais*:

> The One remains, the many change and pass;
> Heaven's light for ever shines, Earth's shadows fly;
> Life, like a dome of many-coloured glass,
> Stains the white radiance of Eternity,
> Until Death tramples it to fragments.

41. See F. W. Dillistone, 1975, *Charles Raven: Naturalist, Historian, Theologian*, Hodder & Stoughton, London.
42. Included in a letter from Dr Stuart Young to JMKS, dated 17 September 2001.
43. The book was published by Basil Blackwell, Oxford, in 1958.
44. NUSGR number 1, p. 1, dated 18 February 1954, and written from 9 South Parks Road, Oxford.
45. Radhakrishnan, 1958, TDU, *op. cit.*, pp. vii–viii. Radhakrishnan was awarded the Order of Merit in 1963. From 1962 to 1967 he was President of India. He died in 1975. The quotation from Whitehead is to be found in *The Philosophy of A. N. Whitehead*, edited by P. Schilpp (1941), p. 698.
46. *The Times*, 17 September 1953.

CHAPTER FOUR

Unfulfilled Plans and Frustrated Aims

Questions of Truth

Using the phrase 'the soul of the East for the mind of the West',[1] some of HN's Indian friends spoke enthusiastically about the *complementarity* of Eastern and Western spirituality. The words were sometimes taken to suggest a prescription for the cure of a uniquely Western *malaise* that was caused by an increasing neglect of the spiritual dimension of human experience. HN thought that there was such a malady, but tactfully declined the suggestion that it was limited to people in the West. He maintained, on the contrary, that the sickness is universal. He agreed, however, that its cure is to be found in the world's great religions, all of which reveal *Truth* to anyone who is disposed to look hard enough. Before it became fashionable to speak about the relativism not only of religious 'truths' but of all 'truth-claims', he sought to defend the notion of *Truth*. Unlike many of his contemporaries he did not regard transcendental truth as a chimera. Nor did he take the easy option of stating that all religious truths are of equal worth. He contended that although the Truth of the sovereignty of God and of the contingency of the created universe is differently expressed, it is universally recognised and capable of being widely understood and shared. This Truth, he argued, can not be 'true' for some and 'not true' for others. To discover the reality of Truth— more strictly, perhaps, to *dis*-cover it—was for him to find the pearl of great price.

For this reason he hoped that the educational curriculum might be broadened in order to allow for much wider searching to ensue. He also felt that there was another potential benefit to accrue from the study of other religions and other cultures. The study might lead to a re-awakening of interest in the spiritual traditions of the West, where religious belief was in decline. A study of Eastern religions might produce a renewed interest and respect for Judaism and Christianity in tired and spiritually deprived Western societies. This might then lead to a renaissance in Europe, which might prove to be comparable to that which followed the scholarly researches of the nineteenth century into Indian history, cultures and religious traditions. The publication of these researches had already stimulated Western interest in Indian religions. It had done something else. It had helped to rekindle the interest of many Indians in their own neglected spiritual inheritance. Could the same be done, *mutatis mutandis*, by reinvigorating the study of the spiritual traditions of the West? And if, as HN believed, people in the West were not the only victims of a debilitating spiritual *malaise*, the 'soul'—not to mention the 'mind'—of the West had much to offer to the East. HN's best and most closely argued book, *Civilization in East and West* records his efforts not only to diagnose this universal sickness but to prescribe its cure.[2] In the Preface to the book that sums up his personal philosophy, he wrote:

> Man is made for happiness, and everywhere he is unhappy. What is wrong with the world? And how can it be made right? Our politics have broken down: nation is turned against nation and class against class. Our religions have broken down: we no longer know what we think about God and man's life in the Universe. And for the first time in history this bewilderment has fallen, not upon one civilization only, but upon all. Yet, if men did but realize it, their resources far surpass their difficulties. Immense treasures of wisdom and imagination (together with much junk) have accumulated through the ages, both in East and West.
>
> Statesmen, poets, prophets, thinkers, seers, this civilization and that, have contributed things rich and strange that contain the clue to the problems that beset us. To appreciate the greatness of human achievement is to see a new dawn break over man, his society and his destiny. And as men grow more sensible and enlightened, science will cease from its menace and bring only its boon: will bring, not death, but life and opportunity to the whole population of the earth.[3]

This approach to the human condition sounds utopian, not to say naïve, today, but Spalding's apparent *naiveté* is balanced by a sense of realism that came from his experience of the world. He was a man who had seen the cosy optimism of late Victorian England, the comfortable assurances of established religion, and the outwardly gentle rhythms of Edwardian life, precipitately disrupted by events and all but destroyed by the bitter conflict and the fearful death toll of the First World War. The Russian novelist Aleksandr I. Solzhenitsyn, who won the Nobel Prize for Literature in 1970, once described the gifted scientist Nikolai Ivanovich Kobozev—a friend, ally, and fellow-prisoner in the Soviet Union—as a man 'acutely aware of the Russian spiritual collapse in the twentieth century, but in religious terms he was a simple Orthodox Christian free of intellectual pretensions'.[4] The deceptive simplicity and lack of intellectual pretentiousness attributed to Kobozev by Solzhenitsyn are also characteristic of Spalding's efforts to try to do something to arrest the spiritual collapse he saw around him. It is surprising that he was able to resist the crushing pessimism that afflicted so many of his contemporaries. HN described himself as a man 'of boundless hope', who believed in 'the triumph of good over evil, the victory of the spirit over darkness'. He had none of the attachment to imprecision in philosophical and moral questions, which sometimes passes in the West for intellectual rigour.

He had long been persuaded that the follies of human beings, which threaten social and political stability and lead all too often to bitter wars, are attributable at least partly to a failure to recognise and to understand the universal beliefs and aspirations which unite rather than divide human beings. He believed that this *religious* unity was being obscured by new forms of Western cultural imperialism, which were essentially secular. The reality, as he saw it, was that the rejection of the wisdom accumulated over centuries in the religions of both East and West, contributed to the conflict and the horror of human conflicts. There was nothing new in this, but Spalding was determined to try to do something about the world in which he lived. At that time the influence of all institutional religion in this country appeared to be waning for several reasons. As in every age, there was the apathy of large numbers of people who, though ignorant of the claims made upon them by religion, were invincibly indifferent to them. HN did not seek salvation in a new universal religion. His approach to the spiritual unity of mankind called, rather, for a recognition that there is a profound sense in which all the great religions of the world are already universal religions. What is needed, therefore, is not a conflation of the 'best' elements in different religions, but an awareness of the underlying unity that is already there, waiting to be discovered.

> Socrates and Plato are the forerunners of Jesus, who emphasized that reason is the inner bond of all synthesis—blessed are they who know and love God and man and Nature. Men are divine, the sons of God, and are destined to form His Kingdom. That Kingdom will be world-wide; 'They shall come from East and West, and shall sit down in the Kingdom of Heaven.' It will not be made up of those who merely call him Lord, 'Not every one that saith unto me Lord, Lord, shall enter into the Kingdom of Heaven, but he that doeth the Will of my Father. Which is in Heaven'—he who knows and loves.
>
> As with space so with time—he gathers all into the Kingdom: 'I am not come to destroy but to fulfil.' Today the so-called non-Christian peoples of the world, accepting the Christian Gospels and rejecting

Christian Theology, are perceiving in Jesus the Universal Lord who can fashion the earth into the Kingdom of God. He belongs no more to the West than to the East, and his rule is a spiritual rule. 'I, if I be lifted up, will draw all men unto me.'

The moment is therefore coming to seek amid the multiplicity of religions the one religion of the One God that is revealed by reason, foreshadowed in the universal religions, and perfected in Jesus Christ; to realize the vision of Ram Mohan Roy, the union of Asia and Europe in which neither shall sacrifice its individuality, but both come together in a 'Church of Brahma', where all may worship the One God. The harvest is ripening but unreaped. Much has yet to be interpreted and developed before the 'one way' is made manifest in its various forms. Beneath the outward multiplicity of religions beats the one religion that is the heart of all.[5]

Unity in Diversity

HN's growing interest in helping to promote an awareness of the unity that underlies an apparent diversity was much more than an interesting intellectual pursuit. There was an element of moral passion in his determined efforts to draw attention to what the great religions had to say about the human predicament. He defended universal moral and ethical values. He sought to encourage a deep respect for the ways in which religious and cultural diversity could enrich our common life.

It is man's task today, while adhering to the inessentials so far as they still help him, to look within and to see the essentials—the Divine Nature and man's Way of Return to It. As we all draw near to the One, though from many different and it may be distant points, we shall all draw nearer to one another. A knowledge and love of the One God will bind the sons of God together in the Kingdom of God. Union with Him and with all things in Him is the goal of mankind and of the universe here and hereafter.'[6]

In the previous chapter HN was described as 'a practical dreamer and a poet'. He held with firm conviction to a belief that the religious experience of mankind, in all its astonishing variety, resembled a multi-faceted jewel through which enlightenment is refracted in a thousand ways. It was the religions of the East, furthermore, which seemed to him to acknowledge most readily the unity that lies beneath the multiplicity of ways in which the reality of the One is variously manifested to human beings. If that was the dream, how could a practical man set about the task of making it real? Long before steps began to be taken to break down the barriers between members of different Christian communities, and long before efforts were made to do the same between members of different religious communities, HN was among the pioneers of inter-faith dialogue, focusing on the upward progress of the human soul to which all the great religions of the world bear witness.

> The soul in its upward progress does not stop even at knowledge and love; it rises to that union with the Godhead and the Universe in which subject and object are united. There is here a spiritual marriage between the soul and the Godhead, an 'intuitive reason' that is also an 'intellectual love of God', a 'knowledge above knowledge', that is the realisation of the Divine.[7]

These words convey a sense of HN's pre-occupation with what he considered to be the relationship between the empirical, differentiated, self or soul, and the undifferentiated Godhead or Absolute. Disunity, division, and conflict, were the bitter consequences of the separation of 'subject and object'. Yet despite the tragic conflict and losses of the First World War, the Bolshevik revolution of 1917, the collapse of the American economy at the end of the 1920s, the Depression at home of the 1930s, and the rise of Adolf Hitler and the National Socialists in Germany, he remained optimistic—even on the brink of the Second World War. In the book that was to be his *magnum opus*, published in 1939, he conceded that order had already broken down, noting that this time the breakdown in social relationships, politics, and religion, was not just local but world-wide. Nation had turned against nation; religions were divided and divisive; and class was ranged against class. What was worse, from his point of view, was that men and women had lost the capacity as well as the desire to think about human existence with reference to God. There was, nonetheless, good reason for hope. Human progress through the centuries, though fitful and marked by notable regressions, was real and demonstrable in his judgement. His book was designed to illustrate this.

> It is the business of this book to survey the marvellous progress towards happiness made by mankind during the last few thousand years, through the definition and development of ideals, as well as to indicate the false ideals that fight against progress, and the fate that has lain in store for them. The past can show the present which road leads to ruin, and which to Renaissance and the goal of its desires.[8]

Re-appraising Christian Uniqueness

As a Christian, however unorthodox his faith may have been, he felt obliged to begin with the primary christological questions recorded in St Mark's Gospel (8.27–9). Jesus is recorded there as addressing two questions to his disciples: 'Whom do people say I am?' and 'Whom do you say I am?'. HN's answer echoes the reply of Peter to the second of these questions, 'You are the Christ'. He believed that these questions were important for Christians to re-consider in the light of the growing evidence that God was at work in and through other religions. He believed that Christians should re-appraise their own attitudes to God's redemptive activity in 'the Christ'. The writer of the New Testament letter to the Hebrews offered some words of counsel against Christian self-assertiveness, presumption, and parochialism.

> So Jesus also suffered outside the gate in order to sanctify the people through his own blood. Therefore let us go forth to him outside the camp and bear the abuse he endured. For here we have no lasting city, but we seek the city which is to come (*Hebrews* 13.13).[9]

At the same time the writer of the letter to the Hebrews, whilst acknowledging that God spoke of old 'in many and various ways', is in no doubt about the finality of Christ in the divine plan of salvation (*Hebrews* 1.1). The writer of the book of the *Acts of the Apostles* went further, recording what Peter said to the Jewish authorities in Jerusalem when he was called to explain his actions since the apparent finality of the death of Jesus: 'There is salvation in no one else, for there is no other name under heaven given among men by which we must be saved' (*Acts* 4.12). It was to such texts as these that Christians turned when confronted with the claims of other religions to be conduits for the waters of salvation. The publication of translated texts from the scriptures of other religious communities confirmed that God had not left himself without witnesses in other cultures. If the comparative study of religion made it reasonable to conclude that all religions may ultimately lead to the summit of the same mountain, though by different routes, it followed that it would be prudent for Christians to be more precise when continuing to urge the uniqueness of Christianity. HN was not a theologian. He did not attempt a systematic answer to questions about Christian uniqueness in the comity of world religions.[10] He chose instead to name Jesus the Christ as his unique religious Master, addressing him in the following terms: 'the Word Divine, the Way, the Truth, the Life, God standest Thou, incarnate Light-Love-Mirth, Jesus, the Reason of the Universe!'[11]

Identities of Meaning

In 1932 the American idealist philosopher, W. E. Hocking (1873–1966), Professor of Philosophy at Harvard from 1914 until his retirement in 1943, had taken a more cautious—and perhaps a more realistic—view of the human condition than Spalding. Like HN he was concerned about the future of religion.

Christianity and the environing religions face at the same moment the same menace, the spread of the secular spirit; the former opponents [i.e. the different religions of the world] have become to this extent allied by the common task

... It takes a determined effort, armed both with sympathy and analysis, to see through the diversities of language, of symbol, of observance, to the identities of meaning. This effort has long been incumbent upon us: it speaks but sadly for the candour and perspicacity of this present religious age that these barriers of expression, all but banished in the scientific unity of mankind, should still hold kindred spirits apart in the field of religion.

... Why compare Mohammed and Buddha, when all the utterances of religious intuition are threatened with discard in the light of practical reason? It is no longer, Which Prophet? or Which Book? It is whether any prophet, book, revelation, rite, church, is to be trusted. All the old oracles are seeing a new sign: the scorn on the faces of students who know the experiments in anti-religion in Russia and non-religion in Turkey, and the actual religionlessness of much western life. The chief foe of these oracles is not Christianity, but the anti-religious element of the philosophies of Marx, Lenin, [Bertrand] Russell. The case that must now be stated is the case for any religion at all.[12]

Spalding took that last sentence of Hocking seriously. He strove to make a case, not for *any* religion but for *true* religion. In doing so he invited the inevitable criticism that anyone who uses the word 'true' needs first to guard against the *petitio principii*. If he was guilty of begging the question, it was because he presumed to see through the diversities of language, of symbol, of observance, to the identities of meaning mentioned by Hocking, and to do it with gentleness and respect. Religion in the West was in decline, but HN insisted that it was far from dead. He was sceptical about the tendency in the West to commend methodological doubt as a means of resuscitating religious belief. The notion that *doubt* (in the profession of Christianity, for instance) is a mark of a maturity is one that he would have found unconvincing. It was one thing to question belief, to subject the claims of orthodoxies (whether sacred or secular) to scrutiny, but another to elevate doubt itself to the status of a reasonable neo-orthodoxy. He would nonetheless have had some sympathy with the English novelist James Hilton, who called for 'the flexible armour of doubt' to be donned 'in an age when too many people are certain'.[13] HN was well aware that fraudulent certainties and licensed insanities emerge in all religions, but the problem, as he saw it, was that many people were becoming too certain—even too dogmatic—about their doubt. There was irony in the fact that doubt was assuming the nature of an alternative religion, with its own unchallenged and unchallengeable assumptions.

Unrealised Ambitions

During the course of his adult life Spalding had the satisfaction of seeing at least a few of his ideas accepted and some of his plans implemented. Several of the generous benefactions made by him and his wife have already been mentioned, but he had plans for two more ambitious projects. The first was the setting up of a Chair in the University of Oxford for the study of Eastern Religions and Ethics. The second was to establish an 'Asia House' in Oxford. Optimistic as ever, he hoped that these plans, when implemented, would help to reduce the misunderstanding and ignorance of Eastern religions and cultures in the West. In his closing years, however, he suffered disappointment over both projects. His detailed plans for the establishment of an 'Asia House' in Oxford were rejected by the University in the years immediately after the end of the Second World War. His plans were designed to replace what he considered to be the existing poorly sited and ineffective Indian Institute in the city with a broader based and more comprehensive establishment for the exploration of Eastern religions and cultures. The second disappointment was the more painful because it came after sixteen years in which his major benefaction to the University had been used—to his obvious satisfaction—to promote the work of Professor Radhakrishnan, the first occupant of the Spalding Chair of Eastern Religions and Ethics. To the gifts that enabled the University to establish the Chair in 1936 HN and his wife had attached certain conditions, which proved to be unacceptable to the beneficiaries who, without wishing to give offence to HN, resisted anything that looked like interference from him with regard to the appointment of a successor to Radhakrishnan in 1952. The high hopes that HN had once entertained for both an 'Asia House' and the Spalding Chair began to be dashed. The last six years of his life from 1947 to 1953 were thus clouded by frustration and even an anger which he did less and less to conceal. His failing health contributed to his discomfiture.

The story of these unrealised ambitions, can be prefaced with a reference to the figure of Edward John Thompson. He played a significant role in Spalding's plans for the two projects just mentioned. Thompson's parents served for many years as Wesleyan missionaries in India. He spent many years there assimilating the local culture and acquiring the knowledge and experience that were to make him an outspoken advocate of Indian independence. Mahatma Gandhi described him as 'India's Prisoner', a man for whom India had become a spiritual home that he could never bring himself to leave.[14]

Although Thompson said repeatedly that he longed to be quit of India, he could not say a final farewell because he was entangled in the network of derivations, aversions, and enthusiasms attached to India's two centuries of involuntary affiliation with Britain. He was not one of those entangled in India's mysticisms, so many of which were (are) constructs of Western wishful thinking.[15]

In 1935 Thompson was elected to a Senior Research Fellowship in Indian Studies at Oriel College, Oxford, thanks to HN's generosity.[16]

In 1935 a new resource appeared in the person of H. N. Spalding, an Oxford graduate and resident with private means. A determined idealist, he was committed to mutual understanding through study of the spiritual heritages of East and West. Like Thompson he 'dreamed that Oxford might become the centre of a new renaissance based on an Honour School of Religion and Ethics'. He dreamed also of an 'Asia House' to revitalise the faltering Indian Institute. Spalding saw immense improvements possible in British-Indian relations 'by public recognition in Oxford of the current intellectual movement in India'. He happily began to devise ways to forward [Edward Thompson's] suggestions to the Rhodes Trustees. He had 'profound admiration for Thompson' and saw him as *kingpin* of the enterprise'. Britons, he said, did not '*despise* India; they are simply indifferent & ignorant about it. Yours is the pen to help', and 'Eastern studies must spring from the universities themselves', Oxford leading.

The Indian Institute was useless. Its building, [Edward said] was 'cumbrous, dark, cluttered up—such a *chawl* [slum] as the Bombay Government might have built and as you know did build. Nor will any Indian ever regard this jail-like structure with anything but horror and aversion, while it is used solely for a modicum of Indian scholarship strictly subordinated to administrative requirements …' Spalding established at Oriel a Senior Research Fellowship in Indian History for Edward at £250 a year for three years. 'Oriel made history a century ago [with Keble and Newman]', Spalding wrote, 'and now would do so again'.[17]

Preliminary discussions between HN, his friends and associates, and the University authorities about a new professorial post at Oxford for the study of Eastern religions began in 1935. HN's plans for the foundation of an 'Asia House' in the city began to develop during the same period.

The Spalding Chair of Eastern Religions and Ethics

In 1936 the Spalding Chair of Eastern Religions and Ethics was established for a trial period with a generous grant from HN and his wife. The first occupant was the Indian scholar Sarvepalli Radhakrishnan, whose name may well have been suggested to HN by the afore-mentioned Edward Thompson. Under the arrangements of the original benefaction made by HN and his wife, the group of electors included a representative of the Spalding Trust. HN had always made it clear that his purpose in founding the Chair was to provide a suitably qualified Asian candidate with a professorial position in Oxford. Such a candidate, he hoped, would lecture and teach from a first-hand knowledge and experience of an Eastern religion, promoting the study of religion and religions along lines suggested in Spalding's own published work. There were two main objectives. First, to provide a position in Oxford from which an eminent Asian scholar could share his knowledge and make his views heard in this country. Second, to produce informed teachers of religion and ethics for the nation's schools and universities, who would approach their work from a less parochial Western perspective. It was clear from the outset that HN expected the University to honour his wishes by appointing 'an eminent Asian' to the Spalding Chair. Radhakrishnan certainly fulfilled the founder's wishes in that respect. His occupancy of the Chair was both distinguished and fruitful. He once observed that when the Indian leaders were discussing whether India should become entirely independent or remain in the Commonwealth, one faction said that Britain had never shown any interest in Indian culture and the other faction replied: 'What about the Spalding Chair of Eastern Religions and Ethics, held by no less a person than Radhakrishnan?' [18]

At first everything seemed to be going well in accordance with HN's wishes. Radhakrishnan, already well-known in Oxford for the four Upton Lectures he delivered in Manchester College to packed audiences in Eights Week in 1926, was the candidate for whom HN was looking. Spalding had listened to Radhakrishnan's Hibbert Lectures in Oxford in 1930, and had been impressed as much by the speaker's personality as by his knowledge. A distinguished Indian academic, Radhakrishnan was to bring distinction and international recognition to the Spalding Chair. At first he was required to spend only two terms each year at Oxford. During the remaining six months he was free to return as a professor to Calcutta. In 1937 the Spaldings made another gift of money to the University, sufficient to extend the duration of the Professorship for another fifteen years. In 1949 they were to endow the Chair permanently. To begin with there was no College Fellowship attached to the Chair, although Radhakrishnan was quickly made a member of the Common Room at All Souls. HN was delighted that his choice for the Chair was likely to be re-elected after the initial five year appointment came to an end. Professor Collingwood had enthusiastically endorsed the extension of Radhakrishnan's tenure of the Chair with the words: 'He is a great man and I love him. I don't know how much effect he is having on Oxford (we are rather a generation of deaf adders) but whatever effect he has can only be good. Let us, I beg, have him amongst us for as long as possible'.[19] HN repeated the words to Radhakrishnan, but not everyone agreed with Collingwood. Some years later, in a note to Tom Knox-Shaw (Master of Sidney Sussex College, Cambridge and Chairman of the Spalding Trust) and to Dr John Spalding, Henderson wrote: 'I saw Evans-Pritchard yesterday. He said Radhakrishnan has been a complete flop as Professor and was very much *persona non-grata* at All Souls.'[20] This would have been news to Radhakrishnan, who loved the College and took every opportunity to re-visit the place whenever his post-Oxford career allowed him time to do so.

Radhakrishnan's contributions to the intellectual and cross-cultural life of India and Britain were acknowledged by the award of several public honours. In June 1931 he had been awarded a knighthood and with it a title that he found useful at times but 'embarrassing on the whole'. In 1938 he was elected to an honorary Fellowship of the British Academy, the first Indian to be so honoured. When President of India he was admitted by Queen Elizabeth II as an Honorary member of the Order of Merit in 1963.[21] Yet his years in Oxford were never easy. He was often discouraged at the reception he received. His loyalty was divided between Oxford and India, between academe and politics. His difficulties were increased by the ambiguity of his position in Oxford. He had no official Fellowship at an Oxford College. His post was linked to Oriental Studies, when HN (and later Henderson) was convinced that it would have attracted more students by being attached to Theology. Professor K. S. Murty of Andhra University, Waltair (Vishakhapatnam, in Andhra Pradesh, where Radhakrishnan had once been Vice-Chancellor), wrote a letter to Henderson many years later asking for details about Radhakrishnan's time at Oxford. The Indian Government was planning a series of monographs under the title, *Builders of Modern India*. Radhakrishnan was to be Murty's subject. Murty went straight to the point

> While he was Spalding Professor what precisely was he doing in Oxford in addition to reading, thinking and writing? Did he take any classes and/or supervise research? In the former case who attended his classes, i.e. were they people reading for a degree, if so what degree, or did he just give public lectures? In either case how many regular lectures did he deliver per week or month and on what subjects? Were there examinations in the subjects on which he lectured, and if so, who evaluated the student performance? Do you know the names and present

addresses of any who took his courses or regularly attended his lectures? Were there any who took Ph.D under his supervision? Was he active in any other way as Professor at Oxford? Would you give me a sort of account of his achievement and impact as Oxford Professor.'[22]

A few days later, in June 1981, Henderson wrote back to Murty, pleading old-age for his inability to engage in such a difficult task. His response was understandable, not to say diplomatic, given the amount of information he was asked to provide. Many have asked similar questions, then and since, about the work of the Spalding Professors.

Who was to succeed Radhakrishnan after his sixteen years of tenure of the professorship? The election to the Chair in 1952 demonstrated that Oxford was not prepared to allow the benefactor's personal wishes to influence the decision about who the new Professor was to be. HN's main purpose in founding the Chair had never been to promote the study of 'Comparative Religion' as a discrete academic subject for an intellectual elite. He wanted people in the West to be informed about Eastern religions in general, and about Hinduism and Buddhism in particular. For this purpose he was convinced that the exposition of these religious systems by a competent Asian scholar was likely to be more authentic than that given by someone born and educated in the West, however able a research scholar that person might be. In a memorandum written in 1953 after his disillusionment with the decision taken by the electors to appoint R. C. Zaehner to the vacant Chair, Spalding recapitulated some of the reasons why he established it. He noted that in any study of 'the Great Religions' Hinduism, Buddhism will 'have a peculiarly important place; for they developed perhaps the greatest religious philosophy and mystical systems in the world'.

> These have been powerfully developed by the great Commentators. From the Bhagavad-Gita onward till today they have given rise to successive devotional movements. They are the source of two of the greatest epics in the world, of dramas and lyrics, of sculpture and painting. In short, these two great related cultures vie with that of Greece itself. It was with these wider studies in view that my wife and I founded the Chair of Eastern Religions and Ethics at Oxford. We did not in terms restrict it to the teaching of these two cultures, or even to a scholar of Asian descent; we trusted to the Electors (unfortunately in vain) to carry out the intentions of the Chair. The Preamble makes them clear:
>
> *'It is a condition of the Gift that the purpose of the professorship shall be to build up in the University of Oxford a permanent interest in the great religions and ethical systems (alike in their individual, social, and political, aspects) of the East, whether expressed in philosophic, poetic,*

devotional, or other literature, in art, history, and in social life and structure, to set forth their development and spiritual meaning, and to interpret them by comparison and contrast with each other and with the religions and ethics of the West and in any other appropriate way, with the aim of bringing together the world's great religions in closer understanding, harmony, and friendship; as well as to promote co-operation with other Universities, bodies, and persona, in East and West which pursue the like ends, which purpose is likely to be furthered by the establishment of a Professorship, which would in the natural course normally be held by persons of Asian descent.' [23]

Growing Disillusionment

It was clear that in normal circumstances—by which he meant the availability and readiness of a suitably qualified candidate—HN expected the holder of the Chair to be an Asian. This had been acknowledged by the University from the outset, when provision for 'normal tenure by a person of Asian descent was substituted at the suggestion of the University for an original draft which precluded Europeans from appointment'. The importance and significance of the *Preamble* was recognized by the inclusion of extracts from it in a footnote to the Statutes. If it were found necessary to appoint a European in the absence of a suitable Asian candidate, the successful European candidate would not expect to hold the Chair permanently. HN recognised (and even hoped) that an Asian candidate, who could 'rely upon returning from Oxford with enhanced prestige to preferment in his own country', would in any case find a short-term professorship more congenial than a European. Things came to a head in 1952 when the electors met to choose a successor to Radhakrishnan. On this occasion they did not choose an Asian. They chose R. C. Zaehner. Spalding was infuriated that an 'unsuitable' candidate had been chosen to fill the post instead. A lasting rift with the University ensued, as a result of which HN decreed that the University was to receive no further grants from the Spalding Trust. He expressed his displeasure in the following terms.

> The election of a highly unsuitable candidate (a philologist, a Christian, and a European) to the Chair of Eastern Religions and Ethics having been arranged without consultation with its Founders, and in the teeth of their own wish for a highly suitable Hindu philosopher, and of the intention and provision of the Statute, no further benefactions are to be made to or in the University of Oxford until these abuses and their cause have been remedied.[24]

The election of R. C. Zaehner was perceived by HN as a repudiation of his ideas and ideals in founding the Chair. Zaehner's inaugural lecture entitled *Foolishness to the Greeks*, was given before the University of Oxford on 2 November 1953, only a few weeks after HN's death. In retrospect it is easy to understand why some of Zaehner's remarks on that occasion gave such lasting offence to the members of Spalding's family who were in the audience. Parts of the lecture were perceived by them and others to constitute a gratuitous insult to HN's memory. The ensuing rift between Zaehner and the Spalding Trust was not to be healed. In fairness to Zaehner some lengthy extracts from his lecture deserve to be quoted. There is no hostility in the following passage:

> The endowment of a Chair in Eastern Religions and Ethics was an act of faith. It was an expression not only of Mr and Mrs Spalding's faith in an ultimate unity underlying all the great world religions, but of their faith in the University of Oxford as a suitable channel through which to make these outlandish systems more widely known. It was, however, more than an act of faith: it was an act of statesmanship. For it showed a keen realization on the part of Mr and Mrs Spalding that any view of world history which was based exclusively on the European contribution must be, to some extent, lop-sided. For they realized, earlier than most of us, that Asia, so long the unwilling ward of Europe, could not for ever be subjected to an alien way of thought. They understood that it is not possible for one culture permanently to be imposed on another, and that sooner or later the cultures of Europe and Asia would have to meet on equal terms.[25]

HN's statement of aims and objectives in establishing the Chair has already been mentioned. It was the subject of comment in the next part of Zaehner's lecture. His remarks were reasonable enough, focusing on the problem that would face any Spalding Professor who attempted to work to Spalding's own blueprint. Zaehner's point was that HN's plans were too wide-ranging and too much for one man to follow, but there was a more serious difficulty. He pointed out that the implementation of HN's plans for the Chair was impossible because 'the secularization of the University has come to stay'. More controversially, and more likely to give offence, were some of the remarks that Zaehner added:

> The promotion of understanding between the great religions can hardly be pursued in a British University, where the non-Christian religions can scarcely be said to be represented at all. Nor do I think that it can be a legitimate function of a university professor to attempt to induce harmony among elements as disparate as the great religions of mankind appear to be, if, as seems inevitable, the resultant harmony is only to

be apparent, verbal, and therefore fictitious. Such a procedure may well be commendable in a statesman. In a profession that concerns itself with the pursuit of truth it is damnable.[26]

There was the challenge to HN's ideals. There was the cause of offence, but before he ended Zaehner added a more conciliatory note:

I think that the University owes a great debt to the late Mr Spalding for endowing this Chair with a view to stimulating interest in what is, by any standards, an important subject. In accepting his gift the University demonstrated that they shared this view.[27]

For the next twenty years Zaehner worked on a number of scholarly publications. In a book that is primarily concerned with Spalding's intentions and aspirations it is only fair to recognise that in choosing Zaehner the electors were clearly of the opinion that they had chosen the best candidate. His academic qualifications for the post were narrow but outstanding. His work at Christ Church, Oxford, had hitherto involved him in the specialised field of Persian Studies, but he soon began to develop much wider interests in the field of Comparative Religion. During his occupancy of the Chair his scholarly output increased at the rate of almost a book a year. One of his close friends at All Souls, a Fellow of the College and also a Catholic, gave a moving address at Zaehner's memorial service in the College Chapel in 1974. In the course of his address Professor Michael Dummett had this to say.

[Zaehner] found himself the occupant of a Chair in a subject which was hardly, if at all, his own, since Zoroastrianism is presumably not an Eastern religion within the sense intended by the title of that Chair, and one that called not only for scholarship but for qualities of insight and synthesis based on, but transcending scholarship.

In accepting the Chair, he knew that his appointment would provoke some indignation in certain circles. A lesser man might have refused the challenge, or, having accepted it, kept very quiet, and behaved in a deferential manner to those already in the field, until he was ready to meet that challenge. Zaehner did neither of these things. As some of you will remember, he made of his Inaugural Lecture an opportunity to issue a manifesto declaring himself independent of those who would use the study of comparative religion to promote a universal syncretism; and he did it in the most abrasive manner possible, by direct and trenchant criticism of the founder of the Chair and of its only previous occupant.

This, his first public act in his new role, was in many ways typical of him. It was an act easy to misunderstand by attributing it to insolence or pugnacity, to neither of which it was due; though he never pulled punches in academic debate, he was not combative by temperament, nor did he take pleasure in wounding others: but it was characteristic of him that, while he was very careful to express his thought without ambiguity, he took no pains to guard against a natural misinterpretation of his motives. This lecture can only have aggravated the affront given to those who deprecated his appointment, and, indeed, he was later to feel some anxiety that, when his period of probation came to an end, he would not be confirmed in the tenure of the Chair. Since he must have known that such an Inaugural would have this effect, its delivery was an act of great courage (perhaps of foolhardiness); and this, too, was much in character, for he never lacked courage and was largely indifferent to the opinion others held of him or of the figure he cut.[28]

Spalding and Henderson both felt that the University of Oxford—and in particular the faculties of Oriental Studies and Theology—had not responded to the new opportunities provided by HN's benefaction by making it easier for Radhakrishnan and his successors to reach more students. Henderson, for instance, was to say that if Radhakrishnan (or Zaehner, for that matter) had been provided at Oxford with some of the facilities afforded to Robert Slater at the newly established Harvard Center for the Study of World Religions, his pupils would be found today staffing departments of Religious Studies all over the world. As a Professor and Fellow of All Souls. Zaehner was not obliged to teach students, but those who did come to him were given the help they sought. In the position he held he could never attract the numbers of students that HN had hoped to see in Oxford. Radhakrishnan was a gifted generalist, well able to consider many different aspects of different Eastern religions and cultures at the required scholarly level. Zaehner was a specialist who gradually increased his range. His work in Persian Studies has already been mentioned, but he adapted himself to embrace wider interests during his occupancy of the Spalding Chair.

Had HN lived longer he and Zaehner might well have discovered some common ground. Both men were criticised for having an 'unscholarly' agenda on the grounds that both were committed to a world-view—though clearly not the same world-view—which rendered the necessary 'scholarly' objectivity impossible for either of them. Spalding never claimed to be a scholar in the narrow academic sense of the word. He certainly had an agenda in that he strove in all he did to try to make the world a better place by taking religion seriously. For Zaehner, the professional scholar, the charge of bias was potentially more injurious. It was often made with reference to his professed Catholicism. The charge levelled against him and against Spalding was an unwarranted slur on their integrity. In more direct terms he was accused of approaching his subject in an 'apologetic' rather than a 'descriptive' way.[29]

There was a quirky side to Zaehner's character, which sometimes left his critics confused about his real motives. One of the best examples of this came when his article 'Why not Islam?' was published posthumously in the journal *Religious Studies*.[30] Some readers took it to signal Zaehner's decision to convert to Islam. Henderson, who had talked with Zaehner about this, knew better. He knew that the article "was intended to lead up to further arguments on the lines of 'Now I'll tell you why not'. His death, although he seems to have foreseen it ('Can't live longer than Aristotle!') left him still on the verge of embarking on a really constructive synthesis. At least I got that idea talking to him the last time we met."[31]

Discussing the development of teaching about world religions in schools, Professor Ninian Smart considered some of the ways in which the study of religion and religions may be approached. He clearly favoured the descriptive approach. As an example of the apologetic approach he cites Zaehner's *Mysticism Sacred and Profane*,[32] adding that 'such a work hovers uncertainly between the A and B group [i.e. the descriptive and the apologetic]. This by itself is no fatal criticism, provided an author knows what he is doing. Since there is a great deal of confusion about the aims of CSR [the comparative study of religion], this is not always a wise assumption to make.'[33] But there was no such confusion in Zaehner's mind. He was well aware of the aims of the comparative study of religion. He was also aware of the limits and the limitations of such study. And he certainly knew what he was doing. In addition to his scholarly writing, of which his small book, *Hinduism*,[34] was described by Sirdar Panikkar as the best available on the subject in English, he was ready to help visiting students with their Persian translation exercises. The same critic, who now said that Zaehner's little book on Hinduism showed an insight deeper than that of any other Western scholar he had encountered, had dismissed Zaehner earlier with the comment 'for him all roads lead to Rome'.[35]

In 1960 Zaehner was uncertain about his future course of action. He was thinking about applying for another position at All Souls College, and hoping that this might be combined with the post of Domestic Bursar. If he were to succeed and be offered either or both of these positions, he would have to resign as Spalding Professor. But should he even contemplate such a move? Would there be alternative opportunities? Would the University of Oxford establish a Chair in Persian, a post for which he was well qualified? Would the Chair of Persian at Cambridge become available to him? During this trying time he wrote a letter to Henderson, with whom he had been establishing friendly relationships for some time. Henderson hoped that the hostility that had arisen between Zaehner and the Spalding Trust after the latter's election to the Chair was being reduced to the point at which Zaehner might be invited to become a Spalding Trustee. Zaehner wrote:

I have now become so intensely interested in the study of religion that only in extremis could I be tempted back to Persian. My heart is not in it. Further I feel that my meeting with Mr Spalding [i.e. Dr John Spalding] has removed a host of misunderstandings and it would be futile to give up at a moment when the atmosphere has, I hope, definitely cleared. I quite see Mr Spalding's point that his father's idea had been for the Professor to interpret the Indian religions from inside, but I wonder how far this can be done in a course of University lectures. This would be rather like my lecturing on 'What the Catholic Church means to me', and I can see many an academic eyebrow being raised if I were to do this.[36]

Meanwhile plans for the rapid extension of higher education in Britain were being made. Among the plans for new universities was one for the establishment of the University of Lancaster in the north of England, on a green field site near the city on the edge of the Lake District. Had he lived to see what was being suggested for the development of Religious Studies there, HN might have chosen Lancaster rather than Oxford for the Spalding Chair.

A New Initiative

It was left to a new university, at Lancaster, to promote the kind of broad study of world religions that HN had hoped to set up at Oxford. Ninian Smart, H. G. Wood Professor of Theology in the University of Birmingham, was appointed to the new Chair of Religious Studies at Lancaster in 1967. The advertisement for the new post was interesting, if not controversial. Applications were invited from candidates 'of any creed or none'. After his appointment Professor Smart was described in the London *Observer* as 'an Anglican layman with a certain affection for Buddhism'. His credentials as a mid-twentieth-century Christian believer were clearly impeccable, but is there (should there) be a place for an unbeliever, for an agnostic, in a department of Theology or Religious Studies? Had Zaehner wished to apply for the Lancaster post, would his Catholicism have excluded him? If an uncompromising believer like him is an unacceptable candidate, would not an uncompromising unbeliever be equally out of place? It is somewhat ironic that as things developed, H. N. Spalding's ambitious plans for the widest possible inclusion of the study of world religions in education were never to be fulfilled in the post he had created at Oxford for precisely that purpose, when his programme was at least partly to be followed thirty years later at Lancaster. Smart was one of the signatories of a memorandum that might well have been written, or certainly signed, by HN.[37]

'We the undersigned, are members of the British Section of the International Association for the History of Religions. We are deeply concerned that there should be a proper expansion of the teaching of comparative religion in our educational system. We take notice of the following facts:

a. There is a great and growing demand for information about world religions.

b. There is in process a wide attempt to re-think the principles of religious education in schools.

c. There is an expansion of Asian and African Studies, which reflects a greater impetus in the social sciences and in the humanities towards a better understanding of non-European societies, cultures, and politics. This in turn reflects the recognition that humanity in this country must concern itself with humanity as a whole.

d. The institution of the degree of Bachelor of Education provides a new opportunity to appraise the place of religious studies in the universities and colleges of education.

e. The expansion of technological education, in the colleges of technology and in the new technological universities, has as a side effect an increasing interest in liberal or general studies, one element of which may be the study of religion.

f. The long-standing popularity of comparative religion in adult education courses is undiminished.

'In the light of the above facts, it is a pity that better use is not made of the existing opportunities for the comparative study of religion in this country. This study in many ways is and has for long been well advanced in Britain. But for various reasons these opportunities have not been properly exploited. In schools, colleges of education, colleges of technology and in universities, there is some shortage of those trained to fulfil the growing demand for the teaching of courses in this subject.

'This is partly at least because this area of study has not an altogether ensured place in curricula, despite the demand. Once the assured place is recognised, there would be a natural increase in those who present themselves for training in this area of study. The training resources, certainly, exist, though in certain respects they need supplementing. There is provision for the subject in a number of universities, including London, Oxford, Glasgow, Manchester, Wales, Leeds, Birmingham and Hull; and there will soon be courses in two or three other universities. As well as research by thesis, there are graduate courses by examination in two or three universities. Research and other activities are in some degree co-ordinated through the British Section of the International

Association for the History of Religions. A substantial amount of publications testifies to the liveliness of the group of scholars engaged in this field in this country. We therefore recommend that the following policies be considered seriously in the planning of religious and allied studies in our educational system.

a. Some teaching of world religions should form a component of the curriculum in religious education in schools, chiefly for the higher age-levels. This, where necessary, should be combined with a broadening of syllabuses in history, art, etc., to include some reference to the history, art, etc., of Asian and African cultures.

b. Comparative religion should everywhere be part of the curriculum in religious studies in colleges of education.

c. Comparative religion should form part of the curriculum in the theological half of the Bachelor of Education degree. It should also form part of the curriculum in theological colleges.

d. To improve the quality of teaching in this subject, teachers both in schools, colleges of education and elsewhere should be granted, wherever possible, encouragement and secondment for courses of training in this subject.

e. There should be an active concern to generate a creative interplay between sociology and social anthropology on the one hand and the comparative study of religion on the other. In general, it is desirable that comparative religion should be integrated into University studies, both in the Social Sciences and in the Humanities.

f. Liberal and general studies in the technological side of higher education should make adequate provision for the teaching of comparative religion.

g. The development of African and Asian studies should increasingly complement existing social and linguistic disciplines with a proper appreciation of the role of the history and analysis of religious ideas and experience.

'It should also be recognised that comparative religion can play an important social role in helping to create a better understanding of the different cultural backgrounds of African and Asian people resident in this country.' [38]

HN would undoubtedly have agreed with the opinions and suggestions included in this memorandum. From his point of view, the new initiative at Lancaster came too late.

Henderson's Reflections on the Work of the Chair

Henderson was well placed to understand HN's intentions for the Spalding Professorship. He was also in a good position to assess what happened immediately before the election of Zaehner to the Chair in 1952. He was also able to reflect on Zaehner's twenty-year occupancy of the Chair and to compare him with his predecessor, Radhakrishnan. In the Summer of 1975, when it was still unclear that anyone would be appointed to succeed Zaehner, Henderson wrote the following note.

> I have been used to think how remarkable it was that a Hindu philosopher should have proved a more successful statesman than Plato or Aristotle, and when I was asked last February to draft a citation for the bestowal on Dr Radhakrishnan of the Templeton Award I tried to illustrate this side of his message by a quotation which I shall repeat below. Its keynote is Relevance, the relevance of reason to the interpretation of religious experience and the relevance of that interpretation to the human condition. Zaehner's last book, *Our Savage God*, stresses both these relevances, ranging as freely through the slums and alleys of our contemporary conturbations as over the high citadels of metaphysics. It is perhaps not strange that two such different men should have reached similar conclusions.[39]

The quotation to which Henderson refers above was taken from something Radhakrishnan said as Spalding Professor elect. In the discussion that followed his talk on *Religion and Religions* at the first World Congress of Faiths (held in London from July 3–17, 1936, and organised by Sir Francis Younghusband), Radhakrishnan said:

> The question has been raised that those who believed in intuition tried to exclude the operation of the intellect. The way the leader of the debate put it was that those who practise do not investigate, and those who investigate do not practise. But if you go to the really great mystics, whether in the Upanishads, or to a man like Buddha, or one like Plato, or any of the great mystics of the world who may be regarded as examples of saintly life, you will find in them an intellectual eminence and comprehensive knowledge. And it would have been impossible for them to practise those things unless their intellects had been satisfied. The life of the spirit is an integral life, a life where you sanctify your body, illuminate your intellect, and obtain a complete kind of manhood. There should, in any complete life, be an equal emphasis on the intellect and the intuitions.[40]

And to this passage Henderson appended some words from Zaehner's *Our Savage God:*

> There is much nobility and probably much truth in the theory of the union of opposites proclaimed by Heraclitus and the Upanishads alike, and Aldous Huxley is not far wrong in calling it The Perennial Philosophy since it crops up everywhere, in every form, and at all times. But it needs to be rigorously checked by the rational mind which it would destroy. If not, then all things are lawful.[41]

A few months later, in February 1976, shortly before the election of Zaehner's successor, Henderson wrote a paper with the title 'Some Reflections on the Spalding Chair':

> For nearly a quarter of a century my work as Secretary to the Spalding Trust and the Union for the Study of the Great Religions has brought me into contact with scholars involved in the study of these subjects in Europe and America and Australia, and in Asia and Africa. Some are specialists in one religion. A Professor of Arabic cannot help being deeply interested in Islam, or a Tibetologist in that brand of Buddhism. It is difficult to avoid such a commitment unless you are dealing with a language like Sanskrit which has an important linguistic role independent of its literature. Some are philosophers, like Hywel Lewis, drawn increasingly into discussion with their Asian counterparts. Some are historians, like the leading continental scholars who still dominate the International Association for the History of Religions, treating religious issues as a human phenomenon, and careful to avoid any controversial comparison of doctrines. Arnold Toynbee was an exceptional example of this point of view because he used religion to illustrate a theory of history.
>
> Some were like George Bell and Charles Raven; some educationalists like Richard Livingstone; some anthropologists like Evans Pritchard; some mystics like Alan Watts and Marco Pallis. A few, surprisingly few, regard religion as a psychological phenomenon, to be treated on the same lines as the sex instinct in man. From this hotch-potch of differing interests and talents there has emerged, increasingly in recent years, a new discipline, the study of world religions—Spiegelberg, Morgan, Eliade, Slater, Cantwell Smith, Huston Smith, Ashby, Bouquet, R. E. Hume, Geoffrey Parrinder, Ninian Smart. Dr Radhakrishnan, for whose gifts the Chair was designed, does not fit exactly into any of these categories. He was a philosopher and a propagandist for Hinduism as the all-embracing mother of other faiths; but his special ambition was to achieve a sort of universal culture based

upon all religions, as European culture was based on Christianity and Hellenism, and Chinese culture on Confucianism and Tao.

Not did the Chair fit exactly into the pattern of Oxford disciplines. It was attached to the Oriental school but drew its rare students mainly from the departments of Theology and Philosophy. When the demand arose for scholars in the field of comparative religion to fill new lectureships and chairs all over the English-speaking world Oxford was not, therefore, in a position to supply them, as it would have been if Radhakrishnan had been equipped with the facilities later provided for the school of world religions at Harvard. His influence depended instead on his writings and his public lectures. The influence of his successor also depended on his writing. The appointment of Robin Zaehner, a lecturer in Iranian studies little known outside Oxford, and a reputedly bigoted Roman Catholic, broke H. N. Spalding's heart and accelerated his death from leukaemia. Zaehner's Inaugural Lecture, 'Foolishness to the Greeks', was interpreted by a leader-writer in the Times Educational Supplement as being a repudiation of all H. N.'s ideas and provoked a storm of protest which the Editor refused to publish. He published instead a letter from Zaehner himself claiming that he had been misinterpreted, but the damage was done and for many years relations between Trust and Professor were strained.

The subsequent development of this supposedly narrow-minded Zoroastrian expert into a scholar of international repute with a remark-able grasp of the scriptural languages and basic ideas of Hinduism and Islam and an insight into the mystical aspects of both, was remarkable, and one can only regret that neither H. N. Spalding nor his wife lived to see it happen. Watching all this going on, from a seat in the gallery rather than the wings, I have found my own attitude changing from one of regret at the failure of the University to provide any supporting research fellowship, such as Spalding understood would be forthcoming, with the resultant transfer of influence from Oxford to Chicago and Harvard, to the picture of the Chair as a cloistered centre where the holder would be free from the distractions of running a university department.

This change of view has altered my attitude to the appointment of an Asian successor. I had become a bit dubious about this, after two contested re-elections [of Zaehner], because I felt that no Asian could hope to establish the Chair as an integral part of the University, existing in its own right and associated with the faculty of Theology instead of being appended to the school of Oriental Studies, providing a useful additional lecturer and tutor in whatever oriental language the holder might profess. If instead the Chair is to remain simply a base for the propagation of ideas through the University Press, any objection to the appointment of a 'person of Asian descent' as prescribed in the preamble [to the Statutes] falls to the ground, save only in the absence of an Asian candidate of sufficiently high calibre or the presence of a European candidate of exceptional eminence.[42]

An Asian Elected

When Zaehner died in 1974 it was by no means certain that the Chair would be offered to a successor without delay. It was a time of financial stringency in higher education. Economies were sought and achieved. With regard to the Spalding Chair the talk was of a moratorium. In the event the post was re-advertised and a candidate was elected in 1976. The successful applicant was Bimal Krishna Matilal, a Professor in the Department of Sanskrit and Indian Studies at the University of Toronto. Matilal was born in 1935 at Joynagar in West Bengal, not far from Calcutta, the only son of a Brahmin family. One of his boyhood companions was Gopikamohan Bhattacharya, who was also to achieve distinction as an interpreter of Indian philosophy. After a brilliant career at Calcutta University, graduating Master of Arts in Sanskrit and Indian Philosophy in 1956, Matilal was appointed to a lectureship at the University's Sanskrit College. From Calcutta he went to the United States, to Harvard where he was awarded his PhD in 1965 under the aegis of Daniel Ingalls. By 1975 he was already a full Professor in the Department of Indian Studies at Harvard and later a professor in Toronto. He was not well known in this country, although he had already made a reputation for himself in the Indian sub-continent and later in North America. Unprepossessing in his manner, Matilal often appeared to be shy and diffident in the company of others. He spoke quietly, rapidly, and indistinctly, so much so, that many who came to hear him speak in lectures or seminars left with the feeling that he had not done himself justice. No-one with whom he worked, however, could question his command of Sanskrit, or doubt his scholarship and erudition.

By the time he took up his new appointment in December 1976 he had already made significant contributions to Indian philosophy, logic, epistemology and ethics. He was Founder/Editor of the *Journal of Indian Philosophy* from 1970 to 1991. From 1971 to 1976 he was Professor of Sanskrit and Indian Studies at the University of Toronto. He acted a Vice-President of the Society for Asian and Comparative Philosophy from 1973 to 1975. He held the Spalding Chair at Oxford and a fellowship at All Souls College from 1976 to 1991. In 1978 he was S. N. Dasgupta Memorial Lecturer at Cambridge University. His arrival in Oxford promised to end the long-standing disagreement between the Trustees and the occupant of the Chair. Here, once more, was a distinguished Asian, whose candidacy HN would undoubtedly have approved. Several weeks before he officially took up the post Matilal was invited to lunch by the Spalding Trustees. This first meeting between them took place on 3 July 1976, at Shotover Cleve, Dr John Spalding's house in Oxford. A cordial relationship was immediately established between the Trustees and the new Professor, so much so that it was not long before he was invited to become a Spalding Trustee. He served in this capacity until his untimely death from a crippling disease at the age of 56. He died in Oxford on 8 June 1991. Despite their admiration for his scholarly competence and personal charm it soon became apparent that Matilal's concerns were very different from those of HN and from those of the two previous occupants of the Spalding Chair. Culturally a Hindu, he had long adopted a secular approach to the study of cultures and religions. For him they were fascinating subjects of historical interest, which had little or no influence on his personal convictions. His approach confirmed what Henderson had noted after visiting India: 'In general, I got the impression that there is a drift away from religion amongst the educated class'.

During a close friendship that developed in Oxford between Matilal and the present writer, I often noticed the way in which he poked gentle fun at those in the West who entertained what he considered to be an unrealistic and romantic view of Indian religions, especially Hinduism. He was forthright in his criticism of Western observers whose characterisation of some Indian religions in terms of *ahimsa*—non-violence—could only be maintained by ignoring, or overlooking, the less congenial aspects of religious belief and practice in those religions. And in company with other Asian scholars he was critical of Radhakrishnan's idiosyncratic and selective exposition of *The Hindu View of Life*.[43] Matilal signalled his critical approach to the study of religions East and West in his Inaugural Lecture, which was delivered in the Examination Schools on 5 May 1977 with the title *The Logical Illumination of Indian Mysticism*.[44] Here, in a lecture addressed to a Western audience, he indicated the lines along which he proposed to follow a determinedly post-colonial approach to Indian Studies, inviting his hearers to look again and see that Indian philosophers and logicians have their own ancient intellectual traditions that parallel those of their Western counterparts. In choosing mysticism as his subject, however, he was at pains to point out that an insistence on the underlying unity behind all the differences of name and form to be found in the great religions is misconceived and even mischievous. Zaehner had drawn attention to the profound differences between the mysticism of the East and the mysticism of the West.

At the beginning of his inaugural lecture Matilal noted that Zaehner had reservations about Aldous Huxley's identification of the universality of a *philosophia perennis*, which can be be detected and acknowledged in the mystical experience of mankind. Matilal spoke of Zaehner, who 'entertained deep misgivings about the implicit amorality of a monistic metaphysical position, which is regarded as the bedrock of eastern mysticism'.[45] That was a moral judgement of the kind that Matilal was not disposed to make. As a logician he sought instead to question the validity of a strictly rationalistic position, whether Western or Eastern, in which the choice had finally to be made between 'the juice of religion and mysticism' and 'that of rationality and scepticism'.

> Buridan's ass was most probably a philosopher, certainly a logician. But an ordinary man even with reason chooses to act randomly under the circumstances. In fact, the ordinary man is worse off than Buridan's ass in this matter. He is torn and tormented by the conflict between the taste of 'the tree of life' and that of the 'tree of knowledge'. And reason cannot show any evaluative preference of one over the other. His condition is comparable to that of one who is placed between two equally tempting glasses of juice—one containing, say, the juice of religion and mysticism and the other that of rationality and scepticism—and being attracted to both, tries, not unreasonably, to partake a little of both. Thus he may ask much in the same way the Vedic seer asked: 'To what god shall we offer oblation?' [46]

Sadly, Matilal was unable to complete the tasks he set himself. It cannot be said that he felt completely at ease in Oxford. He had tempting offers to leave Oxford and return to North America, notably to Chicago in 1982, but he chose to stay. His untimely death came when he was working on the final stages of several future publications. The election of his successor in the Spalding Chair proceeded uneventfully. The successful candidate, already a Fellow of Wolfson College, Oxford, was Alexis G. J. S. Sanderson. Professor Sanderson's research is concentrated on some of the less well-known aspects of *Śaivism*. His is an esoteric field of study. In this selective enterprise there is no room for the kind of broad and comparative approach to religion and ethics advocated by HN and Radhkrishnan. Sanderson remains respectful but critical of his predecessors (and by implication, of HN himself) on grounds that they each had an agenda that was inappropriate in a university setting. The criticism appears to be based on the conviction that each of them, even Matilal, was an apologist. The charge against them, for it is no less than that, is that their work was compromised to a greater or lesser extent by their lack of scholarly objectivity. In the light of what they were able to achieve it is difficult to maintain the charge against them, however. They are no longer in a position to defend themselves against it. Critics, as is often the case, tend to be selective in their judgements, overlooking (or even not noticing) the way in which their own efforts are influenced by subjective opinion and fashion. It is a matter of fact not of opinion that with the passing of time little remains of the original vision of Mr and Mrs Spalding for the development of the work of the Spalding Chair at Oxford other than their name.

Plans for an 'Asia House'

For several years Spalding had expressed his dissatisfaction with the state of the Indian Institute in Oxford, but he had done much more than complain about what he thought was a lost opportunity for promoting the study of Indian religions and cultures. In the late 1940s in Oxford he served as a member of the *Committee for the Promotion of Cultural Relations with India*. Its purpose was explicit, namely, to assist the revival of Indian Studies at Oxford. Radhakrishnan was a member of the Committee. In addition to the Spalding Chair in Eastern Religions and Ethics the University could point to the Boden Chair of Sanskrit, and a Readership in Indian History as evidence of its interest in Indian Studies. This was admirable but not quite enough for HN who wanted much more attention given to the kind of comparative religious studies likely to attract undergraduates. The Committee did not lack support from distinguished senior representatives of the University. Besides Spalding himself, it included as Chairman, Sir W. D. Ross (Provost of Oriel), Professor Radhakrishnan of All Souls, T. S. R. Boase (President of Magdalen), A. H. Smith (Warden of New College), Sir Maurice Bowra (Warden of Wadham), Professor T. Burrow, W. Cohn, C. C. Davies, G. F. Hudson, Guy Wint and W. A. C. H. Dobson, who acted as Secretary. Naturally enough, those already engaged in this work in the University were quick to point out that much had already been done to further this aim. Anticipating criticism that studies in Comparative Religion at Oxford, with particular reference to Indian Religions, were still not attracting large numbers of undergraduates, Radhakrishnan produced a memorandum showing that progress was being made. Headed *All Souls College*, Oxford, but undated, it reads,

Eastern Religions and Ethics

When I came here in October 1936, I found that there was scope for the study of Eastern Religions in the Honour Schools of Oriental Studies and of Theology. In the Honour School of Oriental Studies (Sanskrit) a candidate must offer *one* of four special subjects which are:-

(1) Comparative Grammar of Greek, Sanskrit and Zend.

(2) History of Indian Religions

(3) History of Indian Philosophy

(4) Indian Epigraphy and Palaeography.

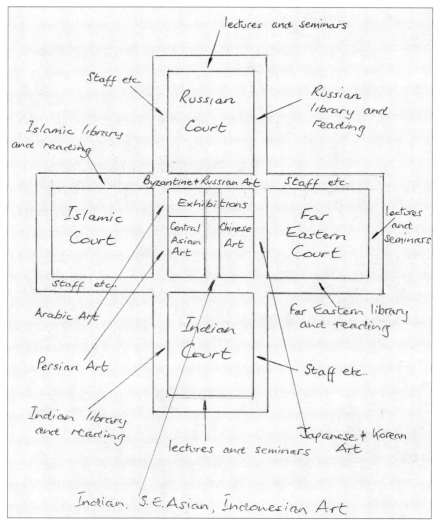

lectures and seminars

Staff etc.

Russian Court

Russian library and reading

Islamic library and reading

Byzantine + Russian Art

Staff etc..

Islamic Court

Exhibitions

Central Asian Art

Chinese Art

Far Eastern Court

lectures and seminars

Staff etc.

Arabic Art

Persian Art

Indian Court

Far Eastern library and reading

Staff etc.

Indian library and reading

lectures and seminars

Japanese + Korean Art

Indian, S.E. Asian, Indonesian Art

From H. N. Spalding's plan for the interior of an 'Asia House' at Oxford.

There were few students for this School and one or two who occasionally turned up were advised to take up the first subject, which is of philological interest. In the Honour School of Theology, there was provision for the study of Comparative Religion but it was very inadequate. Candidates for this School are required to take not less than two of the subjects in Groups B & C.

Group B (1) Ecclesiastical History etc.
(2) The Hebrew of the Old Testament.
(3) The Philosophy of Religion.

Group C (1) Liturgies.
         (2) Sacred Criticism and Archaeology of the Old
              and New Testaments.
         (3) Christian Ethics.
         (4) A special subject which included ten alternatives of
              which Comparative Religion was one. To my knowl-
              edge no one took it up for some years past.

Though my lectures in the first two years were fairly well attended by
students of Theology and Modern Greats I felt that their interest was
not sustained as the subjects of the lectures had no direct bearing on
the examination courses. I spoke to one or two members of the Board
of the Faculty of Theology and through their assistance a few alterations
were made in the courses for Theology, which were intended to increase
the value of the study of Eastern religions from the examination point
of view.

Under *Philosophy of Religion,* a sentence was added: 'The problems of
philosophy of religion may be discussed in the light of other philosophical
traditions than those of "Christendom"'.

'Christian Ethics' was taken over to Group B from Group C and in
its place 'The Comparative Study of Religions' was inserted into Group
C. It is now one of four subjects out of which candidates are required
to take two.

I could not perceive the effect of these changes till I came back in
1946, as the war intervened. I now see that some of the students of
Theology regularly attend my lectures on 'Philosophy of Religion' and
a few students have selected 'The Comparative Study of Religions' as
one of the two subjects of Group C which they are required to take.

I feel that the subject of 'Eastern Religions and Ethics' is slowly getting
rooted in the academic system of the University. One candidate is
working for the D. Phil. degree under my supervision. All the candidates
who attend my lectures on 'Philosophy of Religion' and classes on 'The
Comparative Studies in [*sic*] Religion [*sic*] as well as the candidate for
the D. Phil. degree are British nationals.

I think that the solidarity of the human race which we may hope for
as the ultimate issue of human history may be promoted to some extent
by the building up of academic traditions which are free from pro-
vincialism and prejudice and encourage the study not only of the
languages of other civilizations but of their views of the universe and
ways of life.[47]

When he was an undergraduate at New College, Oxford, HN's knowledge
of the civilizations of Greece and Rome was systematically extended. Having

returned to live and work in Oxford, and having in the meantime become absorbed in a study of Eastern religious thought, he wanted the University to start an 'Oriental Greats', for which students would be required to study not only Eastern religions and philosophies but also other aspects of Oriental civilizations as a necessary prelude to their acquisition of a deeper under-standing of East/West relationships. He wanted Oxford to have a School 'like Greats, to humanize the new learning in all its branches, for he believed it possible to achieve understanding of religions, as he had done himself, by studying their sacred books in translation, under the tuition of scholars with access to the originals.' [48] HN met a number of Rhodes scholars who came to Oxford to continue their studies. Rhodes House was established in Oxford by the will of Cecil Rhodes as a centre for scholars from the British Empire, the United States and Germany. In 1929 it was erected in South Parks Road only a few yards from the Spaldings' house. HN's plans for an Asia House in Oxford were designed to provide a 'Rhodes House for Asians'.

HN saw his plans for 'Asia House' as an important contribution to the development of global unity, believing that if an 'Asian House' were to be established in Oxford it would not merely help to promote but actually *demonstrate* the spiritual unity of mankind. Oxford had been a major training centre for recruits to the Indian Civil Service, although this was not to continue. By 1947 Probationers for the Service were no longer trained in Oxford. HN drafted a memorandum about his plans for Asia House and revised it several times in an attempt to persuade the University to go ahead with the project.[49] The first thing to strike the reader about these plans is the detail that HN includes. He is not content with an outline of what ought to be done. He concerns himself with the practical questions of how the building is to be financed and where it is to be erected. The second thing to strike the reader is the sheer determination shown by HN to press his case when it becomes clear that the University is not prepared to accept his proposal but reluctant to offend an honoured benefactor. The plans are too long and detailed to include here but a summary can be given. They appear under the heading, *'Asia House': The Development of the Indian Institute into an Institute for Indian Studies'*. HN's idea was that Indian civilizations should be studied along the same lines that students at Oxford had traditionally studied the civilizations of Greece and Rome. After a section in which he considered 'Eastern Studies at Oxford' HN proceeded to deal with the design of the new building. It was based on the lay-out of a museum in Honolulu. His sketch-plan of the interior shows 'approximately what Asia House might look like.' The drawing shows a cruciform structure, separated into discrete courts, with surrounding areas for libraries, private study, seminars, lectures, exhibitions, workshops for 'crafts and folk-art' and staff accommodation. A representation of his hand-drawn sketch for the layout of the building appears in the illustration on page 129. He added that the plans he had in mind would also make an important contribution to Adult Education.

Where was Asia House to be built? In HN's opinion the Indian Institute building, situated on the corner of Broad Street and Holywell Street in Oxford, could no longer serve. The site as well as the building were unsuitable and would have to be sold. The proceeds from the sale would help to finance the new development. HN's first choices were Balliol or Merton playing fields. He noted sadly that the University had already 'lost' possible sites in Mansfield Road 'through lack of foresight'. It is difficult to understand how he expected his proposals to be accepted by the University, not to mention Balliol or Merton. The 'Newman site', some 3½ acres along Manor Road was a distinct possibility for Spalding, although this clashed to some extent with his designs for improved sporting facilities for Oxford students. His unfavourable comparison of the facilities available to students in the United States with those available to students in Oxford has already been noted in chapter three. These memories of his extended visit to America had not faded, so the apparent digression was justified in case the University had overlooked his earlier recommendations. The 'Newman site' seemed to be admirable for the construction of sporting facilities. What, specifically, did he consider was necessary? In the first place there would have to be an athletic centre. Exercise for sedentary students was the thing. There would have to be a swimming pool. a gymnasium, racquets courts, areas for wrestling, judo and boxing. Eton Fives would feature. What he simply called 'a Physical Training Centre' would also have to be built. He had no shortage of ideas for promoting this side of the development of students and for at least some of their teachers, for that matter. To what extent this might be seen as part of the plans for Asia House was left undisclosed.

None of these plans could have been implemented without adequate finance. HN had some ideas about how the money could be raised. The sale of the Indian Institute site and building would help, but a much more ambitious money-raising campaign would have to be organised. HN suggested that a start be made by appointing a committee consisting of 'leading figures from East and West'. The Committee would have the responsibility of contributing or soliciting contributions for the development fund as soon as the project 'was costed'. *'Asia House', an Institute for Asian Studies* would be the result. The response to his memorandum dated 6 June 1947 was courteous but lukewarm. His speedy revisions of the memorandum, dated 10 and 18 June respectively, fared no better. Two items of correspondence effectively killed off HN's proposals, The first, dated 30 June 1947, was a note from Sir Richard Livingstone, sometime President of Corpus Christi College, Oxford and at that time the University's Vice-Chancellor. His note to Spalding on this occasion was friendly in tone, but noticeably unenthusiastic about Asia

House. Livingstone was a personal friend, who was to become Chairman of the Union for the Study of the Great Religions, which Spalding founded in 1950. In the absence of Livingstone's unqualified support, it would have been difficult for HN to press the matter further, not least because he was suffering increasingly from an as yet undiagnosed illness.

Spalding had tried to get help from the British Government, urging that the Indian authorities be urged to make a grant to help finance the project. The timing was unfortunate. 1947 was the year in which India gained her independence from British rule. It was the year when ethnic and religious differences there led to partition and to a period of unrest and wholesale murder in the sub-continent. A characteristically terse note from the Prime Minister, Clement Attlee, dated 15 July 1947 and written from 10 Downing Street to Sir W. D. Ross, the Chairman of the *Committee for the Promotion of Indian Culture* on which HN served, describes the suggestion that His Majesty's Government approach the Indian Government about Asia House as 'inopportune'.[50] Even these discouraging responses did not quite extinguish HN's hopes, but the subject was not to be raised seriously again.[51] It was not his proposals that offended members of the academic community in Oxford. It was the explicit agenda that he attached to his plans. He was in the habit of attaching conditions to the benefactions he made. It is natural for benefactors to make their wishes known, but when the conditions seek to direct the present and future course of the work for which the money is donated, tensions inevitably arise.

The work HN started goes on, although circumstances have changed. To say that he had an agenda is to state the obvious. To repeat the statement in criticism of his efforts, on the grounds that he was more interested in *pre-scription*—especially in education—rather than *description*, is to pretend that a clear line can be drawn between commitment and neutrality in any human enterprise. Others, more inclined to insist on the need for scholarly objectivity also had world-views, religious beliefs, agnostic or atheistic persuasions, which influenced what they said, wrote, and taught, in ways that they were less prepared to concede. Spalding and Henderson both encouraged the study of World Religions as an instrument for promoting justice and peace. At the beginning of the twenty-first century their vision has lost none of its importance.

Notes and References

1. A phrase used by Professor Krishna Satchidananda Murty of Andhra University in India. He was Vice-President of the Indian branch of the Union for the Study of the Great Religions.
2. HNS, 1939, *Civilization in East and West: An Introduction to the Study of Human Progress*, Oxford University Press.
3. *Ibid*, 1939, p. vii.
4. Aleksandr Isayevich Solzhenitsyn, 1997, *Invisible Allies* (*Nevidimki*), translated by Alexis Klimoff and Michael Nicholson, The Harvill Press, London, p. 27.
5. HNS, CEW, pp. 322–3.
6. HNS, 1958, *The Divine Universe*, Basil Blackwell, Oxford, p. 354.
7. HNS, 1939, CEW, p. 325.
8. CEW, *op. cit.*, p. vii.
9. See also Roger Hooker, 1973, *Uncharted Journey*, Church Missionary Society, London.
10. A discussion of this subject is contained in Gavin D'Costa (ed.), 1990, *Christian Uniqueness Reconsidered: The Myth of a Pluralistic Theology of Religions*, Faith Meets Faith Series, Orbis Books, Maryknoll, New York.
11. In the fourth part of IPL, entitled 'Portrait Gallery', Spalding included a sonnet, 'The Incarnate Reason' that ends with these words. The poem appears on p. 101.
12. W. E. Hocking, 1932, *Re-Thinking Missions: A Layman's Inquiry after One Hundred Years*, Harper, New York, pp. 29, 32, 33.
13. James Hilton (1900–54); see, for example, his novel *Knight Without Armour* (1933).
14. Thompson's novel *Farewell to India* was published in 1925.
15. Mary Lago, 2001, *India's Prisoner: A Biography of Edward John Thompson (1886–1946)*, University of Missouri Press, p. 1.
16. HN's generosity in enabling Oriel to renew the Fellowship after the initial three year period is recorded in the Oriel College Minute Book (1926–41, p. 251): 'It was agreed to accept with thanks Mr H. N. Spalding's generous offer to renew for 3 years from 1 January 1939 his grant to the College to enable it to elect Mr Thompson to a Senior Research Fellowship; and it was resolved to re-elect Mr Thompson for the period.'
17. Mary Lago, *op. cit.*, p. 263.
18. It seems that Edward Thompson is the only person who could have passed on this comment to Spalding.
19. See Sarvepalli Gopal (Radhakrishnan's son), 1992, 'The Spalding Chair', in *Radhakrishnan, A Biography*, Oxford India Paperbacks, pp. 145–62.
20. Letter dated 17 August 1959, STP.
21. S. Gopal, 1992, *op. cit.*, pp. 323–4.
22. STP, letter, Murty to Henderson, 27 May 1981.
23. My italics.
24. This extract from HN's original memorandum of 1953 was quoted again by KDDH in a letter to the Spalding Trustees, dated 8 July 1981, when an application to finance a visiting lectureship or fellowship in Indian Philosophy and Religion at Wolfson College, Oxford, was received. The Trustees decided that by that time the 'abuses' had been 'remedied', so the visiting fellowship was financed for a trial period of three years.
25. R. C. Zaehner, *Foolishness to the Greeks*, published at the Clarendon Press in Oxford, 1953, pp. 3–4.
26. *Ibid*, p. 5.
27. *Ibid*, p. 22.

28. M. A. E. Dummett's address was given in All Souls College, Oxford on 15 February 1975, during the memorial service for R. C. Zaehner. The quotations are from pp. 5–6 of the limited printed edition.

29. Not long before he died Zaehner acknowledged that his critics were not all of the same stamp. He had just been accused by one of them of elevating Aristotle above Jesus, an odd thing to do—even for a Catholic.

30. R. C. Zaehner, 'Why Not Islam?', in *Religious Studies*, volume 11, number 2, June 1975, pp. 167–79. Bishop Kenneth Cragg's thoughtful response with the title 'How Not Islam?' was published in the same journal (volume 13, number 4, December 1977, pp. 387–94). He regrets that the debate 'cannot now be joined', noting that Zaehner 'appeared to be withholding his own position by the very form of his advocacy. The article could equally be read as a subtle dissuasive' (p. 387).

31. Letter dated 5 September 1975 from Henderson to Professor Dorothy Emmett, HFP, Box 4, file F2/6.

32. R. C. Zaehner, 1957, *Mysticism Sacred and Profane: An Inquiry into Some Varieties of Praeternaturalism*, Oxford University Press.

33. Ninian Smart, 1970, 'The Structure of the Comparative Study of Religion', in *Comparative Religion in Education*, edited by John Hinnells, Oriel Press, Newcastle upon Tyne, pp. 20–31. I am grateful to Penny Thompson, whose analysis has been of great assistance to me in understanding the development of Religious Education in British schools since World War II.

34. R. C. Zaehner, 1962, Oxford University Press.

35. NUSGR, number 23, February 1967, p. 1,

36. 7 March 1960, STP.

37. NUSGR, number 23, February 1967, pp. 1–3.

38. The memorandum was signed by E. O. James, E. G. Parrinder, R. A. Barclay, John Bowker, S. G. F. Brandon, Rundle Clark, Raymond Hammer, H. D. Lewis, Trevor Ling, Ninian Smart, John Taylor, and C. G. Williams.

39. NUSGR, number 32, Summer 1975, p. 1.

40. Sarvepalli Radhakrishnan, 'Religion and Religions' in *Faiths and Fellowship* (undated), edited by A. Douglas Millard, J. M. Watkins, London, pp. 119–20.

41. R. C. Zaehner, *Our Savage God*, p. 102.

42. The paper, dated 25 February 1976, is in the Henderson Family Papers (HFP), Box 'Talks and Tours'.

43. Radhakrishnan, 1961, Allen & Unwin.

44. Published at the Clarendon Press, Oxford, 1977. I located a copy of the lecture In the Indian Institute, Oxford, ref: Hindu B366, 9401 e. 140.

45. *Ibid*, p. 3.

46. *Ibid*, p. 34.

47. OCA (Oriel College Archives) PRO 46 [uncatalogued], Sir W. D. Ross, Box 4 (misc. papers and letters).

48. K. D. D. Henderson in *The Oxford Magazine*, 21 January 1954, p. 145.

49. The original draft is dated 6 June 1947. It was revised four days later, and again on 18 June 1947, marked 'Urgent'.

50. HN's plans for Asia House, from which the brief account given above is taken, are to be found in OCA PRO 46 [uncatalogued], Sir W. D. Ross, Box 4 (miscellaneous papers and letters).

51. There is an interesting footnote to the story of HN's plans for an 'Asia House'. On 18 July 1955 the Warden of New College, Oxford and the University's Vice-Chancellor,

A. H. Smith, gave an address of welcome to the members of the Association of British Orientalists assembled in Oxford. After referring to his long friendship with H. N. Spalding in warm terms, he expressed his belief that the proposed new Institute of Oriental Studies to be erected on a site adjacent to the Ashmolean Museum would at last fulfil HN's dream of an Asia House in Oxford. He added that although its proximity to the home of Occidental Classical Studies was better attuned to his own than to HN's conception of the ideal site for such an Institute, he was confident that HN would have approved of it and that it would lead to a revival of Oriental Studies in Oxford. (NUSGR, number 5, October 1955, p. 3).

CHAPTER FIVE

The General Secretary, the Union, and the Trust

Putting Heart Into a New Service

In 1953, shortly after Henderson had retired from the Sudan Political Service, he was invited by Mrs Emma Spalding (HN's widow) to become Secretary of the Spalding Trust. He and HN had known each other since 1922 when they met in Oxford—Henderson as an undergraduate at University College and Spalding, a frequent visitor to the city where he had been admitted as a member of the Senior Common Room at Brasenose College in 1919. Their paths diverged soon afterwards. Henderson's career took him to the Sudan in 1926, the same year that Spalding and his family moved to live in Oxford at 'Shotover Cleve'. In recognition of his twenty-seven years of service to the Sudan, from being a Probationer in Khartoum in 1926 to appointment as Governor of Darfur Province in the Western Sudan in 1949, Henderson was gazetted a Companion of the Order of St Michael and St George (CMG). He also enjoyed the distinction of being invested as an Officer of the Order of the Nile. The statutory age of retirement for members of the Sudan Political Service was 50. Henderson was still fit and active. In the Spring of 1953 he decided to accept an appointment in London. Within a few days he was decidedly unhappy about the decision he had taken. He did not find it congenial to have to work in the capital, but the real problem was that he was obliged to work in the Central Office of Information in Baker Street for someone whom he described as 'a high-powered female civil servant'. He found the attitudes of his colleagues 'intolerable'. After living as Governor with considerable authority in a remote region of the Sudan he found his subordinate position in the COI to be irksome. In fact, he loathed the job and faced a disconsolate summer.

Within a few weeks Mrs Spalding's invitation arrived. At first Henderson was uncertain about whether or not to accept. While he was deciding what to do he remembered the words of a Sudanese friend, the elderly Sheikh Abdel Bagi Muhammad el-Bahr, an historian with a compelling presence, a keen mind and an ability to describe the events of the eighteenth century as though he had been present. Henderson used to visit him frequently, fascinated by his humanity and wisdom. The two men became close friends. Henderson recalled their first meeting, and their last.

> Early in my career I was sent for a week to a village called Managil to brush up my colloquial Arabic. One evening I was button-holed by an old man, who was sitting by his door chatting to a friend. [The man] was the descendant of a 17th-century religious leader ...[1] The years rolled by and at last the time came for my transfer. I went to say my last farewell to Sheikh Abdel Bagi. 'I am getting old', he said, 'and I don't think we shall meet again in this world. As for the next, my faith tells me—and doubtless yours tells you—that there is no place for unbelievers in Paradise. Still, there is a warrant in the Koran for thinking that this view may be mistaken. And I shall pray to God to make an exception in your case. Let us hope, then, to meet again after all.'
>
> And he blessed me. The blessing of a patriarch is a moving thing, and Sheikh Abdel Bagi's farewell came back to me a quarter of a century later, when I had been offered the Secretaryship of the Spalding Trust, which works for understanding between faiths. There were so many reasons for accepting the offer other than the right one—and I wanted to be sure. The old man's words played a large part in convincing me that I could 'put my heart into the new service.'

David Henderson, KDDH's son, quoted these words during his father's funeral service in Steeple Langford parish church on Ash Wednesday, 30 March 1988. The experience of meeting the Sheikh and of sharing a belief in the ultimate mercy of God despite differences of faith left a lasting impression on Bill Henderson, who came to believe that although he had much to learn about the religions of the world, he could work for inter-faith understanding with a clear conscience. For almost thirty years he had devoted himself to the service of the Sudan. He now accepted Mrs Spalding's invitation and began the thirty-five years of his new service with the Union for the Study of the Great Religions and the Spalding Trust. It can not be doubted that he put his heart into the work he did in both parts of a distinguished career.

A Scottish-Australian Background

Kenneth David Druitt Henderson's father, George Gilfillan Henderson, came from Dundee. He was named Gilfillan after a close family friend, a radical who was well-known as an evangelical preacher in the city. In the closing years of the nineteenth century, whilst George Henderson was still a student reading Law at the University of Edinburgh, his father died. Profoundly affected by his father's death, he decided to change from the study of Law to the study of Medicine. The Medical School at Edinburgh already had a world-famous reputation for excellence. Sir Arthur Conan Doyle (1859–1930) had studied medicine there as a pupil of the renowned surgeon Joseph Bell, who is said to have been the inspiration for the creation of Conan Doyle's master sleuth, Sherlock Holmes. It appears that one day George Henderson's father was asked by a friend to do him a favour. The friend had been told that some Australian cousins had come to Edinburgh on a visit. Unable to meet them himself, he invited George to take his place. It was by this fortunate chance that George met the Australian who was to be his wife. She was soon to return to Australia. He still had three more years of medical studies to complete in Edinburgh. After he qualified as a doctor he married his Australian bride in London in 1899. With the marriage, a strong and lasting family link with Australia was established.

Dr George Henderson soon went to work as a general practitioner in London. He chose to set up a practice in the East End, in Bethnal Green. His life-style was a little eccentric. During the week he lived above his surgery, returning home to his wife at the week-ends. Each Tuesday, however, he allowed himself a break from work, taking his wife to a London show before returning once more to his solitary apartment above the shop. In due course, in 1903, his wife gave birth to a son, to be named Kenneth David Druitt. It was the year in which the British conquest of Northern Nigeria was completed. A few months before, in December 1902, the Durbar in Delhi had celebrated the coronation of Edward VII, King and Emperor, and the achievements of the British Raj in India.[2] In the absence of his father, who was otherwise engaged for most of the time, the boy was brought up by his mother. A succession of maids helped her as best they could. One of them, Alice, was to become a much-loved member of the family. England and London were all very well but the proud traditions of a Scot were not to be overlooked. In order to ensure that Henderson junior understood his Scottish background, his father sent him, aged 13, to Glenalmond, a small public school situated at the edge of the Scottish Highlands, some ten miles north-west of the ancient city of Perth. The year was 1916, the year of the Battle of the Somme.

Glenalmond had a wide curriculum and good tutors, especially in the Classics, a subject that was to be of lasting interest to KDDH. At school, Henderson was to show his prowess as a fine shot, a talented rugby player, and a courageous boxer. He was at the school until 1921, when he left to go up to University College, Oxford. At this point in his life a chance encounter with another undergraduate and a trivial exchange of pleasantries with him were to change the way in which he was to be called. There are several slightly differing versions of what happened. His son David provides the one given here. On his first day in College KDDH was shown to his rooms and he proceeded to make himself at home. When the bell went for Hall, he came out of his rooms, to be met by the figure of a larger-than-life fellow freshman emerging from the rooms opposite. This young man greeted him, speedily introduced himself, and asked 'What's your name?' KDDH just had time to say, 'Henderson', but before he could add, 'Kenneth', the other man interrupted, saying 'Ah! *Bill* Henderson!'. It transpired that the speaker had just been reading a novelette, popular at the time, in which the hero was called Bill Henderson. KDDH was swept into Hall for dinner, where his new acquaintance promptly introduced him to the company as 'Bill' Henderson. From that moment the name stuck. Thereafter, to his family (though rarely to his wife), to his friends, and his colleagues he was to be known as 'Bill'

Oxford

Oxford always meant a great deal to Henderson. He was an undergraduate at University College from 1921 to 1925. Towards the end his fourth year he was given to understand that the College would like him to become a member of the Senior Common Room as Junior Dean, but there was an important condition. He was told that he would have to get at least a second in the Schools. The final examinations came, but when the results were posted he saw that he had been awarded a third. His prospects of starting a career as a young don disappeared. He had failed to meet the Dean's requirement and failed to do himself justice in the process. In some respects he had only himself to blame. He had never cared much for Logic and he had not worked hard enough to prepare adequately for the Schools. His fourth year at Oxford found him without most of the friends he had made in the first three. They had already taken their degrees and gone down. He got idle. Still involved in sport, he entertained hopes of a rugby Blue. Had he been in training he might have been chosen to play in the University match against Cambridge. In the event a fitter wing-forward was preferred, but when this player broke a leg three weeks before the University match, there was still an outside chance of selection. Henderson was not fit enough to be considered. He did play for the Oxford Greyhounds, but always regretted that he never got the Blue he coveted. Having failed the first test, he faced another. At school he had thought of the Sudan as a country in which he might be able to serve. His College tutor encouraged him to apply for appointment to the Sudan Political Service. In 1924 he decided to apply for admission.

He presented himself for interview and was greeted by a serving Governor, two senior District Commissioners, and the Sudan Government Agent from London. His interlocutors had been discussing a question about Biblical texts with a previous candidate. They were still discussing the unresolved question when Henderson walked in. He was invited to sit down. The first question put to him was on the subject of the disputed Biblical text. Looking at him expectantly, one of his interviewers asked, 'Can *you* help us?' He could, and he did. In speaking about this incident later, Henderson gave only the barest details of the exchange, choosing modestly to remain silent about the question or his answer. His reply, whatever it may have been, seems to have been sufficient to convince the members of the board that he had the right stuff because they asked him few other questions. On occasions he would recall what took place, not to demonstrate his knowledge of the Bible (which, in the King James Version, was considerable), but out of astonishment that the answer he gave was the only concrete fact he had to provide during the course of the interview. Accepted for a cadetship, he next spent six months at London's School of Oriental and African Studies, studying basic law, the language and religion of the Sudan. R. A. Nicholson, who subsequently moved to Cambridge as Sir Thomas Adams Professor of Arabic, was the tutor he remembered best. Henderson finished his course in 1925 and was accepted for service in the Sudan that year. He left England for the Anglo-Egyptian Condominium in 1926, to begin his service in the Sudan as a Probationer in Khartoum.

The Sudan

Henderson's progress in the Sudan Political Service was steady. He went out as a Probationer from 1926 to 1927. The next three years were spent at Wad Medani in Blue Nile Province. From 1930 to 1936 he was District Commissioner at Nahud in Kordofan Province. This was followed by two years at Kosti in White Nile Province. The period from 1938 to 1944 brought him increasing responsibility and a variety of tasks in Khartoum, in the Civil Secretary's Office. In addition to this he was Secretary to the Council and Commanding Officer of the Sudan Auxiliary Defence Force.[3] A generation younger than Spalding, he had been too young to serve in the First World War. In the Second World War he was too distant from any theatre of operations to gain personal experience of combat, but the strategic location of the Sudan made it vital that military measures were taken there to counter any possible threat to the Allied cause from German or Italian incursions. The Sudan was to become a supply base for three armies, the British, the Indian and the Ethiopian. British administrative presence in the region was depleted by the departure of many able personnel to other theatres of war. Henderson subsequently recalled the efforts to contribute to the war effort of the small force he commanded. He remembered their readiness to use bows and incendiary arrows in the Baro salient against any armoured force that dared to appear, and how at one time they attempted to produce a fast

dye for camouflaging white camels in the desert. His sense of humour rarely deserted him.

His military service entitled him to wear the appropriate campaign medals awarded to members of the armed forces. For his part in gathering intelligence he earned a Mention in Despatches in 1942. From 1940 to 1944 he was Liaison Officer with the Free French Forces. These military, or quasi-military, responsibilities added to his work as Editorial Secretary of the Sudan Notes and Records. The research for his two major publications was started during this period.[4] In 1944 he was appointed Principal of the School of Administration and Police before moving in the same year to Kassala Province, where he spent two years, latterly as Deputy Governor. He then returned to Khartoum as Assistant Civil Secretary (Political), where he worked until 1949. In 1947 he was a member of the Sudan Government's delegation to the United Nations' Security Council session at Lake Success, New York, for the hearing of Egypt's claims for sovereignty and the Sudan's aspirations for freedom and independence. The position of the Condominium Government was not enviable at this time, as he noted.[5] In 1949 came the crowning moment of his career in the Sudan Political Service. 'To his unconcealed delight' he was appointed Governor of Darfur Province, one of the eight provinces into which the Sudan was then divided. It was to be his last appointment. He retired in 1953.

K. D. D. Henderson reviewing a farewell parade at El Fasher, on his retirement as Governor of Darfur, Western Provinces, the Sudan, in 1953.

Family Connections and Marriage

The Henderson link with Australia has already been mentioned. It had been strengthened in a somewhat roundabout way at KDDH's christening. His godmother, whose name was Charlotte Druitt, lived in Christchurch (then in Hampshire, now in Dorset). Her surname provided Henderson with the third of his Christian names. She belonged to an eccentric family of solicitors, related to Henderson on his mother's side, some of whom had emigrated to Australia. An interesting family link between Henderson, who spent many years in the Sudan, and the Revd Eric F. F. Bishop, sometime lecturer in Arabic at the University of Glasgow, came to light in the letters between the two men that were written in the 1960s. Bishop, a notable authority on Islam, had also worked in the Near and Middle East. Henderson provided some information about their shared ancestry in a letter to Bishop dated 12 June 1963. The link was established through the name *Druitt*.

> Our common ancestor was Sacheverel Druitt of Wimbourne, Surgeon, born 1719, died 1795; married in 1739 Sarah, daughter of Nettleham Tory, by whom he had several daughters and three sons, Philip of Christchurch (1744–1804), Thomas of Wimbourne (1750–1814) and

William of Winchester (1756–1821). Thomas was my great-great-grand-father and William was yours. The line of Philip is extinct. Further details on request.[6]

Henderson's own family association with Australia was through his mother, but the strongest link of all with that part of the world was forged when he met the woman who was to become his wife. To recall this event it is necessary to go back to 1935, when he was still serving as District Commissioner in Nahud. He was advised to take some leave so he decided to take the opportunity to visit some of his relatives in Australia. He left for Port Sudan and joined a ship bound for Sydney. Having embarked and found his cabin, he went off to the bar. There he met his future wife. He wasted little time in proposing marriage. In due course she accepted. Margery Grant Atkinson was on her way back home to Australia after training as a remedial gymnast (what would now be called a physiotherapist) at Guy's Hospital in London. There was good company on board ship. The members of the D'Oyle Carte Opera Company were sailing on the same voyage. Most of them turned up to the wedding when Bill and Margery were married in Sydney, in the middle of his leave, in 1935. He gained the impression that his new Australian relatives did not accept him at first but relationships improved after subsequent visits. From the outset, however, he established a close rapport with his mother-in-law, Mrs Ethel Atkinson. During this first visit to Australia Henderson went to a conference in Canberra. There he met Raynor Johnson, the author of several works on mystical theology, who was to influence the development of his ideas and beliefs.[7]

A Fresh Start

From the moment the decision was taken to accept Mrs Spalding's invitation things moved quickly. David Henderson recalls his return home from his preparatory school in December 1953 to find that his father had already started work for the Trust in an office provided for him in the Spalding house in South Parks Road, Oxford. The Henderson family spent the Christmas holidays that year with friends in Harpenden. They spent the Easter holidays in Great Milton, occupying the coachman's accommodation of the manor house. It was there, in the Spring of 1954, that they had their first experience of a televised University Boat Race between Oxford and Cambridge. During the Summer holidays that year the family moved to number 42 Park Town in Oxford. The house was purchased by the Trust. Until it was ready for occupation the family stayed in Harpenden with one of Bill Henderson's old Oxford friends from days at University College. Henderson quickly began to co-ordinate the work of the Spalding Trust and the Union for the Study of the Great Religions. On behalf of the Union, which was soon to be organised into discrete sections in different parts of the world, each with its own organising Secretary, it was necessary for him to make extensive trips abroad.[8] He was away from home in America, Australia, India, Pakistan, the Middle East and West Africa, sometimes for up to two or three months at a time.

Henderson was already involved in several kinds of activity related to his work for the Union and the Trust. In many ways Oxford was the ideal place for the headquarters of the Trust, but he realised that it had changed since his days as an undergraduate. He was disappointed to discover that the kind of academic mentors he had respected in the 1920s seemed to have disappeared. In place of the senior members of the University he had known, who carried their knowledge lightly and whose erudition was borne with commendable modesty, he found young men who were self-confident, assertive, aggressive, and too clever by half in his opinion. Typical of those whose company he found uncongenial was a don in University College, the future Prime Minister, Harold Wilson, whose approach to life was so different from his own. No doubt he was prejudiced in his assessment of the situation, but the perception served to increase his disenchantment with Oxford as a place in which to live and work.

'Orchard House', Steeple Langford

The house in Park Town, Oxford, was clearly not the place for the Henderson family to be, although his dissatisfaction with life in Oxford was not the only reason for wanting to move. The house at number 42 Park Town was terraced, with several floors, and it presented problems for a couple who were getting older. Henderson himself was increasingly troubled with arthritis. In 1965 he was admitted to the Nuffield Orthopaedic Centre in Oxford for a hip-replacement operation. The procedure was successful, enabling him to move about much more easily. After the years of comparative isolation in that part of North Oxford Mrs Henderson was looking, as she put it, for 'normal company'. On a journey down to Dorset to visit family and friends she and her husband stopped in the Wylye valley in Wiltshire, as they often did, to have lunch with Pat and Joan McDowell, friends from days in the Sudan Political Service. During the course of conversation it emerged that there was something the Hendersons might care to see in the nearby village of Steeple Langford, a few miles West of Salisbury, before continuing their journey to Dorset. The object of curiosity was a house, *Orchard House*, which the owner wanted to dispose of in a quick sale. The visit was made. Mrs Henderson walked into the hall and said, 'This is it'. The house was to be their new home, but not before a number of things had to be settled.

The Park Town house, which belonged to the Trust, had to be sold. The Trustees then agreed to purchase 'Orchard House', after receiving assurances from Henderson that links with Oxford would not be broken by the move. Oxford, as he put it, was 'not that far away'. It was, in fact, some 65 miles away, but 'only two hours by road'. The choice of the village and the house was the right one. He and his wife left Oxford for Steeple Langford in 1963. They were to enjoy 25 years of great happiness there. In 1974, with the approval of the Trustees, they purchased Orchard House by private treaty. Advising members of the Union in February 1963 of the impending move, Henderson wrote,

> This will be the last News Letter to be sent out from Oxford. From March 15th 1963 the address of the Union and of the Spalding Trust will be Orchard House, Steeple Langford, Wiltshire [tel. Stapleford 388]. The reason for the move is that 42 Park Town has too many floors to be easily handled by people of advanced years. It was built just over 100 years ago in the heyday of domestic service.[9] ... A good train service from Salisbury will make it reasonably easy for the Secretary to meet people in London or welcome them in Steeple Langford for a more leisurely visit than the usual brief encounter amidst Oxford's many distractions. Nor does Oxford command any longer the major share of the Trust's activities.[10]

He and his wife were generous hosts. Of his resilience and good humour there was never much doubt. My less formal memories of him include one in which he appeared at speed over a crest of the garden lawn at Orchard House, careering towards me behind the wheel of a four-wheeled motorised lawn-mower and bouncing up and down in the driving seat. He sped past me, waving a greeting with one gnarled hand, and disappeared suddenly behind a row of bushes as if he had chosen to vault over a tricky fence.

During this period he attended countless conferences on aspects of religious studies and inter-faith dialogue in Britain, continental Europe, and much further afield. He took an interest in the appointment of Professor Ninian Smart to the Chair of Religious Studies at Lancaster University. He visited the department on several occasions. An important link with the Sudan was retained with Richard Hill. Hill ran Sudan Railways, but he was a distinguished historian, an archaeologist, and an academic, who had assembled a collection known as the *Sudan Archives*. For some reason, not made clear, this collection was eventually lodged in the University of Durham. It may be that Durham was chosen because Professor T. W. Thacker, a Spalding Trustee, was building up the Middle Eastern and Oriental Studies departments there.

Mr and Mrs Henderson at 'Orchard House', Steeple Langford, 1983.

The Union for the Study of the Great Religions (USGR)

The two original documents, dated respectively 16 January 1923 and 18 July 1928, were the Trust Deeds of what were to be known collectively as the Spalding Educational Trusts.[11] As the years passed they became known jointly as the Spalding Trust. The 'Movement Trust', had been formed to administer the affairs of the Union for the Study of the Great Religions, but was finally absorbed into the parent Spalding Trust, which had originally endowed it and financed its projects. In the Autumn of 1950 Spalding, his brother K. J. Spalding, and two of their distinguished friends, Professor Sarvepalli Radhakrishnan and Canon Charles Raven, began to plan for the creation of 'the Movement', which was later to become known as the Union for the Study of the Great Religions. They 'met in a bedroom that overlooks the heart of Oxford'[12] and drew up the statement of aims which was the beginning of the Union. It was incorporated by a Trust Deed after HN's death in 1953. The purpose of the Union was to help promote what would now be called 'a wider ecumenism'. In the service of the Union, Henderson was to travel

K. D. D. Henderson at work on the text of his book *The Sudan Republic.*

extensively and to spend long periods away from home, co-ordinating the work of local area committees and attending numerous conferences in different parts of the world. He was the Union's first, and only, General Secretary. In the Autumn of 1979 he wrote the following paragraphs in response to the questions he was being asked about the origins of the Union.

> 1936 the year of Francis Younghusband's first World Congress of Faiths,[13] was also marked by the appointment of Sarvepalli Radhakrishnan to the new Spalding Chair of Eastern Religions and Ethics at Oxford. In 1942 Sir David Ross, Vice Chancellor, laid before the General Board of Oxford University proposals drafted by Spalding for a new graduate School of Ethics, Philosophy and Religion, for which the Board decided the time was not ripe.
>
> In October 1943, George Bell, Bishop of Chichester, gave an address to the World Congress of Faiths which was published in *The Fortnightly Review* in February 1944. It constituted a plea for religious toleration as a vital ingredient in post-war plans for a peace settlement. The League of Nations had failed, he said, precisely because it failed to recognise the strength of spiritual authority. On the vexed question of the right attitude to be adopted by a devout person to devotees of a different faith he quoted Jacques Maritain's dictum that while a certain compatibility of principle is essential for the common pursuit of a terrestrial

goal, complete identity of doctrine is not. He stressed the importance of the experience of seeing men of a different faith living better and holier lives than many members of one's own spiritual family.

In October 1949 Charles Raven, who had just completed his term of office as Vice-Chancellor of Cambridge, attended a meeting arranged by the W. C. F. in London to discuss the possibility of setting up some sort of institution to handle religious affairs under the United Nations Organisation in default of any such action by Unesco. At his suggestion Sir John Stewart Wallace, the Chairman, wrote to enlist Spalding's help, with a supplementary letter from Raven himself in which he stressed the folly of supposing that any institution could handle education on a world scale in a strictly secular context.

H.N. had just handed over full control of the Spalding Chair with an endowment to Oxford University. He was also subsidising a lectureship in Eastern Orthodox Culture at Oxford and lectureships at Durham in Indian Religion and Philosophy, and Chinese Literature and Civilisation. At his instance George Bell's brother-in-law, Sir Richard Livingstone, put forward proposals during his Oxford Vice-Chancellorship (1945–47) for the inclusion in every B. A. syllabus of a basic course in Science, Philosophy and Religion. Spalding's main objectives were:

(1) the recognition of the study of world religions as a basis of education all over the world.

(2) the foundation of some sort of international institution of religious studies, to provide the necessary research, teacher-training and materials.

(3) the formation (as a pre-requisite) of a society or union of influential people who would pledge themselves to work for a change in the hostile climate of opinion at Unesco, in the academic world, and above all amongst the religious hierarchies, without whose co-operation the whole project was doomed to failure.

He envisaged this union as playing a co-ordinating role in the subsequent activities, academic and non-academic, of societies, universities, and individuals working in this field. It was decided to make one more attempt to persuade Unesco to admit that the duty prescribed in Article I of its Constitution 'to preserve the independence and integrity of the diverse customs of its members' involved the recognition of religion as the underlying factor in many of them. Within a few weeks Spalding had drawn up and circulated a draft note on *The Promotion of Religious Education and Culture by Unesco* (dated Nov. 29th, 1949) which would be presented, it was hoped, by Radhakrishnan and Sir John Maud, who was at first reasonably optimistic. Support was expected from the

Bishops of Chichester and Winchester, Canon Ramsey at Durham, Israel Mattuck, Canon Anson Phelps Stokes in America, and a number of leading academics.

The suggestion was that after learning the principles of his hereditary faith the average child, as his mind developed, could be interested in the teachings of the other great religions. Like all H.N.'s memoranda, the paper was not content with the expression of long term aims, but included detailed suggestions for curricula, training teachers, inter-disciplinary co-operation at Universities, research, visiting lecturers, adult education courses, broadcasting, and the provision of materials, visual aids and, where necessary, new translations of the sacred books. It concluded with a list of institutions, societies, and eminent persons in Europe, Asia and America whose co-operation could be anticipated.

A series of approaches to Unesco followed, but were nullified in turn by Communist opposition and Catholic suspicion. Spalding never allowed his failing health to suppress his energy and enthusiasm and returned to the attack again and again despite periodic visits to hospital. But his attention was concentrated more and more upon his other two aims, an Institute of Religious Studies and a Society for the propagation of the Idea. Sites for the Institute were suggested at Durham, at Madingley [Cambridge], and at Manchester College, Oxford (the closing of which was under discussion at the time) and funds were sought from the Ford Foundation and other great charities. A series of memoranda and statements of aims were drafted and circulated to sympathisers and re-drafted in the light of their comments.

As Unesco remained obdurate, another attempt was made to persuade the parent authority to set up an independent World Council of Religions, more or less on the lines of the 1936 World Congress but meeting at regular intervals and with a permanent secretariat at Geneva or elsewhere. A proposal on these lines was submitted by Radhakrishnan on his election as President of Unesco at the end of 1951. Late in October 1952 the members of the U. N. Sub-Commission for the prevention of discrimination approved by nine votes to nil with two abstentions (Russia and Poland) a motion recommending Unesco to support the comparative study of religions as a means of promoting understanding and abolishing prejudice. Dr Rezasada Shafaq of Iran, who moved the resolution, said that it was his object to secure the issue by Unesco of explanatory literature to stimulate the understanding and mutual acceptance of the religions of other races and nations.

H.N. immediately drafted a letter to the Secretary General which was sent off over the signatures of Raven and Radhakrishnan before the end of the month. Dr Adenauer, President of West Germany, and the Pope himself had adopted a sympathetic attitude in conversations with Radhakrishnan. At the same time a new and longer memorandum was drawn up and addressed to the Director General of Unesco over the signature of Richard Livingstone. The situation at the end of 1952 was therefore not unfavourable, and on January 27th, 1953, an article about the proposed *Union for the Study of the Great Religions* was published in *The Times*. No financial help had been forthcoming, but Spalding hoped that by diverting to the Union the whole remaining funds of the Spalding Trust it might be possible to attract a man of the calibre of Sir John Maud or Sir Oliver Franks as its Secretary General. But the work involved had taken its toll of Spalding's failing health and the various submissions to UNO and Unesco were talked out. A draft deed of incorporation for submission to the Charity Commissioners was drawn up in the spring of 1953, but proved unsatisfactory. Spalding and his legal advisers were busy on a re-draft when he was overtaken by his final illness. He died in September 1953.

The Spalding Trustees met in November and decided to proceed with the embodiment of the Union as a charitable trust albeit of a much more modest nature, with a general secretary and committee in Oxford, and branches, which it was hoped would be largely self-supporting, in other parts of the world. Livingstone agreed to be Chairman of the co-ordinating committee and the five original area secretaries were W. A. C. H. Dobson at Toronto, T. M. P. Mahadevan in Madras, Lev Gillet in the Near East, Itrat Hussain Zuberi at Rajshahi, and Kenneth Morgan at Colgate University, New York. Later Dr F. H. Hilliard was appointed as secretary for West Africa. (He was succeeded by Dr Geoffrey Parrinder.) [14]

The signatories and supporters included the Anglican Bishops of Winchester, Durham and Chichester, the Primates of Sydney and New Zealand, Deans Inge and Matthews, Canons L. W. Grensted and Anson Phelps Stokes, the Vice Chancellors of the Australian National University (Sir Douglas Copland), Delhi (Sir Maurice Gwyer), Durham (Sir James Duff), Benares (Radhakrishnan) and Rajshahi (I. H. Zuberi), in addition to Livingstone, Raven and Ross. [15]

In June 1954 Henderson published a leaflet about the Union. As a summary of the aims and objectives of the Union it was never to be replaced. The object of the Union was defined in the original Statement of Aims as being to promote ethical, philosophic and religious education and culture through the study of the great civilizations of East and West, with a view to better social and international understanding between the peoples of the world, and to enrich their spiritual life. An element of unreality was allowed to creep into the explanatory leaflet when it was stated as an aim that *every* student ought to spend some time studying aspects of the religions of the world. The programme was flawed from the outset, however, by its assumptions about the methodology as well as the scope of what was to be studied.

> The founders' belief was that just as European civilization achieved unity in diversity on a basis of Christianity and Hellenism. so a world culture could be built up and a world renaissance made possible if educational institutions throughout the world were re-inspired by a common study of the spirit of man as reflected in his approach to God. The great cultures and religions of East and West—of the Far East, India, Islam, ancient Greece and Palestine, Slav, Latin and Nordic Europe, and North and Latin America—should be impartially studied and compared in their independence, integrity and fruitful diversity.[16]

Three lines of approach were to guide the work of the Union. The first was the systematic study of religions and religion by competent scholars who would produce authoritative texts and commentaries designed to assist others to begin and to further their own studies. The second approach was through inter-faith dialogue at a personal level. This, it was affirmed, would increase mutual understanding 'among men of faith'. The third approach was based upon an appeal for co-operation between those concerned to combat secular materialism. This appeal was directed especially to the leaders of religious communities. Under the four sub-headings *Study, Worship, Leaders,* and *Organization,* the leaflet added the following details:

> **Study** The Union's immediate academic aim is to further the study of religions in universities, where the student should obtain an outline knowledge of the great cultures as a whole and a more detailed knowledge of one, or a group. His studies would be cultural rather than philological and sound translations will have to be provided where they are not already available. Use should also be made of the appeal to eye and ear of art, architecture and music in specimen, picture and record. The importance of studying the arts as a means to the understanding of a religion was stressed by the founders. The recommendations of the Radhakrishnan University Education Committee for India,[17] which have been accepted by the Indian Government, and have commended themselves to high educational authorities elsewhere, are that all university students should study, in their first year, the lives of the great religious leaders; in the second, selections from the scriptures of the world; and in their third, the central problems of the philosophy of religion. This scheme also provides a guide for the ordinary person who wishes to study religions as a part of his general education ...

The section of the leaflet on the subject of 'Worship' is brief to the point of ambiguity. Henderson was always a little uncertain about the value and the purpose of joint services of public worship involving adherents of different faiths. Some twenty years after he penned the rather vague paragraph that follows, he was to express his reservations more explicitly. On 12 June 1972 he attended an 'All Faiths Service' organised by the World Congress of Faiths (WCF) in the Central Baptist Church in Bloomsbury. The WCF was founded by Sir Francis Younghusband in 1936.[18] Both HN and Henderson supported its work. Henderson, who was to become its Associate President in 1966, was not opposed to inter-faith services of worship but he felt that in the absence of an agreed order of service for such occasions there could be no satisfactory focus of attention for the participants.[19] In 1972 he wrote, 'There is certainly a need for a joint emotional approach to supplement intellectual ecumenical exchanges'. He found it difficult to see how far 'these joint services are genuine acts of worship and not facades of wishful thinking. When concepts of God differ so widely, is a joint approach really possible?'. Having raised the question, he added, 'Those who believe in the validity of joint services might well argue that God is not a concept but an objective reality, whose existence does not depend upon our ideas of him. He must be the object of all worship because he is the only worshipful object'.[20] In 1954 he was not yet ready to voice his concerns. His leaflet proceeded:

> **Worship** Where inter-religious collaboration in meeting, prayer or celebration has begun the Union will encourage it in every way, bearing in mind its founders' beliefs that the best illumination of another religion is a strong faith in one's own.

Two further important issues were mentioned in the introductory leaflet—leadership and organization.

> **Leaders** Efforts to obtain, ultimately, recognition by international authorities and the support of national governments, are dependent upon the combined, continued and active support of religious leaders and religious bodies throughout the world. In its inception the Union has had the support of many such leaders. Its success is dependent on the continuance of their support, both as individuals in their own country and faith and in combined approach to international institutions and combined resistance to international materialism.

> **Organization** The Union has a Council of eminent men in different countries. It proposes to work on a basis of local autonomy, with Area Secretaries and Committees, backed by local members of Council, working to further the general aims of the Movement in whatever manner is best suited to the Area's culture, needs and financial re-

sources.[21] Where organizations are already operating in the same field the Union will keep in touch with them and avoid duplicating their work. There is no hard and fast definition of Areas; they will develop or be sub-divided as seems natural and convenient at any time. The Area Committees are responsible for making regulations to cover temporary and permanent membership of local branches or centres, and for the raising and expenditure of funds.

The Area Committee for the United Kingdom acts (under the advice of members of the Council) as a Co-ordinating Committee for the work of the Union as a whole and as an information centre for the other Areas. It is hoped that this information service may be extended to cover what is being done in the universities and also the work of as many as possible of the other organizations and societies which are working for similar ends. The General Secretary of the Union is responsible for maintaining these contacts and for the production from time to time of news-letters and reviews of progress. He also acts as Area Secretary where no Area organization exists.

Anyone wishing to support the work of the Union was invited to apply for full membership by writing to the General Secretary at 9 South Parks Road, Oxford. There was no fixed membership fee. Subscriptions and/or donations could be sent for use by a designated Area, or by the Union as a whole, as means may allow or conscience dictate. In view of the work being undertaken it is astonishing that the average voluntary subscription in Great Britain, mentioned by way of example, was shown to vary between five shillings and one pound sterling. No willing helper was to be excluded by lack of funds, however: 'It is a principle of the Union that where no money is available voluntary service is an acceptable alternative'. Nor was anyone excluded who had enough and to spare: 'Benefactions by wealthy persons for general and specific purposes will, of course, do much to further the objects of the Movement'.[22] In the event few sought membership and no benefactors answered the call for substantial subventions.

Journeys on Behalf of the Union

Henderson's indefatigable work for the Union for the Study of the Great Religions took him to many different parts of the world. There is not space in this book even to chronicle his extensive itineraries. His reports on these foreign visits, his assessment of their value, and his circulars to Trustees were models of careful documentation and incisive comment. A brief account of his activities overseas can be given by way of example. It provides details of his itinerary and his engagements in Pakistan, India and Ceylon (Sri Lanka) from December 1956 to February 1957.

After noting that the total cost of his trip should amount to little more than £610, excluding personal expenditure, he itemised his itinerary: December 19–20, Bombay; 23–26, Madras; 27, Bombay; 28, Karachi; 29 December to 2 January, Lahore; 3–4, Rawalpindi; 5–8, Peshawar and Swat; 9–14, Karachi; 15–19 Dacca; 20–23, Rajshahi; 24, Calcutta; 25–29, Delhi; 30 January to 4 February, Benares and Allahabad; 5–6, Calcutta; 7–9 Waltair; 10–12, Madras; 13–15, Bangalore; 16–18, Ceylon; 19–21, Bombay. His hosts were uniformly hospitable, courteous and receptive to his words. He was already three years into his retirement from the Sudan Political Service but still indefatigable and of indomitable spirit. Everywhere he went he gave talks about the work of the Union and offered advice about how the study of World Religions might be encouraged, even in the Indian sub-continent in which religious and cultural diversity had been part of the fabric of daily life for centuries. He met with local dignitaries, Vice-Chancellors, faculty members, teachers, students, politicians, leaders of industry and commerce, and a host of others. He gave a public lecture at the Union seminar at Vivekananda College, Madras on 26 December. The meeting was chaired by Dr Leon Roth. On 18 January he gave a talk to students of Dacca University in Dacca Hall, 'a residential hall for members of mixed religions', as he put it. The warden of the Hall was Dr G. Chandra Dev, a member of the Union Council. On 23 January he spoke to undergraduates and members of the Faculty at Rajshahi. A week later he was in the Hindu University of Benares, addressing students of Philosophy and members of the Union. Andhra University at Waltair was the venue for his discussion with members of the Faculty of Philosophy on 7 February and his lecture to members of the Union and students a day later. He noted that unlike the Benares branch of the Union that at Waltair was 'very active'. On 17 February he gave a lecture to undergraduates at Paradenia. Finally, in Colombo on 18 February, he gave another public lecture at which, he noted, 'most of the audience were undergraduates'. Even he found it impossible to include in his report all the visits he had made during the visit, although in Benares he found time to call on the Maharajah,

> who is in progress of founding a Trust for the advancement and propagation of Sanskrit language and learning and of Indology in general. He is anxious to keep in close touch with our activities, and suggested that the Union might hold a seminar in Benares in May to coincide with the inauguration of his Trust by the President of India, The All-India Kashiraj Trust, as it is called, is employed at present in editing and publishing a complete edition of the *Puranas* with a translation into Hindi. *It occurs to me that an English version of one or*

The General Secretary of the Union, K. D. D. Henderson (*right of picture*),
about to present the Mace donated in memory of Mr and Mrs H. N. Spalding to
the Chancellor of the University of the Punjab, Lahore, at the special
Convocation of the University held on 30 December 1957.

*more of these volumes might be suitable for inclusion in our series of Sacred
Books.* The Maharajah has asked me to stay with him during my next
visit to India.[23]

Henderson had always echoed Spalding's call for a recognition in the East
of the West's rich spiritual traditions, but there were moments when his
comments sounded uncharacteristically critical and out of place in the light
of his efforts to promote understanding by means of inter-faith dialogue. A
little earlier in the report from which the previous extract is taken, he agreed
that the work of the Union should be developed in the Indian sub-continent,
but on certain conditions. The relevant passage in the report is revealing, not
for any lack of charity it may be thought to betray but for the frankness with
which its author expressed his concerns. So, for example, after his experiences
in India during this visit he sensed that in some places there was 'a
mid-Victorian complacency about the atmosphere' in which politicians and
press seemed to be more interested in pursuing expansionist political aims
than in furthering the causes of justice and peace.

The conclusion I draw from all this is that high as Hindu philosophy may reach, and remarkable as the coincidence may be between ancient Indian thought and the results of modern psychical and psychological research, yet the hundreds of saintly persons who form a background to Indian life today and for thousands of years past do not appear to have made any difference to the national psychology. The undoubted enthusiasm everywhere for movements such as ours is due, of course, partly to the opinion of these men and the philosophy which produced them, but is also, I think, being used for less worthy expansionist aims. The best examples of East–West understanding I found were two fully Westernised lawyers in Bombay and Allahabad whose contacts have been frankly materialist.

None the less I think our work there should continue, on the understanding that we in the West have a spiritual contribution of our own to make and also that by the re-discovery and utilization of truths over which India has dreamed ineffectually for thousands of years we may succeed where she has failed in extending the ethical principles to cover the relations of societies and nations as well as individuals. Our work in Pakistan must at first be confined to increasing the knowledge of non-Islamic religions by any method that comes to hand. In India it is to use their interest for the purposes which H. N. foresaw but not to allow ourselves to be used by any so-called peace movement aiming at the promotion of Indian national interests under a cloak of Hindu philosophy.[24]

As if this hectic activity were not enough, he agreed to go to Australia after receiving a letter when he was in Madras inviting him to do so. First, however, he had to return to Oxford. An Australian visit starting in October 1957 was finally agreed. The invitation came from the Charles Strong (Australian Church) Memorial Trustees, who asked him to advise them on the best way to utilise their limited income for increasing knowledge of World Religions in Australia. This Memorial Trust, named in honour of its foundation minister the Revd Dr Charles Strong (1845–1942), was set up in accordance with the provisions of a Trust Deed executed in 1944 and amended in 1956. The Australian Church in Melbourne, founded in 1885, sought to contribute to the 'liberalising of Christianity'. It was closed in 1955. The Memorial Trustees were looking for ways to use the remaining Trust funds by helping to promote the study of Comparative Religion.[25] Their funds were modest, amounting to an annual income of £1,000. Henderson, unable to go until a date could be arranged for the end of 1957, asked if the Memorial Trust would pay his expenses. A compromise was eventually reached. The Spalding Trust would meet the cost of his forthcoming visit to Pakistan on Union business. His Australian hosts would meet the costs of his travel from

Karachi in October 1957. The Spalding Trustees had given Henderson permission to take a month's holiday whilst in Australia. He intended to visit his relatives there. This, he suggested, would help to reduce the cost of his accommodation. In any case he was being encouraged to use his visit to go to a number of universities, including the Australian National University in Canberra. He and Mrs Henderson arrived in Sydney on 16 October.

In Sydney he noticed 'a growing public interest in the Asian world, but a tendency to concentrate Government aid upon the graduate National University at Canberra'. In a letter dated 7 October to Henderson from Radhakrishnan, then Vice-President of India, the former Spalding Professor at Oxford wrote: 'I do not think that India will be able to finance any endowment for a lectureship on Indian religions in Australia', noting at the same time, 'it is true that Australia is geographically a part of Asia, and I am glad that some leaders recognise that'.[26] There seemed to be no departments of Comparative Religion at Sydney, where 'lecturers aren't necessarily attached to Chairs' and where it was clear that inter-disciplinary tensions were rife. In Henderson's view, Sydney 'did not appear to offer a very promising field', confirmed perhaps by his experience at the headquarters of the Royal Empire Society, where he gave a talk about the objectives of the Union 'to a formidable assortment of dog-collars'. In Melbourne a few days later he met the Charles Strong Memorial Trustees. He was warmly received. He had two interviews with Sir Douglas Copeland and two with Sir George Paton, the Vice-Chancellor, whom he had met in Pakistan the previous year. He also had discussions with Raynor Johnson, Master of Queen's College. 'Melbourne has some constitutional bar to the study of Theology, which could be circumvented if necessary. They would welcome a lectureship in Islamics attached to this Chair [Semitic Studies], and they have staked out a claim against Canberra for Sanskrit and Indology … At Melbourne again there was a demand for the sort of lectureship we favour; but not for the lectureship in World Religions which is the objective of the Strong Trustees.'[27] He left Melbourne for Canberra by car, where he was met by the professor of Social Philosophy, P. Partridge. He began a series of conversations with senior members of the University. Canberra was ready to have a research fellowship in the field of World Religions, but the Charles Strong Trustees were not able to finance it from their limited resources. Another question was forming in Henderson's mind. Had the time come to appoint an Area Secretary for the Union in Australia? After his visit Henderson was not sure. The idea was shelved.

There was little rest for Henderson. The Australian interlude was followed by further visits to Pakistan and India. One important occasion for the Spalding Trust and the Union may be mentioned. A special Convocation of the University of the Punjab was held on 30 December 1957 for the purpose of laying the foundation stone of the new University buildings some miles outside Lahore. Delegates to the Colloquium, members of the Diplomatic Corps, and representatives of other universities attended. Henderson was honoured by an invitation to represent the University of Durham at the proceedings, which opened with a reading from the *Qur'ân*. After this Henderson was called upon to present the Mace to the Chancellor of the University, the Governor of West Pakistan. Henderson has left an account of the event:

> I said 'Mr Chancellor, on behalf of the Spalding Trust and in memory of Mr and Mrs H. N. Spalding I have the honour to present this Mace as a token of good will to the University of the Punjab and the Islamic Republic of Pakistan.' The Chancellor made a suitable brief reply, after which the President of the republic laid the foundation stone and the university representatives read messages and presented scrolls or gifts. In the circumstances our presentation was happily timed and incidentally stole the thunder of other gift bearers. The Mace itself is a handsome piece and was later in display with other presentations.[28]

Henderson's delight in recording the manner in which he perceived the gift to be received reveals his enduring boyish enthusiasm rather than any inclination to be competitive. Quite apart from his exhausting official visits to Union conferences and other meetings in parts of Asia, America and North America, he wrote—sometimes in great detail and at length—to correspondents who asked him for advice and guidance, or merely for financial assistance from the Spalding Trust. He prepared meticulous records of his various activities, leaving this researcher with a voluminous collection of papers that await the attentions of a qualified archivist. He received innumerable invitations to speak to groups of people about the work of the Union. He spoke to teachers, parents, children in schools, and students in universities. He addressed more formal gatherings through his association with numerous groups involved in inter-faith dialogue.

As early as November 1954 he attached to the Union's third News Letter a list of societies and organizations with which he had made contact. The list included the *World Congress of Faiths* in London, founded by Sir Francis Younghusband in 1936 'to promote a spirit of fellowship among mankind through religion and to awaken and develop a world loyalty'. Next came the *World Alliance for Friendship through Religion*, founded by the philanthropist Andrew Carnegie in 1914 with the aim of working through religious bodies and agencies for the establishment of enduring peace. The *World Brotherhood* was instituted in Paris in 1950. It was an educational association for individuals who believed in a spiritual interpretation of the Universe. The *World Spiritual Council* based in Brussels was founded in 1946 by ex-Senator Wittemanns to bring together men and women of goodwill, and of all beliefs, to seek solutions for human problems without abandoning their own religious and philosophical convictions. Its specific purpose was to help displaced children and its Vice-President at that time was the distinguished conductor, Sir Adrian Boult. Next on Henderson's list was the *Society for the Study of Religions*, founded in London by Sir Denison Ross to promote the study of religions and, in particular, 'their origins, nature ideals and inter-relation, and to ensure mutual understanding and the dissemination of accurate information in respect thereof'. New York's *Fellowship of Prayer* was an organization founded 'to promote the practice of prayer among all religious faiths whose fundamental belief is in God, regardless of race, creed, or colour, that thereby there may arise a closer relation to God and a deeper spirit of fellowship among mankind'. The last group to be mentioned in Henderson's 1954 list was the *Council of Christians and Jews*. Under the presidency of 'the heads of the Christian Churches and the Chief Rabbi in the United Kingdom', its objectives were 'to combat all forms of religious and racial intolerance, to promote mutual understanding and goodwill between Christians and Jews, and to foster co-operation in educational activities and in social and community service'. With all these different groups Henderson retained cordial relationships.

Links with Other Societies and Groups

Over the years the number of kindred societies with which Henderson was involved in the service of the Union grew. He was an active member of the *Centre for Psychological and Spiritual Studies*, an inter-faith association, convened and administered by Miss Alison Barnard. Like other similar groups it welcomed speakers and participants from Eastern as well as Western religious traditions. It attracted men and women from all walks of life. The members held their annual meeting in Brighton and then in Hove, gatherings in which Henderson often exercised a moderating influence. 'KDDH was an active supporter, very often laying the stamp of his character on the meetings and recalling them to their senses if enthusiasms tended to leap too far forward'.[29] Henderson took an interest in the professional bodies working in the widening field of World Religions, for example, the *International Association for the History of Religions*. He attended academic conferences in Holland and Germany. For several years he was a member of the Shap Working Party on World Religions in Education, of which Professor Geoffrey Parrinder and Professor Ninian Smart were founder members. The initiative for the establishment of 'Shap' came from the University of Newcastle through the work of John Hinnells, later to be Professor of Comparative Religious Studies at the University of Manchester. Hinnells subsequently moved to the School of

Oriental and African Studies in London, and thence to the department of Religious Studies in the new University of Derby.[30]

'Spiritual Summit Conference' in New York

In 1975 Henderson attended the remarkable 'Spiritual Summit Conference', *One is the Human Spirit* organised in New York City by the Temple of Understanding to mark the thirtieth anniversary of the founding of the United Nations. The present writer was also there on that occasion, having been invited the previous year to help to plan the event.[31] The guiding spirit behind this venture was the Temple's American founder, Mrs Judith Hollister of Greenwich, Connecticut. The week-long Conference was based at the Cathedral Church of St John the Divine, the largest cathedral building in the world, prominently situated in New York City at Amsterdam Avenue and 112th Street. The final session was chaired by the then Secretary-General of the United Nations, Dr Kurt Waldheim, in the United Nations building on the East Side. It brought together a number of representatives of the world's religions, including American Indians from the reservations in Arizona with their unique 'Prophecy'. Srimati Gayatri Devi addressed us as a Hindu, Lord Abbot Kosho Ohtani spoke as a Buddhist, Rabbi Robert Gordis spoke as a Jew, Professor Seyyed Hossein Nasr spoke as a Muslim, and Mother Teresa of Calcutta spoke as a Catholic nun.[32] Most of the dignitaries attending the Conference were accommodated in the Waldorf-Astoria, a luxury hotel situated in the block behind an imposing façade on Park Lane in mid-town Manhattan. There, in the Grand Ballroom of the hotel on an upper floor, several hundred guests (and many who just turned up for the occasion) met on the evening of 23 October for the reception and the 'Thirtieth Anniversary Banquet'. Dinner was accompanied by entertaining contributions on the elevated stage to the left of the crowded dining tables from a number of artistes, including the *sitar* virtuoso Ravi Shankar. One of my memories is of Henderson at midnight, clad immaculately in old fashioned dinner jacket, wing collar and black tie, leaning reflectively on his walking stick in a door-way leading into the ballroom and watching with a mixture of curiosity and puzzlement as Miss Black America stood on the huge stage and sang one of his favourite songs 'Night and Day, You are the One …' to a piano accompaniment, as the diners finished their meal in a cacophony of clattering crockery. The following morning, in a basement café, I joined Henderson for breakfast during which he asked the busy elderly waitress for her views on religion and peace. Though obviously pre-occupied with her own immediate concerns, she replied by simply re-stating the Golden Rule about 'doing unto others …'. Henderson declared afterwards that in saying so little she had succeeded in saying more than all the official speakers at the Conference.

Archimandrite Lev Gillet

One of the lesser known but most devoted servants of the Union's cause was
Henderson's colleague, Fr Lev Gillet, 'a Monk of the Eastern Church'. It
was he who was responsible for producing the 'Book Lists' and the book
reviews, which first appeared as appendices to so many of Henderson's Union
News Letters and then as publications in their own right. The amount of
reading necessary to fulfil this task, in what Fr Gillet was in the habit of
calling 'the world of compared religion', was prodigious. His last contribution
to the series appeared shortly before his death on 29 March 1980. Fifty of
Fr Lev's 'Book Lists' were to appear. A highly competent linguist, he was
able to review books in several different languages. He set out to provoke
discussion as well as to inform. The subject of Comparative Religion intrigued
him. His sixteenth Book List, published in May 1962, contains a review
prefaced with questions for which answers are still being sought:

> What is Comparative Religion? How is it approached today? What
> challenge do the Asian religions present to the Western or Semitic
> faiths? What have been the numerous causes of intolerance? Are there,
> or are there not, points of contact between Christianity and other
> religions? Is a man in a position to judge between his own religion and
> his neighbour's? How do the problems of conversion, mission and
> propaganda confront us now? Is a syncretist amalgamated creed possible
> and desirable? To what extent can adaptation be relieved? Are religions
> complementary? What use may be made of criticism? [33]

For some years the Trust had helped to provide him with accommodation
in retirement in St Basil's House, Ladbroke Grove, London, where he died
peacefully whilst dozing over a copy of *The Times Literary Supplement* after
conducting the evening liturgy in the house. He was 86 years old. For some
time he had been assisted by Miss Joan Dopping, librarian of the World
Congress of Faiths and a keen supporter of the Union for the Study of the
Great Religions. In the 1950s Henderson arranged for Fr Lev to help her in
the library at Younghusband House in Norfolk Square. She developed a deep
affection for Fr Lev, appointing herself as his cicerone. She looked after his
domestic needs, even providing him with a new umbrella from time to time.
She also provided him with an outlet for the puckish side of his nature that
was seldom seen by those who benefited from his spiritual counsel. 'For her,
and her alone, would he sit down at the piano and sing the *poilu* songs of
the '14–18 War.' [34] In recognition of Fr Lev's services it was proposed to create
an archive of his writings in St Basil's House, and to institute an annual
memorial lecture. The first such lecture was to be given on the anniversary
of Fr Lev's death by Lord Ramsey, a former Archbishop of Canterbury.

Like Fr Teilhard de Chardin, Fr Lev served in the trenches in World War I. He survived the conflict, being saved on one occasion from certain death when the New Testament he was carrying in a breast pocket stopped an enemy bullet. Despite this chilling experience he never forgot the *camaraderie* of the soldiers with whom he served. In moments of relaxation and nostalgia, he would reflect about his experiences as a soldier. 'Characteristically he did not conclude, as some did in similar circumstances, that he had been singled out for preservation, but only that his future life should be an act of gratitude.'[35] He chose, in consequence, to dedicate his life to the service of God as a Catholic priest, although his understanding of the word 'Catholic' in that context was not to endear him to those of a more traditional Latin persuasion. He set out to explore what it meant to be a member of the Holy Catholic Church of Christ, committed to the search for unity between the two branches of Christendom, East and West, that were separated by the great schism of 1054. And more than that he was committed to the ecumenical movement, constantly striving to bring closer together all those who believed in God. As 'a pilgrim of the Absolute', in Elizabeth Behr-Sigel's phrase, he was well qualified to serve the interest of the Union for the Study of the Great Religions.[36] He hoped like Henry IV of England to be allowed to die in Jerusalem. He was not permitted that wish. The King died in the Jerusalem Chamber at Westminster. Fr Lev's life ended quietly in Ladbroke Grove.

> For all his distinction as a theologian and a scholar, his first interest was bringing people together, especially young people. In the early [nineteen] fifties when we [i.e. he and Henderson] first became associated, his efforts were primarily directed to the Christian and Muslim youth of Beirut and Alexandria, and the Christian, Muslim and Jewish youth of Jerusalem. The consummation so devoutly wished has since receded from sight, and his last visits to the Lebanon were not to cities but to an abomination of desolation, where none the less, in the Bible Lands settlements and homes, and doubtless elsewhere, the indomitable spirit of man has risen to meet it, as it did in the trenches of the first world war and the concentration camps of the second.[37]

His spiritual crisis came in 1927–28 when he decided to enter into communion with the Orthodox Church. At the end of the First World War he had entered the Benedictine Abbey at Farnborough. In the Autumn of 1924 he chose to make his solemn profession at the Lavra of Uniov in the eparchy of Lvov. This was an Eastern-rite monastery of the Ukrainian or Ruthenian Church, which was in union with Rome. For some years he had felt what he called 'a violent attraction' for the Slav world and for Russia in particular. This was the land of Tolstoy, Dostoyevsky, Soloviev and other writers, whose works he so much admired. The conviction grew in him that he was called to work for the restoration of unity between Eastern and Western Christians. Much of his life henceforward was to be spent in the Ukraine, France, Switzerland, and other parts of the Near and Middle East. His work as a spiritual counsellor and a leader of retreats was highly regarded. Few in this country knew of his tireless efforts with the Uniate Churches, with Youth movements in the Near East, with the World Council of Churches, with the World Congress of Faiths, or of his personal contacts with men such as Louis Massignon and Martin Buber. Massignon's approach showed how a Christian could understand what it meant to be a Muslim.[38] Buber's approach demonstrated how a Jew could understand what Massignon himself had earlier identified as the spiritual patrimony, inherited from the patriarch Abraham by Jews, Christians and Muslims.[39] Henderson wrote:

> Gillet never pulled his punches but (except for one or two dyed-in-the-wool prejudices) he did not allow his enthusiasm to over-ride his judgement. His criticism of 'ecumania' was founded, for instance, on a lifetime of constructive work in the ecumenical field ... In his funeral testimony Metropolitan Anthony Bloom quoted one of [Fr Gillet's] 'spiritual daughters' as having said that, '*Les conseils du pere Lev ont la pureté, mais aussi la dureté du diamant*'. His Book Lists ranged across Europe, in several of whose languages he was fluent. Time and again he was able to confute a modern writer from personal knowledge of the subject of his critical biography. (Can *any* biographer or historian write knowledgeably about a generation he did not know?). I got to know him best in his hours of relaxation, where his extraordinary humility of mind was accompanied by a puckish wit, a love of anecdote, and an encyclopaedic erudition. I was never privileged to hear him crooning his beloved Ukrainian folk-songs but I have sat opposite him in front of one of the log fires he enjoyed so much, and listened to his reminiscences of life with the Russian émigré community in Paris, or in the peace of the Lebanon before it was shattered. His conversation was a perpetual delight, breaking into French on occasion—and increasingly in his later years. And he was a very present help in trouble, always.[40]

Henderson's *News Letters*

The News Letters that Henderson wrote for circulation to members and friends of the Union for the Study of the Great Religions now constitute a collector's item. One complete set is retained in the Spalding Trust Papers, together with the Book Lists compiled originally by Henderson himself and later in collaboration with Fr Lev Gillet, whose work for the Union is considered above.

The first News Letter appeared on 18 February 1954, sent out from 9 South Parks Road, which was still the Trust's headquarters after the death of H. N. Spalding the previous September. The last News Letter, number 39, was despatched from Orchard House, Steeple Langford, in Autumn 1982. News Letter number one set a pattern that was to be followed throughout, although the style was to change over the years. With the exception of the sixth, the series appeared on typed, duplicated, foolscap sheets. Number 6, dated June 1956, was handsomely printed on foolscap sized paper of superior quality, but the experiment was not repeated, principally because of the costs involved. The function of the News Letters remained the same throughout, namely, to keep those members (especially 'isolated members') informed about what was going on in the Union. Brief reports were given about aspects of the work of the Union in different parts of the world, about policy decisions, about relations with other groups involved in inter-faith activity, about grants solicited and made, and about useful publications.

The News Letters were of uneven length. From the seventh issue (November 1956) they are often more discursive in treating the issues thought to be of interest to readers. The style became more personal, more conversational and informal. The eighth issue (June 1957), the first to be sent out from 42 Park Town, included Henderson's own comments and reflections about 'Religious Studies in the United States', about Unesco, and about his recent visit to India, Pakistan and Ceylon. The tenth (July 1958) provides a typical example of his tendency to include controversial comments of his own, although it should be said that he did this in the hope that others would be encouraged to respond with comments of their own.

> Muslims believe in a God who actively participates in the affairs of men. This differentiates them from both the Humanists and the Marxists. On the economic side, their prohibition of lending at interest ranges them against capitalism, and their respect for private property makes them allergic to socialism. So runs the argument. What is needed here, I submit, is again a definite attempt to work out what this means in practice—to produce a new *Wealth of Nations* embodying Muslim economic theory and a new philosophy of life incorporating the Muslim sense of spiritual values.[41]

The shift in emphasis from reportage to critical—even polemical—engagement is more pronounced by the time the series came to an end in 1982, so much so that a 'Quaker Unitarian' correspondent resigned from the Union, citing Henderson's unsolicited and idiosyncratic comments on a variety of religious, philosophical, and ethical topics as evidence of a Protestant Christian bias, inappropriate in what ought properly to be a publication of scrupulous objectivity. Henderson was clearly affected by what he thought of as an undeserved criticism, noting plaintively that he found it difficult to believe that anyone could accuse him of such bias when he had always seen himself as something of a heretic, albeit a Christian heretic. As for his collaborator, Fr Gillet, how could he possibly be accused of Protestant Christian bias? He was an Orthodox priest! Even so, Henderson was ready to concede that the News Letters were 'no longer a chronicle of events' but 'a series of random reflections'. His comments irritated some readers whilst merely amusing others, but there were many appreciative letters from a wide range of correspondents.[42] As he grew older he found, not surprisingly, that his pages included increasing numbers of obituary notices of his friends and associates. Another feature of the later News Letters was his inclusion of short quotations, which might more appropriately have been kept in his Commonplace Book. Reading the News Letters today, however, one is struck by their breadth of vision, their understanding of the human condition, and by the humility of the man who wrote them. It is difficult to think of anyone else who might have written them with such a combination of wit and wisdom. But by early 1980s he was getting short of inspiration and enthusiasm. Shortly after receiving wounding criticisms of his efforts, and finally realising that the work of the Union had effectively come to an end, he decided not to write any further News Letters. He signalled the end of the Union in his News Letter of September 1976. His regret and his disappointment at the end of an era were difficult to conceal. He chose to write about the Indian Branch, but by that time there was little, if anything, left of the co-ordinated regional work he had once undertaken on behalf of HN's initial vision for a world-wide organisation. After recording the appointment of Professor Matilal to the Spalding Chair, he included the following paragraphs.

> For 21 years the Indian Branch of the Union has been administered by Professor T. M. P. Mahadevan, of Madras University. The Branch was inaugurated by Dr Radhakrishnan at the Indian Institute of Culture in Bangalore on 29 May 1955. This was followed by a Six-Day Seminar on *The Great Scriptures* of the Hindus, the Jains, the Buddhists, the Christians, Muslims and Zoroastrians. Raymond [*sic*] Panikkar and Dom Bede Griffiths were among the Christian speakers on this occasion. The proceedings were subsequently published, as were those of the *Seminar on Saints*, held the following year in Madras, at which public lectures were given by Sri Jayaswami Aiyar, Maharajah and Governor of Mysore, Leon Roth, and the General Secretary of the Union.[43] The opening address was again from Dr Radhakrishnan; and the fifty-odd speakers included leading experts of India.

> Now Professor Mahadevan has written to recommend that the branch be wound up in view of the many organisations in India which are

conducting similar activities. The Co-ordinating Committee of the Union has agreed, since indeed the same thing applies everywhere. The work of the Union has been accomplished and its membership is confined to the recipients of this News Letter and of Father Gillet's Book Lists. When these are no longer available the Union will cease to exist with them. Its work is being carried on by others in a completely different climate of opinion to that which obtained in 1953.[44]

After the death of H. N. Spalding, who was the prime motivating force and the principal source of its inspiration, and despite the continuing heroic efforts of Henderson to maintain enthusiasm for its cause, the Union gradually declined. The end came quickly, to the great disappointment (not to say the annoyance) of Henderson, who had devoted so much time and energy as its General Secretary to the pursuit of its aims in various parts of the world.

Nothing Here for Tears

Henderson's declining years were spent in quiet, if not always comfortable, retirement because he was increasingly plagued by infirmity. In the Spring of 1988, he died. He was full of years. His mind was still keen but his body was burdensome. He was ready and glad to go. His life, as already noted, was divided into two parts. There was his service in the Sudan and his service to the Spalding Trust. He put his heart into both. E. J. Bickersteth, a colleague in the Sudan Political Service, spoke movingly about Henderson's life at the funeral service in All Saints Church, Steeple Langford on Wednesday, 30 March 1988, emphasising that there was an integrity about 'Bill' Henderson that linked all the phases of his life. It is appropriate to quote from what was said on that occasion.

> The first part of his working life lay in the Sudan. He joined the Service in 1926 just after the General Strike, during which he had been a dock labourer at Hay's Wharf. He first thought of serving in the Sudan while still at school at Glenalmond. He was a successful schoolboy—Head of School and Captain of the XV—and went up to University College, Oxford ... He loved Oxford, then and always, and he greatly enjoyed his years an undergraduate. He played rugby for London Scottish and read Honour Mods and Greats ... In 1926 then, he was selected for the Sudan Political Service and travelled out to Port Sudan with a dozen other probationers.

The progress of Henderson's career in the Sudan, summarily recapitulated by Bickersteth, has already been described earlier in this chapter. There is little to add, other than Bickersteth's confirmation of Henderson's delight on being appointed Governor of Darfur province in 1949. It was the highpoint in his career.

> I know about his delight because I was at the time District Commissioner at El-Fasher and I rode with him on horseback across the sandy *goz*, as the new Governor made his traditional entry into his capital. And a few weeks later, I escorted him on a 10-day camel trip into the foothills of Jebel Marra. During that journey, I learned to appreciate two more things about my new Governor. One was his fortitude in the face of pain, pain especially from an old hip injury, which was sometimes so severe that he had to be lifted into the saddle. And secondly, his marvellous sense of humour, sometimes sardonic, more often tinged with tenderness.
>
> Many years later he wrote to me about a sense of humour as 'the characteristic without which the whole corpus of Christian virtues is apt to become a sounding brass and a tinkling cymbal'. Tolerance and a sense of humour he valued very highly. Bill stayed in Darfur for four years—his CMG was gazetted while he was there—until he retired in 1953 at the statutory retirement age of 50, after 27 years' service.

Bickersteth then considered Henderson's appointment to the Spalding Trust and his work for the Union, pointing out his suitability for the post.

> All this was congenial and fairly familiar ground to him. He was a practising Anglican, not of the demonstrative sort but with a quiet, firm conviction, and he was already familiar with Islam from his experience in the Sudan. He began to widen his reading, his travel and his contacts, so that soon the other great religions were equally familiar, if not all equally attractive. He looked at these things, I think, more with the eye of a historian than a theologian, and I am quite sure that nothing he met on this extensive pilgrimage ever weakened his faith in God. He became well-known and highly respected in these circles and the World Congress of Faiths elected him a Vice-President in 1966.

It is one thing to describe what a man has done in his career. It is a much more difficult thing to say what kind of a man he was. Bickersteth ended his remarks at Henderson's funeral service with a personal appreciation of the man he had known so well.

> I mention first his love of family—starting with his father, the doctor, who put up his plate in Harley Street but spent most of his time in Bethnal Green; and then Margery. Bill and Margery met on a boat going out to Australia in 1935, she on her way home and he spending a leave from the Sudan visiting some of his relations out there. Like

many of us who worked in the remote and masculine Sudan, he did not dally in his courtship. He and Margery were married in Sydney a few weeks later and he brought his bride straight back to Nahud in Western Kordofan. She did not meet her in-laws until a year later.

So began a golden partnership, the like of which is best described by Robert Louis Stevenson—'In the closest of all relations', he wrote, 'that of a love well-founded and equally shared, speech is half discarded, like a roundabout infantile process or a ceremony of formal etiquette: and the two communicate directly by their presences, and with few looks and fewer words contrive to share their good and evil and uphold each other's hearts in joy'.

With the arrival of the children—Jane and David and Charlotte and later their spouses and children—the web of family relationships grew ever wider and the old spider at the centre looked on them all with love and amusement and pride: and, if he seemed to them sometimes to be a little old-fashioned and set in his ways, they knew that he was a rock to which they could cling in any emergency.

The second attribute of Bill was his capacity for friendship—not surprising, really, when you remember what good company he was. You can see him, can't you, looking at you quizzically under lowered eyebrows. teeth clenched on an empty pipe, his mouth pulled into fantastic contortions, quoting aptly from his capacious memory, limping over to the bookshelf to check a reference, spoiling his own stories by being overcome with laughter long before the punch-line. Though he had no patience with those who are too clever by half, he loved good company whether at home or at the local pub or at some great international gathering. He made close friendships with people of many races, particularly in the Sudan but also in India and elsewhere ...

The third and last facet of the diamond that was Bill that I want to mention—and there could be many others—was his love of good literature, to read it and to write it, to remember it and to quote it. He wrote clever and amusing doggerel with apparent ease and, to my untutored eye, some of his more serious poetry sings with an authentic voice. His prose style was clear and uncluttered, as you can see from innumerable letters and reports from his three major books on the Sudan: *Set Under Authority*, published last year, to tell the story of the ordinary District Commissioner; *Sudan Republic*, published in 1965, which does so much to unravel the tangled skein in the Southern Sudan today; and *The Making of the Modern Sudan*, published in 1953, in which he wove the history of that country since the first war around the career of his friend and mentor, Douglas Newbold.[45] Bill loved beautiful English, which is why he mourned the disuse of the incomparable cadences of the Book of Common Prayer.

I think one of the happiest periods of Bill and Margery's lives began when they moved into Orchard House exactly 25 years ago this month.[46] Bill loved being part of a village. Each year on 1 January the date of the Cricket Club's Autumn Supper was firmly written into his new diary. During the Summer, much of the weekend was spent watching the cricket team, with plenty of pithy comment on its performance. Down at *The Bell*, he discussed local history and horse-racing, both of which fascinated him. He kept himself informed of local opinion on such issues as the re-opening of the gravel-pits; or car-parking for the anglers fishing the lakes; and above all, the village by-pass. As Chairman of the Parochial Church Council he had to respond to consultation documents about it, or write to the Salisbury Journal: and he knew exactly what the village felt. So the arrival of the surveyors last Autumn to peg out the line of the by-pass gave him great satisfaction, a final wish fulfilled.

So, nothing is here for tears: nothing but well and fair. And this is not the last time that I shall think and talk about Bill Henderson. I shall remember him as long as I live. And so will you.[47]

With that sentiment 'Bill' Henderson's surviving relatives and friends will certainly agree. In his later years his contributions to the village life of Steeple Langford were many and varied. He was Chairman of the Parish Council for many years. He served as Chairman of the Wylye and Wilton Deanery Synod, as Chairman of the South Wiltshire branch of the Council for the Preservation of Rural England, and President of the Salisbury branch of the Classical Association. He was also President of the Wessex branch of the Oxford Society. At the time of his death he was working on a detailed history of his adopted village. For those who never knew him, just as for those who never knew H. N. Spalding, the pages of this book give an all too brief account of what they both attempted, accomplished, and failed to achieve.

Notes and References

1. The religious leader mentioned here was Ibrahim el-Ferdi, whose descendants were known locally as the *Ferdieen*.
2. Lawrence James, 1997, *Raj: the Making and Unmaking of British India*, The Softback Preview edition, p. 317. The durbar mentioned above was organized by Curzon, Viceroy of India. In the king's absence, Curzon rode in his place, seated high above the crowds on an elephant.
3. For details of the origins, personnel, and work of the small Sudan Auxiliary Defence Force, see K. D. D. Henderson, 1953, *The Making of the Modern Sudan: the Life and Letters of Sir Douglas Newbold KBE*, Faber and Faber, pp. 116, 144, 152, 168, 183.

4. The first of these is named in footnote 3 above; the second, *The Sudan Republic*, was published in 1965 by Ernest Benn, London.

5. Henderson, 1965, *The Sudan Republic*, pp. 96–7.

6. HFP, Box 'Correspondence: KDDH'. From this date letters from Henderson to Bishop began 'Dear (or My Dear) Eric'. Bishop's replies were prefaced with phrases such as '[My] Dear Kinsman' and 'Dear Cousin Druitt'. Bishop also used some typically Arabic honorific titles that recognised the close kinship and venerability of the addressee. These included Ibn 'Ammi al-'Aziz, Ibn 'Ammi al-Muwaqqar, Nasibi al-Karim.

7. Dr Raynor C. Johnson was Master of Queen's College, Melbourne. He was a physicist by training. His case-study approach to the experience of mystics focuses not on the great 'classical' mystics but on ordinary people who provide him with accounts of the existence of a God who is 'infinitely beyond us and yet infinitely near'. Of his several essays into the subject of mysticism the one entitled *Watchers on the Hills* (Hodder & Stoughton, 1959) may be given as an example. The title refers to the 'lonely watcher on the hills who has a momentary glimpse of infinitude and feels the universe reaching at him'. This, says Johnson, is 'the only news of interest'.

8. See Appendix 2.

9. The houses were built to accommodate young dons who were allowed to marry and live outside their respective Colleges in the early part of the nineteenth century.

10. NUSGR, number 17, February 1963, p. 1.

11. KDDH's outline of the history of the two Trusts was given in a lecture at Younghusband House, the centre of the World Congress of Faiths in Norfolk Square, London, on 1 December 1968. It was published in *World Faiths*, Spring number (79), 1970.

12. As recalled in *The Times*, 27 January 1953.

13. For an account of the contribution of Sir Francis Younghusband to inter-faith dialogue see Marcus Braybrooke, 1996, *A Wider Vision: A History of the World Congress of Faiths*, Oneworld Publications, Oxford.

14. See Appendix 2.

15. NUSGR, number 36, Autumn 1979, pp. 9–11.

16. From page 1 of the leaflet, *Union for the Study of the Great Religions*, STP.

17. For an account of the work of this Committee under Radhakrishnan's chairmanship, see Sarvepalli Gopal, 1992, *Radhakrishnan: A Biography*, Oxford India Paperbacks, pp. 207–12, 214.

18. See *Faiths and Fellowship, Being the Proceedings of the World Congress of Faiths held in London, July 3rd–17th, 1936*, edited by A Douglas Millard, published for the WCF by J. M. Watkins, London. Sir Francis Younghusband contributed the Foreword. H. N. Spalding was a member of the Continuation Committee.

19. He was sometimes referred to as a 'Vice-President' of the WCF. The Inaugural Younghusband Memorial Lecture was delivered by Henderson in King's College, the Strand, London, on 11 May 1976. The title of the lecture was 'Francis Younghusband and the Mysticism of Shared Endeavour'.

20. NUSGR, number 29, Summer 1972, p. 3.

21. For names of the original members of the Co-ordinating Committee and Area Secretaries see Appendix 2.

22. All the quotations are from the leaflet, *Union for the Study of the Great Religions*, STP, pp. 1–3.

23. HFP, Box 4, Pakistan, 'Report on Visit to Pakistan, India and Ceylon, December 1956 to February 1957', p. 4. The italics are his own. The other details in the paragraphs above are from the same source.

24. *Ibid*, p. 2.

25. STP, Australia file, volume 1 (1949–57). This correspondence was initiated by the Memorial Trustees, Margaret Robertson, A. W. R. Vroland, and W. J. Drummond. In 1958 the Trustees decided to establish a lectureship, to be given biennially by a distinguished scholar working in the field of Comparative Religion. The Inaugural Charles Strong memorial Lecture was given in the University of Melbourne on 14 June 1961 by Dr Huston Smith, Professor of Philosophy at the Massachusetts Institute of Technology.

26. Radhakrishnan's brief *Aerogramme* was returned to its sender in New Delhi on 11 October. The postal authority in Bombay marked it 'Understamped. Returned to sender for making up the deficiency, Rs. 0.10, and Re-posting'.

27. STP, Box: *Australia*, 'Australian Visit (1957), p. 1.

28. HFP, Box: *Pakistan*, [Australia] Pakistan and India Visit (1957), pp. 4–5.

29. In a letter to this writer from Dr M. A. N. Loewe, dated 30 September 2001.

30. This department was closed in 2002.

31. My account of this unique and unquestionably eccentric event is still in preparation.

32. A report of the Conference appeared in *The New York Times*, on Saturday 30 October 1975, p. 31.

33. USGR Book List number 16, May 1962, p. 1. The book under review was Geoffrey Parrinder's *Comparative Religion*, Allen & Unwin, published in 1962.

34. KDDH in a letter to the Spalding Trustees, 8 May 1984. In the same year Miss Dopping bequeathed the sum of £1,000 to the Spalding Trust to support the USGR.

35. NUSGR, number 37, Autumn 1980, p. 5.

36. See Elizabeth Behr-Sigel, 'The Concelebrant at Clamart: Lev Gillet in the Year 1927–28', in *Sobornost, incorporating Eastern Churches Review*, volume 3 number 1, 1981, pp. 40–52; see also the *Revue Francaise de l'Orthodoxie*, 'Contacts', 4th Trimestre, 1981, which devotes the issue to the memory of Fr Gillet, 'un moine de l'église d'Orient'.

37. NUSGR, number 37, *loc. cit.*

38. See L. Massignon, 1969, 'Les Trois Prières d' Abraham', in *Opera Minora*, tome III, Presses Universitaires de France, pp. 804–16.

39. The present writer met Fr Gillet, a small bird-like figure, in 1974 in the home of Professor Gorodetskaya, 94A Banbury Road in North Oxford, during one of the priest's infrequent visits to the city. I asked him several questions about the Jewish philosopher Martin Buber, who died in 1965, and whom he had known in the Holy Land. I was primarily interested in hearing about Buber's pioneering work to bring Jews, Christians and Muslims together, but Fr Gillet did not answer directly. Instead he paced up and down the room for a while before permitting himself a single observation, spoken with considerable passion, 'Buber was *obsessed* with *Catholicisme*'.

40. NUSGR, number 37, Autumn 1980, pp. 10–11.

41. NUSGR, number 10, July 1958, p. 6.

42. A collection of appreciative letters about the contents and style of the News Letters is to be found in HFP, Box 4, file F2/6.

43. i.e. Henderson himself.

44. NUSGR, number 33, September 1976, pp. 2–3.

45. Sir Douglas Newbold completed his long service in the Sudan as Acting Governor-General in 1945, a few months before his death.

46. Orchard House is in the village of Steeple Langford, Wiltshire, a few miles West of Salisbury.

47. A copy of E. J. Bickersteth's remarks is kept among the STP.

CHAPTER SIX

Continuing the Work of the Trust

Taking Stock

What has the Trust been able to achieve, and what remains for it to do? The leading figures have left the scene. It is almost fifty years since Spalding died; Henderson died in 1988. The unique blend of enthusiasm, commitment, and advocacy which they brought to the cause they espoused is not easy to find today. In the Summer of 1973 Henderson quoted once again from a prospectus of the Union, drafted in 1954. He mentioned the three lines of approach needed to promote international understanding between the peoples of the world: 'through the study of religion and religions; through increase in mutual understanding among men of faith; through the co-operation of religious leaders in combating materialism'. He continued:

> Spalding did not, of course, foresee the perversion of educational theory and practice to conform to political ideologies. He was disappointed when Unesco sheered away from the universalist approach for fear of giving offence to the Latin-American bloc. He was delighted when the Indian Government accepted the recommendation of the Radhakrishnan Commission, which provided that all university students should study world religions. He hoped that other countries would do the same. His immediate aims were to encourage the foundation of new centres of learning, the building up of libraries, the exchange of personnel between existing centres, and the encouragement of scholars.[1]

After twenty years as a servant of the Union and the Trust, Henderson went on to ask about the achievements of both foundations:

> What has been achieved in the twenty years since [Spalding] died? Not much, compared with the spread of smog across the sky. But it cannot be denied that there has been progress of a kind. In 1954 we were offering to provide universities and schools with lecturers on any cognate subject at our expense. To the best of my recollection only one university took advantage of the offer, and only one school. Nor were some of

Anne C. Spalding, grand-daughter of H. N. Spalding, and now Chairman of the
Spalding Trust.

the proposed lecturers any more enthusiastic. One eminent Orientalist to whom I had written at the suggestion of my Chairman, Sir Richard Livingstone, sent my letter back with the laconic comment scrawled across it 'A. W. is not interested'.

Things are very different now. More applications [to the Trust] pour in than we can hope to satisfy, and the British Association of Orientalists has included the following paragraph in its statement of aims:-

> Since the knowledge of Asia and its peoples is at present almost exclusively confined to the universities, and since universities and the nation at large have the most compelling reasons for encouraging the pursuit of Asian studies on a broader front, it falls upon the Association to promote a vigorous growth of interest in Asian studies not only in our schools, colleges of education and universities, but also among the general public.

There is still a long way to go, but other vehicles are now available—at Harvard and Melbourne and Ibadan, at Lancaster and Birmingham and London. If the Shap Working Party [on World Religions in Education] can raise the money which it needs so badly, I can see no reason why it should not implement H.N.'s aims in this country.[2]

A few years later, in the autumn of 1980, Henderson wrote a short piece under the heading *Stock-Taking: The Study of the Great Religions.* Reviewing the short history of the Trust, he wrote:

> What about our own performance? Have we any real achievements to record after a quarter of a century? Obviously there has been an improvement in the academic sphere, due at least in part to other factors, notably the large-scale migration from the Third World into the First ... But the study of the Great Religions was never intended to be more than a means. The end was always harmony—harmony between religions and races and nations. How far have we progressed in that direction?'[3]

His somewhat rueful conclusion was that very little had been done with regard to the implementation of HN's ideals, but there were in fact several achievements to note. HN's wider vision was still far from being realised, but 'the study of religion and religions', to repeat the phrase he often used, had developed in the West on a scale that was gratifying. The Trust had played a practical part in the development of a much more comprehensive study of the religions of the world. Few question the value of such study, especially in multi-racial, multi-ethnic, and multi-faith societies such as are now to be found in Europe and the United States. In his inaugural lecture

half a century ago Professor Zaehner described the initiative taken by Mr
and Mrs Spalding in establishing the Oxford Chair as a praiseworthy effort
to make Eastern religions—'these outlandish systems', as he put it—more
widely known.[4] His phrase was not well chosen, but today it would be
factually incorrect as well as unacceptably insensitive to speak of any religion
in such terms. Since the end of the Second World War many immigrants
have arrived and settled in this country from different parts of the world.
Among them are Hindus, Buddhists, and Sikhs, as well as Jews, Christians,
and Muslims. They contribute to the religious diversity of the country they
have made their own. In the literal sense of the word the religions represented
in this cultural mix are no longer 'outlandish', no longer 'exotic'.

Frustratingly, however, it did not seem that efforts to develop interest in
different religions and cultures were reducing inter-religious disputes. Henderson quoted from a letter he received from an American scholar and friend,

> As you recount your struggles to gain a place for the study of religions
> in your universities I perceive that we have had much less resistance
> here—even in the introduction of Asian religions. Yet the outcome here
> is not the ideal that was dreamed. Religions are not visibly growing
> together, tempered by each other. Asian movements have used the
> opening for the beginning of great missionary drives. We have a revived
> fundamentalist Christianity on the other side, and a people now being
> divided in religion as in everything else.[5]

A generation after HN's death, Henderson looked at the world and saw
no respite from conflict and hatred, especially in the parts of Africa he knew
best. As a Christian he could not but grieve over what was happening in the
Holy Land. As an admirer of Islamic culture it was a matter of particular
anguish for him to observe the situation in the Sudan, where increasing
tensions between Muslims in the north of the country and Christians in the
south were increasingly leading to persecution and death. I once asked him
what would convince him, if he ever returned to the Sudan, that there was
hope for that country. He replied that if he heard the women singing as they
walked back in the evening to their villages carrying water from the well, he
would know that there was hope. He added, 'But they are not singing now'.
He saw similar conflicts in Iran and Libya, emerging from what he called 'a
reversion to bigotry in Islam which goes back to the Assassins, while
paradoxically flouting the oldest Semitic traditions of the right to sanctuary
and the obligations of the host to those who have eaten his salt.'

The Provision of Aids to Study

Apart from the numerous small grants in aid to individual applicants, both the Union and the Trust may be credited with at least two major initiatives in recent years, one in the field of publishing, the other with the provision of Visiting Fellowships at two of this country's major universities. From the earliest days HN and his associates understood that one of the most practical ways of encouraging the study of the great religions of the world was to assist in the publication of readable, but scholarly, works. Many such works were already available and countless numbers have been independently published since. HN's support for the publication of suitable teaching material, 'visual aids and where necessary, new translations of sacred books' was recalled in a memorandum written in 1979 by K. D. D. Henderson in answer to queries he was receiving from correspondents about the origins of the Union for the Study of the Great Religions. It was through the work of one of the most prominent of the Spalding Trustees, Professor A. J. Arberry, that the Trust was linked with the publication of a series of monographs.

The Ethical and Religious Classics of East and West

Professor Arberry was appointed General Editor of this series of monographs. The books were to be published by George Allen & Unwin Ltd, London. By May 1954 eleven volumes had appeared, with two more named for impending publication. Two of the books were written by Arberry. One was published as the second in the series. It was called *Sufism: An Account of the Mystics of Islam*. His second book, the ninth to be published, bore the title, *The Holy Koran: An Introduction with selections translated by A. J. Arberry*. This was the book that was subsequently expanded and published in 1964 by Oxford University Press in *The World's Classics* series with the title *The Koran Interpreted*. The general introduction to the series included a statement of aims and objectives which coincided with the aims and objectives of the Union and the Trust:

> It is the object of this Series, which originated among a group of Oxford men and their friends, to place the chief ethical and religious master-pieces of the world. both Christian and non-Christian, within easy reach of the intelligent reader who is not necessarily an expert—the ex-Service man who is interested in the East, the undergraduate, the adult student, the intelligent public generally. The Series will contain books of three kinds: translations, reproductions of ethical and religious art, and background books showing the surroundings in which the literature and art arose and developed. These books overlap each other.

Religious art, both in East and West, often illustrates a religious text, and in suitable cases the text and the pictures will be printed together to complete each other ... Mankind is hungry, but the feast is there, though it is locked up and hidden away. It is the aim of this Series to put it within reach, so that, like the heroes of Homer, we may stretch forth our hands to the good cheer laid before us. No doubt the great religions differ in fundamental respects. But they are not nearly so far from one another as they seem.[6]

The Journal *Religious Studies*

The journal *Religious Studies*, published twice each year by Cambridge University Press, was supported by the Spalding Trust from the start. The first issue appeared in October 1965. The editor was H. D. Lewis, Professor of the History and Philosophy of Religion, King's College, London. The editorial Board included four members with Spalding links: Professor A. J. Arberry (a Spalding Trustee), Professor R. C. Zaehner (the Spalding Professor), Dr Geoffrey Parrinder (sometime Secretary of the West African Area Committee of the Union), and K. D. D. Henderson (the Secretary of the Union and the Trust). The purpose of the journal was clearly stated at the outset. It was to provide readers with a forum in which 'the main problems that present themselves in various fields of religious study' could be discussed in a sustained and scholarly manner. The prospectus promised that 'Issues sharpened by the course of recent philosophy and by the new findings of the historical and comparative study of religions' and by 'the psychology and sociology of religion, as they bear on major religious questions' were also to come 'within its scope'. No shade of opinion was to be barred from the journal, 'provided the highest standards of competence and scholarship are observed in presenting it. No relevant topic will be excluded, the overriding aim being only the pursuit of truth'.

Religion in the Middle East

Another publication supported by the Trust was also associated with Professor Arberry . He was invited by the Cambridge University Press to be the General Editor of a large two-volume work with the title *Religion in the Middle East*. Both volumes appeared in 1969. Volume one was devoted to a survey of Judaism and Christianity. Volume two was concerned with Islam. There were three sub-editors, Dr E. I. J. Rosenthal for the sections on Judaism,[7] the Revd Dr M. A. C. ('Max') Warren, for the chapters on Christianity,[8] and Professor C. F. Beckingham, for the sections on Islam.[9] The work was never accorded the critical appreciation for which the Trustees hoped. Dr Warren wrote about his own contribution to the project in his autobiography.

I had to persuade a Roman Catholic, an Orthodox, a Syrian Orthodox, an Armenian, a Lutheran, a Calvinist, and several Anglicans to produce something which was recognisably Christian. To all but the Anglicans I was a complete stranger. As Christians, they all responded nobly. But they were also authors and, as such, had no idea whatever how to restrict the flow of ink off their pens. In some cases I had to insist on 'cuts' running into thousands of words, in one case to more than ten thousand. That to a measurable degree I succeeded, and retained the friendship of all concerned, was in a modest way a diplomatic triumph. After all it was the Middle East.' [10]

Bell's Commentary on the *Qur'ân*

A more recent publication for which the Spalding Trust provided financial support was the Revd Dr Richard Bell's *A Commentary on the Qur'ân*. The editors of the two-volume work, Professor C. E. Bosworth, a Spalding Trustee, and M. E. J. Richardson, both of the University of Manchester, described Bell as 'a rigorous and accomplished scholar of the finest Scottish type'. Bell was born in Dumfriesshire in 1876 and after working as a minister in the Church of Scotland he was eventually to become Reader in Arabic at the University of Edinburgh. He died in 1952.

> A microfilm of the typescript of a commentary on the Qur'ân, written by the late Richard Bell D. D., was entrusted to Professor C. Edmund Bosworth some twenty years ago, with a grant of any future publication rights, by the then Secretary of the Edinburgh University Press, Mr A. R. Turnbull. The Press must, at some point in the past, have had the idea of publishing it, but nothing in fact ever came of this, and the microfilm was taken home by him and lay forgotten in a cupboard until a chance remark by Professor Josef Van Ess, who happened to be staying with him at the time, regretting the fact that Bell had never completed the promised commentary to accompany his *Translation*, brought the existence of the microfilm back to mind; *habent libelli fata sua* indeed.[11]

At the end of their Introduction the editors of Bell's work record their gratitude to HN and to Henderson.

> Finally, there remains to thank the Spalding Trust, which was formed by the late Mr and Mrs H. N. Spalding to promote a better under-standing of the great cultures of the world by encouraging the study of their underlying religious traditions, for a generous grant towards the cost of publication ... Having spent so much of his life in an Islamic country and having acquired so many Sudanese Muslim friends

in the course of his career in Africa, [Henderson] had a special interest in and empathy for Islam. The publication of a work like Bell's *Commentary*—the work. moreover, of a fellow-Scot—would surely have been particularly close to Bill Henderson's heart, and in this wise it is here offered as a tribute to his memory.[12]

Many other examples of the grants made by the Trustees to assist the authors of articles and books to undertake their work and publish the results of their research could have been mentioned. The provision of this help, though modest in most cases, remains one of the ways in which the Trust can continue to promote the work to which Spalding and Henderson devoted their efforts.

The Spalding Visiting Fellowship at Wolfson College, Oxford

The Trustees have always been open to suggestions about the ways in which the available funds can be used to best effect. In recent years the Trustees have provided a measure of financial support for two Visiting Fellowships, one at Oxford and the other at Cambridge. The first was the Spalding Visiting Fellowship in Indian Philosophy and Religion, tenable at Wolfson College, Oxford. The proposal to establish this Fellowship came at the end of 1980 from Professor Bimal K. Matilal, the Spalding Professor at All Souls College, and a Spalding Trustee. An agreement was made with Wolfson College to give a sum of money sufficient to enable a visiting scholar to reside in the College for part of one academic year. The Trust was unable to finance the Fellowship in full. The costs were to be shared with the College. The arrangement began in the academic year 1981–82 and lasted for more than a decade, during which time a number of distinguished scholars were brought to Oxford for one or two terms to continue their research and to help with seminars and lectures in their chosen fields of study. The Trustees hoped that by supporting the Fellowship they would be providing some additional support for the work undertaken by Professor Matilal. He died in 1991. The Trust was then left without influence in the Fellowship election and, although the arrangement was continued for some years after his untimely death, the absence of a Spalding representative made it less likely that the Trustees would make it permanent. In 1995 this link with Wolfson College was broken.

The first Spalding Visiting Fellow at Wolfson College was Prabal Kumar Sen from the University of Calcutta. In the second year Professor Padoux of the University of Paris was elected. He was followed in the third year by Professor Robert Goldman of the University of California. At the Annual General Meeting of the Trustees, held on 23 April 1994, the Fellowship was reviewed. They took note that the grant they had been making had reached its final year. Subject to certain provisions, hitherto operative, but which the Trustees felt should be stated formally, it was agreed to continue the arrangement with Wolfson for the academic years 1995–6, 1996–7, and 1997–8. Of the various provisions made explicit at that time, the following were the most significant:

(a) The Fellowship will be tenable not more than once by the same scholar, and by one whose subject of research is not within the study of the religion of his or her own persuasion.

(b) At least two members of the appointments committee will be nominated by the Spalding Trust

(c) Notices and advertisements for applications will include the stipulation that the Fellow will be required to take an active part in presenting aspects of religious studies to a wide audience, not restricted to members of the University.

The Spalding Visiting Fellowship at Clare Hall, Cambridge

At that meeting of the Trustees in April 1994 there was some discussion about the desirability of continuing the Fellowship at Wolfson. It was suggested that in future years the Trustees might decide to support a similar initiative elsewhere than at Oxford. This was the way that things turned out. The proposal to make a grant to support a Visiting Fellow at Cambridge was made in 1989. At the suggestion of two of the Trustees, Dr M. A. N. Loewe and Dr Julius Lipner, an approach was made to Clare Hall, Cambridge, with a view to ascertaining whether or not there was any interest in an arrangement with the College similar to that previously made by the Trust with Wolfson. There was an interest. It led to an arrangement by means of which the Spalding Visiting Fellowship in Comparative Religion was set up on a trial basis at Clare Hall. A Fellow would be elected every two years for one academic year. On 14 May 1990 the College's Governing Body warmly approved the proposal for a Spalding Fellowship subject to a number of conditions, among which were the following:

(a) The tenure of the Fellowship would normally be for one academic year. To avoid confusion with other types of Fellowship already established at the College, the term 'Spalding Visiting Fellow' should the adopted.

(b) The fellowship would usually be held by a comparatively junior scholar, perhaps at post-doctoral level. Such a person would be expected to provide a series of public lectures or seminars for the University, on an approved subject in the field of religious studies.

More senior scholars would not be excluded from consideration, however.

(c) The stipend of the Fellow would be fixed at the rate of the stipendiary Research Fellows elected by the College.

(d) The Spalding Trust would be represented on the committee responsible for recommending candidates for election.

(e) Two-thirds of the costs of the Fellowship would be borne by the Trust and the remaining third by the College for a trial period of four years.

The closing date for applications for the first Fellowship election was 30 March 1991. On 20 May the sub-committee met to consider the short-list of five candidates, four of whom were interviewed. The fifth candidate was unable to attend. After the discussion it was unanimously agreed to recommend the election of Dr David L Gosling for the academic year 1991–92. The arrangement with Clare Hall has continued to the present, to the general satisfaction of the Trustees and the senior members of the College. There have been four other Visiting Fellows, among whom were Dr Ram Prasad and Dr Jonardon Ganeri, both of whom had been pupils of the late Professor B. K. Matilal.

Suggestions for Other Spalding Awards

The suggestion that the Trust make awards to individuals for outstanding contributions to religious studies has been put to the Trustees on several occasions. There is nothing against the idea in principle, but difficulties arise when it comes to choosing those who should benefit. In 1991 the present writer suggested that in addition to making provision for the normal run of small grants made to students at various stages of their progress it was worth considering the provision of much larger grants for a limited number of major projects. Some Trustees were concerned that although increasing numbers of applications were being received from undergraduate students, few applications were coming in from established academics engaged in advanced research. The Trust has been listed in the Directory of Grant-Making Trusts for many years, but its existence was (and still appears to be) unknown to many of its potential beneficiaries. The suggestion was that annual cash prizes might well be established for significant achievements in the field of religious studies, enabling students who had performed with promise if not distinction in their undergraduate courses to proceed to study for higher degrees, aided by substantial bursaries. University departments would be invited to submit the names of their ablest students on the basis of final honours school results. Another Spalding prize might be awarded for outstanding achievement in post-graduate studies. A third Spalding prize might be offered for published work. By advertising such awards and prizes, and by soliciting the help of the appropriate University departments in the initial selection of suitable applicants, the Trustees would need to spend less time on deciding how small sums of money for relatively unimportant projects were to be disbursed. In the event a decision about such awards and prizes was postponed. In 1994 a proposal to establish an annual Spalding Postgraduate Scholarship was made. The Scholarship was to be awarded on a competitive basis. Outstanding students, supported by references from their supervisors, might well include those who were unable to finance their final year of work for a PhD from regular sources. The idea was discussed and applications invited. It was agreed that the success of the scheme be reviewed after three years. In 1996 three candidates were considered, of whom Miss Elizabeth English was appointed for the academic year 1996–97. No applications were received in 1998. For the time being the scholarship idea has lapsed, more probably from a failure on the part of the Trust to make its intentions better known than from any lack of interest on the part of potential beneficiaries. In the future the Trustees will no doubt look for other ways of providing a limited number of larger awards for major projects, without neglecting to make many smaller grants available for deserving applicants.

Limitations and Constraints on the Trust and its Work

The activity of the Spalding Trust, like that of other charitable foundations in Britain, is monitored by the Charity Commissioners, to whom a copy of the audited accounts has to be submitted annually. They also ensure that the Trustees are operating in accordance with the provisions of the original Trust Deeds and with the *Directions* subsequently given to Trustees by the founders.[13] In comparison with the pioneering days when Spalding and Henderson were intimately involved with the day-to-day management of the enterprise, the work of the Trust today looks rather mundane. Once established, the everyday work of a small charitable Trust will seem to be repetitive and scarcely worth recording. The Trust is not now in a position to do more than provide small grants to individuals and groups involved in the study of the religions of the world. The income of the Trust depends upon the interest received from investments. It is unlikely that there will ever be any substantial sums of money added to the capital already invested. In the nature of the case the existing investments are subject to the fluidity of the financial markets. In times of recession, economic uncertainty and political instability, income is inevitably reduced. The Trustees have always preferred prudence to speculation. For many years the greater part of the capital has been invested in the Charities Official Investment Fund (COIF) and in a portfolio of Treasury

Stocks. The policy of the Trustees is reviewed in the light of changing circumstances. The grant-making work of the Trust may prove to be even more important in the future than in the past. The costs of higher education, and especially the costs of research for higher academic qualifications, are not likely to fall. In this situation the resources of the Trust will continue to be stretched to provide a measure of assistance for suitable applicants, not least for those who apply from less affluent countries abroad.

Applications for Assistance from the Trust

Publicising the existence of the Trust may be made easier now that the Internet is so widely used as a source of information. Prospective applicants may know little or nothing about HN's own efforts to promote world peace through a study of the religious experience of mankind, but they can be informed. A brief explanatory statement of the founder's intentions and the purpose of his foundation could be sent to each applicant as well as posted on any future web-site the Trustees may wish to have designed. The careful scrutiny of the applications, submitted in the first instance to the Secretary of the Trust, occupies the attention of the Trustees each month. In most cases applicants are required to nominate at least one academic referee. The assessment of applications continues until the Trustees have reached agreement. The criteria, by means of which grants are made to applicants, are reviewed from time to time. At a time when more and more individuals are seeking financial support for their work, the Trustees are obliged to make clear their priorities and their criteria for deciding how the available funds are to be divided among applicants. Requests for grants-in-aid are received each month from individuals and groups who do not qualify for assistance because their applications have nothing to do with the study of the great religions. Such requests are usually dealt with by the Secretary, and rarely brought to the attention of the Trustees. Applications which do qualify for consideration are treated on their merits. In the case of post-graduate applicants a number of suggestions have been made recently about the type of application that merits priority. Senior academics in British universities were consulted on the question. Their answers tended to reflect the existing range of requests that come from applicants themselves. Priority should be given:

1. To research students from overseas, who need to be supervised for one or two terms in a British university and who should qualify for help.

2. To research students applying for necessary expenses that are not already covered by grants and who should be encouraged to apply to the Trust. One correspondent said that such students would not

include those seeking funds to visit India (for example) because the Indian National Trust for Art and Cultural Heritage (INTACH) has a great deal of money available for such students, and a shortage of applicants.

3. To students of 'neglected religions', as were singled out in another reply. The phrase specified the following: Buddhism, Zoroastrianism, Mandaeism, Gnosticism, Manichaeism, Eastern Christianity, Jewish Christianity, and 'certain traditions of Islam'.

4. To students studying part-time at their own expense.

5. To 'post-third-year students'.

6. To 'graduate students who have used up their statutory grants on other subjects'.

7. To 'graduate students, especially those from third-world countries, who have inadequate grants'.

8. To applicants with good (i.e. first or upper-second) degrees who, despite their achievement, have not obtained British Academy funding.

9. To applicants who are producing 'photographs and/or videos', and to those who are engaged in 'short-term fieldwork, and/or intensive language courses'.

The 'Home and Away Rule'

The Trustees apply what has become known as 'the home and away rule'. It simply means that the Trustees look first to see if an applicant is seeking assistance from the Trust in order to begin (or to continue) a piece of research in the field of a religion other than his or her own. Applicants who are proposing to work on an aspect of their own religion are not excluded, however. In the days when there was considerably less knowledge than there is today about what are described in point number 3 above as 'neglected religions', it was reasonable to encourage those already familiar with Christianity to look beyond the religious tradition in which they had been nurtured. Today the situation has changed. The 'home and away rule' may have to be modified at a time when Christianity—especially Christianity as a major *world* religion—is in some danger of becoming a 'neglected religion'. It should be remembered that neither the Union nor the Trust was ever intended to be a foundation for the study of any religion or culture from the perspective of an outsider. From the beginning HN's ecumenical spirit encouraged not only an exploration of the religious traditions of others through inter-religious dialogue, but also a wider study of one's own by means of *intra*-religious dialogue. The latter may open up hitherto unsuspected riches of experience and belief which are to be found within one's own religious tradition. The study of aspects of Buddhism by a Buddhist, of Hinduism by a Hindu, of Judaism by a Jew, or of Christianity by a Christian, may also be encouraged, provided that the approach taken by an applicant acknowledges the pluralism to be found within his or her own religion. Each of 'the great religions' presents evidence of considerable antiquity, theological development, and cultural adaptation.

A Continuing Challenge

Living with the old certainties of institutionalised religion in the nineteenth century proved to be impossible for many who concluded that advances in scientific knowledge and technological development rendered the claims of revealed religion not only unreasonable but absurd. For reasons given earlier in this book, uncertainty about religious truth in HN's early days went hand in hand with a growing optimism about the future of mankind in which men and women would be liberated from the shackles of religious creeds. He sought to challenge an exclusive religiosity as vigorously as he challenged the incipient agnosticism and the militant atheism of his day by demonstrating—to his own satisfaction at least—that the core teachings of all great religions of the world are, on the contrary, life-enhancing and liberating. Faith in 'humanity', in 'the human spirit', and in the capacity of human beings to solve their problems without recourse to deity, has not survived the events and experiences of the twentieth century.

It is not just religious certainties which have been largely abandoned. Many thoughtful people have given up living with any certainties, whether religious or secular. In the first decade of the twenty-first century the struggle for peace and justice has entered a new phase. Enemies are less easy to identify when conflicts are conducted by groups of terrorists operating across the world. The concluding paragraphs of this book are being written only a few weeks after the acts of terror committed in the United States on Tuesday, 11 September 2001, acts which brought death and destruction to the World Trade Centre in New York City, to the Pentagon in Washington D.C., and to a civil aircraft that was brought down in Pennsylvania. Quite apart from raising anguished questions about who was responsible for such wickedness and how the perpetrators are to be brought to justice without inflicting more suffering on the innocent, these events raise wider questions about the use and misuse of religion in the modern world. Terrorists and their apologists all too readily invoke the sanction of religion for their actions. Distinctions need to be made between the insanities for which religion of one sort or another is claimed to provide a licence and the life-enhancing options still

The Spalding Trustees, on the occasion of the retirement of Dr John Spalding and his wife, Dr Elizabeth Spalding, photographed after lunch in Robinson College, Cambridge, after the fifty-second Annual General Meeting, 13 May, 2000. From left to right: Dr John Spalding, Dr. Julius Lipner, Dr Elizabeth Spalding, Professor Edmund Bosworth, Professor Edward Hulmes, Dr Michael Loewe (in front), Dr Humphrey Fisher, Professor John Emerton.

available in an age of crippling uncertainty, whether they are explicitly 'religious' or not. In defending the life-enhancing aspects of religious belief and practice against those who argue that religions of all kinds serve only to poison the body politic (and must, therefore, be eliminated in a 'civilized society'), the Spalding Trust may be called upon to use its resources to meet the changing needs of a society that is increasingly anti-religious in a way that the founder would scarcely have conceived.

The aims of the Trust have not changed since its work began, although the world has changed dramatically since HN and his wife began to devote their time and resources to the promotion of the study of the great religions. The problem he identified as a critical challenge to civilization—East as well as West—remains largely unsolved. Humanity is still threatened by conflicts, not least by those conflicts occasioned by differences of religion and culture. The history of the second half of the twentieth century was marred by several armed conflicts of a conventional kind, but more disturbingly by the emergence of individual zealots prepared to perpetrate acts of terror at the cost of their own lives. The unpredictability of the time, scale, and location of such violence makes prevention more difficult and punishment for personal guilt more problematic. The first war of the twenty-first century is, apparently, to be a world-wide campaign, undertaken against international terrorism. It is likely to be a protracted war from which there may be no discharge.

Spalding's own work may be largely forgotten but his beliefs and principles are no less important today than they were in his own time. The sickness about which he spoke, wrote, and for which he presumed to prescribe a cure, remains universal and contagious. He had his critics but some people, at least, may consider that his prescription has been neither sufficiently acknowledged nor replaced by anything more salutary and effective.[14] This book records something of his vision, his achievements, his disappointments, and his failures. It is not difficult to forget the benefactor whilst continuing to enjoy his benefaction. For HN's memory to be honoured, it is fitting that his wishes be respected, called to mind, and re-stated from time to time. The duty to see that this is done devolves on the Trustees. It was for this reason that they commissioned this memoir from one of their number as a tribute to the founder.

A Note of Optimism

Two quotations about the essential though as yet the unrealised unity of humanity appear at the beginning of this book. The first was written by H. N. Spalding. The second was written by the German/Swiss writer Hermann Hesse, who was awarded the Nobel Prize for Literature in 1946. Both men were born in the same year, 1877. Both men were to be profoundly affected by the two wars between the countries of their birth. Both men addressed repeated appeals for peace in the aftermath of war, pointing to the essential unity they claimed to detect beneath the outward differences of religion and culture. There is no evidence to suggest that either ever knew of the other's existence. Their lives followed very different courses, but they shared and expressed common beliefs about the human condition, urging their contemporaries to reflect about the ways in which a serious reconsideration of the religious experience of mankind could contribute uniquely not just to peaceful co-existence but to international co-operation. Both men left to the world a vision of harmonious relationships that was religious in the widest, most inclusive, and supra-national sense. This memoir concludes appropriately on a note of optimism with a final quotation from H. N. Spalding:

> The men of the Kingdom of the future will thus be able to note the stages of man's advance: the insane raving, then the stammering speech, the clear talk, then the great song. In the Buddha's image they will see society, as they will see the soul, beginning in the darkness of the mud,

growing up through the twilight of the water, expanding like the bloom of the Lotus under the light of the Sun. They will see the story of mankind, like the story of the soul, as a Divine Comedy in three Acts; the animal beginnings, the moral and spiritual development, the return of the creature to its Father and its bliss.[15]

Notes and References

1. NUSGR, number 30, p. 15
2. *Ibid*, p. 15. The Shap Working Party, of which both Henderson and the present writer were members for several years, was chaired at the time by Professor Ninian Smart. For five years the Spalding Trust provided an annual grant to cover the cost of its expenses.
3. NUSGR, number 37, Autumn 1980, p. 2.
4. R. C. Zaehner, *Foolishness to the Greeks*, published at the Clarendon Press in Oxford, 1953, pp. 3–4.
5. NUSGR, number 30, p. 4. Henderson did not name his American friend.
6. See, for example, F. H. Hilliard's contribution to the series in 1956, *The Buddha, the Prophet and the Christ*, pp. 5,7. Hilliard, an educationalist, was at one time Area Secretary of the West African Section of the USGR. He served as a Spalding Trustee, 1972–75.
7. Reader in Oriental Studies, University of Cambridge, and Fellow of Pembroke College.
8. For the last decade of his ministry before retirement (1963–73) Dr Warren was Canon of Westminster. He is remembered best, perhaps, for his twenty-one years of service as General Secretary of the Church Missionary Society (1942–63). He was a prolific author and a convincing (and sometimes passionate) apologist for evangelical Christianity and the modern missionary movement. He was also a sensitive partner in inter-faith dialogue and a keen supporter of the wider ecumenism.
9. Professor of Islamic Studies, University of London.
10. M. A. C. Warren, 1974, *Crowded Canvas: Some Experiences of a Life-time*, Hodder and Stoughton pp. 229–30.
11. From the editors' Introduction to Richard Bell, 1991, *A Commentary on the Qur'ān* (in two volumes), edited by C. Edmund Bosworth and M. E. J. Richardson, University of Manchester, (*Journal of Semitic Studies* Monograph 14), p. xiii.
12. *Ibid*; the quotation is from the editors' Introduction, pp. xiii, xviii.
13. See Appendix 1.
14. See chapter 1, p. 9.
15. CEW, p. 334.

APPENDIX ONE

Directions to the Trustees,
written by HN on 1 January 1953

(a) Together with a copy of the *Directions,* shown in section (b) below, the Chairman, Dr J. M. K. Spalding, sent to the Trustees an additional explanatory note in December 1992. Confirming that many parts of the original documents were now irrelevant to the present work of the Spalding Trustees, he added some points of historical interest.

> H. N. Spalding's mother died in 1938, leaving him the sum of £3,000. On 27 August 1938 a Memorandum was endorsed on the Settlement of 18 July, 1928. The Memorandum added this sum to the 1928 Settlement in order to provide a memorial to his mother. The Memorandum states that the Trust fund 'shall be held ... by way of memorial to ... Ellen Rebe Spalding for the purpose of forming a collection of works of Eastern Art for some educational purpose or for such other purpose falling within the charitable trusts of the Settlement as the said Henry Norman Spalding during his life or after his death the said Nellie Maud Emma Spalding and Kenneth Jay Spalding or the survivor of them or after the death of such survivor the Trustees for the time being of the said settlement shall direct'.

The Chairman added: 'My father lived fifteen years after signing the Memorandum and found no suitable memorial. He wanted something of the sort described in the Memorandum, which would have been of interest to his mother. His mother, however, had had almost no interest in such matters so an impasse arose. After my father's death it was remembered that my grandmother's great interest had been in the welfare of women and children. The fund [the Ellen Rebe Spalding memorial Fund] has therefore been used to help women and children in need, and this was started when my mother and my uncle K. J. Spalding were Trustees and therefore approving this use. For many years this has been done through the Oxfordshire Department of Social Work. I have dealt with it, with Elizabeth's [1] advice.'

With reference to section 1 paragraph 3 of the *Directions* shown below, the Chairman wrote: 'K. J. Spalding was H. N. Spalding's brother, a research fellow of Brasenose College, Oxford, and previously Professor of Classical

Literature and Philosophy at Queen's College, London. The trusts of 1923
and 1928 and the Directions make frequent references to his work and enjoin
Trustees to support it. K. J. Spalding was a Trustee until his death in 1962
and therefore had ample opportunity to put forward his views. Some Trustees
have had difficulty in deciding how his views could be further promoted and
though I knew him well I am unable to make any suggestion.'

(b) The following extracts are taken from the *Directions to the Trustees of
the Spalding Trusts*, circulated on 1st January 1953, and based on the documents
dated 16 January 1925, 18 July 1928 and 27 August 1938.

I. **The Spalding Educational Trusts.** The two original Trust Deeds of
16th January 1923 and 18th July 1928, the Memorandum dated 27th
August 1938 containing Trusts of the Ellen Robe Spalding Memorial
Fund, the Deed dated 12th March 1949 appointing Douglas Veale
CBE, Sir S. Radhakrishnan D. Litt., and K. J. Spalding as new Trustees
and cancelling the powers of revocation contained in Clause 8 of both
Trusts, and the Deed dated 17 April 1953 appointing Professors
A. J. Arberry and T. W. Thacker as further Trustees are in the custody
of the National Bank Ltd, 13 Old Broad Street, E.C.2. The Trust of
18th July 1928 (Clause 6) reads: 'The objects of both Trusts are the
same but are herein more fully and clearly stated for the guidance of
the Trustees of both Trusts', and the two Trusts should be administered as one, the wording of the second making clearer the meaning
of the first. The Trusts of the Ellen Rebe Spalding Memorial Fund
form part of the Trust of 18th July 1928. All the papers relating to
these Trusts are in the chest outside H. N. S.'s [H. N. Spalding's]
study.

Until recently part of the income derived from the securities of the
Trust of 16th January 1923 was remitted to the National Bank Ltd
(Spalding No. 4 Account) and the remainder of the income from that
Trust and the whole of the income from the Trust of 18th July 1928
and from the Ellen Rebe Spalding Memorial Fund was re-invested
by the Official Trustees. On the advice of Dr Knox-Shaw the income
from all three is now remitted to the National Bank for the No. 4
Account, in order to save the expense of a number of small investments. When the balance of the No. 4 Account becomes larger than
is necessary, the Trustees, in consultation with Dr Knox-Shaw, should
arrange for re-investment. A list of the securities in both Trusts whose
income was until recently accumulating, with the income from them
for each calendar year since 1944, furnished by the Charity Commissioners are to be found tagged together. With them is a list of the
securities whose income was until recently alone remitted to the No. 4
Account. There are also valuations of the capital dated 16th January

1951 and 16th June 1953.

Reference is made in the Trusts to the philosophy of K. J. Spalding. This refers (a) to the new form he has given to St Anselm's and Descartes' ontological argument for the Existence and Nature of God (see his 'Talks on Philosophy' and the description given by H. N. S. at the end or Part Two of his book 'The Divine Universe'; see also K. J. S.' 'Three Chinese Thinkers'); and (b) to his study of the development of character (see the brown folders containing records of conversations on the subject, together with a typed summary of these arranged in proper order. (Professor Thacker has consented to preserve the folders and summary in Durham University Library.) It is hoped that three books on character may still be written.

2. **Trustees.**   The Trustees may be of 'any number not exceeding nine' (Clause 6). The following are now Trustees: H. N. Spalding, N. M. E. Spalding, Dr Thomas Knox-Shaw (Master of Sidney Sussex College, Cambridge), to whom were added (by the Deed of Appointment dated 12th March 1949) Douglas Veale, CBE, Sir S. Radhakrishnan, F. B. A., and K. J. Spalding, and by Deed of Appointment dated 17th April 1953 Professors A. J. Arberry (Cambridge) and T. W. Thacker (Durham). When a further Trustee is appointed, the qualifications or Colonel W. A. C. H. Dobson, Head of the Department or East Asiatic Studies and Professor of Chinese in the University or Toronto, should be carefully considered. He is endeavouring to promote Indian studies there, centring on Indian philosophy and religion. Except for strong overriding reasons, no Roman Catholic, though some are themselves most sympathetic to the objects of the Trust, should be appointed a Trustee, as his actions would be liable to control by the hierarchy behind him.[2]

The Trustees will be entitled to charge the usual out-of-pocket expenses for their services, including (for instance) the payment now made to Professor Arberry for clerical assistance in editing 'Ethical and Religious Classics of East and West'. Remuneration cannot of course legally be paid to Trustees for their services as Trustees. But we hereby direct as provided in Clauses 2 and 3 that remuneration may be made to any of the Trustees in respect of any office they may hold or service they may render outside the duties that would ordinarily be expected of Trustees, if and when in the opinion of the Trustees other than the one to be remunerated, payment or such rernuneration will best promote the objects of the Trust. For instance, if a Trustee is the best man to promote the objects of the Trusts in some particular way, but has to forego other remuneration that he needs in order to do so, he should be remunerated from the Trusts.

Without such consent no Trustee shall have power to charge for his services except in the case of out-of-pocket expenses. (Messrs. Haslewood, Hare think this provision is not wholly free from doubt from the legal point of view. But only the Charity Commissioners could challenge it (when the annual return of expenditure under the Trusts is made to them), and it can and should be defended on the ground that the objects of the Trust can in this way be best promoted.)

The holders of the settled funds are technically the Official Trustees of Charitable Funds, Charity Commissioners, Ryder Street, St James's Street, S.W.1 ... Yet changes in investment and so on are made on the directions of the Educational Trustees above mentioned, though the Official Trustees insist: that the actual investment shall be made by them. This works well at present, since Dr Knox-Shaw is a former Treasurer of the University of Cambridge, and a financial expert ... But should the Educational Trustees hereafter not include a financial expert, they should appoint (if this can legally be done) financial. experts as Holding Trustees, to advise them on the management of the settled funds. Messrs. R. Nivison and Co., 6 Threadneedle Street E.C.2 ... have always been most kind in helping in this matter, and may perhaps be willing to supply one or more Holding Trustees, if the Educational Trustees see fit ... If no Holding Trustees or Trustees be appointed, financial experts should be consulted in the sale or investment of the settled funds.

3. **Use of the funds.** We direct our Trustees (in all of whom we have the fullest confidence, and to whom we feel the deepest gratitude) to use the income, and if necessary the capital, of the Trust funds in the following ways:

(a) To honour existing obligations: [A list of several confidential grants to individuals, groups, and institutions follows at this point. All the 'existing obligations' were honoured.]

(b) To promote the Movement for ethical, philosophic and religious education and culture, as far as possible throughout the world, through the comparative study of the great religions (the aims of which are outlined in the Statement of Aims dated 28th January 1951, and the means in the Memorandum on the 'Constitution and Work' of the proposed Union dated 3rd August 1951). The Spalding Trustees shall supplement funds received from other sources in whatever ways seem best to their discretion. Teaching posts and (where necessary) building should as a rule if possible be endowed or paid for from other sources, such as the State, Foundations or Societies, or benefactions. We should be glad if as far as convenient

the income from the settled funds of these Trusts should be devoted
to Grants to promising young men to be known (if the Trustees
see fit) as 'Spalding Students of Religions', for the study of 'the
essentials of religion', namely, the Divine Nature and man's way
of approach or return to It, moral, rational and mystical. Those
should be selected who seem likely to become leaders of religion,
whether in thought or action. It is to be hoped that a number of
such students may eventually become teachers in Universities and
elsewhere throughout the world (compare the early Dominicans
who exercised their influence over thought and action from University Chairs in many countries).[3] Grants may be made during a
Sabbatical year or other period of leave or on retirement, especially
to those who have had experience of (for example) an Eastern
religion, and wish to study it further for its contribution to living
faith. In suitable cases the income from the Ellen Rebe Spalding
Memorial Fund may be given in Grants to women as 'Ellen Rebe
Spalding Students of Religions'. Grants should be made to students
irrespective of country, race or religion (save in so far as it is desirable
that there should be a due proportion between the students and
teachers of the various great religions), in whatever way the Trustees
consider that the aims of this Movement may best be furthered.
The students should throughout life try to work and (where not
too expensive) to meet together. When financial help is given by
the Trustees, it may be given in the name of Spalding or of the
Union or both, as the Trustees may consider will best promote the
objects of these Trusts.

(c) If the Movement should fail (which God forbid) or should otherwise
have insufficient funds for its needs, the Trustees should promote
any educational purposes specified in the two Trusts (Clauses 2, 3
and 4). (Under Clauses 2 and 3 payments can be made to other
than educational charities only by the Founders and K. J. Spalding.)

4. **Indian and Chinese studies at Oxford.** The election of a highly
unsuitable candidate (a philologist, Christian and European) to the
[Spalding] Chair of Eastern Religions and Ethics having been 'pre-
arranged' without consultation with its Founders and in the teeth of
their known wish (for a highly suitable Hindu philosopher of Asian
descent) and of the intention and provisions of the Statute, no further
benefactions are to be made to or in the *University of Oxford* until
these abuses and their cause have been remedied.[4] Papers will be
attached on this subject, and the Founders earnestly hope that, in
furtherance of the Movement, their Trustees will do all that lies in

their power to carry out the recommendations made in them (the creation of an Asian Board, the reorganization of Hindu, Buddhist and Chinese studies, and the revision of the Statute creating the Spalding Chair so as to guard against further abuses), in such manner as may seem wisest to them, if this has not already been done. Individual members of the University may however be helped, it they are likely to prove useful to the Movement. Nothing shall be required of Mr Veale that he considers might embarrass him as Registrar.

5. **Non-use of the funds.** [The directions are too specific and confidential for publication here]

6. **Power of surviving settler.** The power given by Clause 3 to the survivor of the Settlers 'to direct the Trustees' remains of course unimpaired by the foregoing directions.

7. **Permanence of the Trust.** In view of the guarantee given to Allen & Unwin, one or more of the Trusts should remain in force for from ten to (we hope) twenty years. It may well be found desirable in any case to keep them in being permanently.[5] ... Should the University of Oxford agree to the Spalding Trustees appointing one of the Electors to the Spalding Chair at Eastern Religions and Ethics, it will be necessary for one or more of these Trusts to remain permanently in existence. It will also be necessary for one or more of them to remain in existence while the Area Committee for Great Britain of the Union for the Study at the Great Religions still exists ... [If the work of this Area Committee were to fail, the directive goes on to state that the capital sum of £10,000 paid to the Area by the Spalding Educational Trusts would revert to the latter Trusts.]

The Solicitors of the Founders are Messrs. Haslewood, Hare, Shirley Woolmer and Co., 139 Temple Chambers, Temple Avenue, E.C.4.[6]

Notes and References

1. Dr Elizabeth de Carteret Spalding, the Chairman's wife; STP, circular letter, January 1993.
2. Fortunately for the present writer and another Trustee, both Catholic laymen, this part of the directive has been tactfully forgotten or quietly ignored. In a memorandum to Spalding Trustees, dated December 1992, Dr J. M. K. Spalding, Chairman of the Trust and son of the founder of the Trust, commented: 'I think that this interdiction is untypical of my father'. He added: 'Such strong overriding reasons have already been found'.
3. A somewhat ironic point to make by way of clarification after the earlier exclusion of Catholics!
4. The 'highly unsuitable candidate' in this instance was Professor R. C. Zaehner who, by coincidence, was a Catholic. There is no doubt that his appointment soured the

relationship between the Spalding family and the University of Oxford. See chapter 4, pp. 114ff.

5. George Allen & Unwin had agreed to publish the series *Ethical and Religious Classics of East and West*, edited by Professor A. J. Arberry, with subventions from the Trust. The guarantee was an expression of the Trust's goodwill in supporting the venture. The ninth volume to be published in the series was Professor Arberry's celebrated English version of *The Holy Koran*. See chapter 6, pp. 177–8.

6. STP, circular letter, January 1993.

Members of the Co-ordinating Committee of the Union for the Study of the Great Religions (June, 1954)

Sir Richard Livingstone, DLitt, LLD, Oxford, (Chairman)

Professor A. J. Arberry, LittD, FBA, Cambridge

Canon C. E. Raven, DD, DSc, FBA, Cambridge

K. J. Spalding, MA, Oxford

Professor T. W. Thacker, MA, Durham

K. D. D. Henderson, CMG, MA (General Secretary)

K. J. Spalding and Canon Raven were co-opted as members of the committee in 1954. In 1950 Canon Raven, Professor Sarvepalli Radhakrishnan, H. N. Spalding, and K. J. Spalding, were the founders of 'the Movement' that became the Union. In 1961 Dr J. M. K. Spalding was appointed to succeed Sir Richard Livingstone as a Union Trustee.

Area Secretaries of the USGR (June 1954)

Canada	Professor W. A. C. H. Dobson, MA, Professor of Chinese, and Head of the Department of East Asiatic Studies, University of Toronto.
India	Professor T. M. P. Mahadevan, MA, PhD, Professor and Head of the Department of Philosophy, University of Madras.
Middle East	The Very Revd Lev Gillet, Lic. Phil, Archimandrite of the Orthodox Patriarchate of Constantinople, c/o St Basil's House, 52 Ladbrooke Road, London W 11.
Pakistan	Dr I. H. Zuberi, MA, PhD, FRSL, Vice-Chancellor, Rajshahi University, Rajshahi, East Pakistan.
United States	Professor the Revd Kenneth W. Morgan, STB,

University Chaplain and Professor of Philosophy and
Religion, Colgate University, Hamilton, New York.

West Africa   Dr F. H. Hilliard, BD, PhD, Senior Lecturer in the
Institute of Education, University of the Gold Coast,
Achimota.

Advisory Council and Founding Members of the Union (June 1954)

Dr W. G. S. Adams

Dr A Altmann

Professor E. E. Aubrey

Dr Frank Aydelotte

Dr Maulana Azad

Dr Arnold Baké

Dr J. S. Bezzant

Mr H. O. Bhattacharya

Mr Basil Blackwell

Dastur Framroze Bode

The Revd Dr A. C. Bouquet

Sir Reader Bullard

Dr Victor Butterfield

The Lady Chalmers

Dr G. Chandra Dev

Dr S. C. Chatterjee

The Bishop of Chichester

Sir Douglas Copeland

Mr A. E. K. Cull

Professor D. M. Datta

Sir James Duff

Rabbi Leslie Edgar

Professor Sir Alfred Egerton

The Hon. Lady Egerton

Professor T. Finnegan

Mr C. J. Galpin

Dr Mortimer Graves

Mr Theodore M. Greene

Canon L. W. Grensted

Miss Linda Grier

Professor W. Ernest Hocking

The Revd R. V. Holt

Canon R. W. Howard

Dr Zakir Hussain

Dr L. P. Jacks

Dr J. M. Mackenzie

Dr S. K. Maitra

Professor T. W. Manson

Sir John Marshall

Dean W. R. Matthews

Mr Christopher Mayhew

Mr P. Mehta

Dr Nathaniel Micklem

The Hon. Nurul Amin

Lord Pethick Lawrence

Canon Anson Phelps Stokes

Sir Sarvepalli Radhakrishnan

Dr Leon Roth

Mr B. Seebohm Rowntree

Viscount Samuel

Dr Gregg M. Sinclair

Professor Wilfred Smith

The Revd Sidney Spencer

Professor D. T. Suzuki

Professor George F. Thomas

Sir Douglas Veale

Mr H. R. Wade

The Bishop of Winchester

Professor Herbert G. Wood

Professor W. P. Yetts

Spalding Trustees and Secretaries of the Trust, with dates of service

Spalding Trustees

Arberry, Professor A. J., DLitt, FBA, 1953–1969

Bosworth, Professor C. E., MA, PhD, FBA, 1984 to date

Chadwick, the Very Revd, Henry, DD, FBA, 1970–1976

Davies, Oliver, MA, DPhil, 2001 to date

Emerton, Professor J. A., DD, FBA, 1972 to date

Fisher, H. L., MA, PhD, 1992–2002

Hilliard, Professor F. H., MA, PhD, 1972–1975

Hulmes, Professor E. D. A., KCHS, MA, BD, DPhil, 1985–2002

Knox-Shaw. Thomas, CBE, MC, MA, (Chairman, 1953–1971)

Lipner, Julius, MA, PhD, 1992 to date

Loewe, M. A. N., MA, PhD, 1983 to date

Matilal, Professor B. K., MA, PhD, 1977–1991

Mitchell, Professor B. G., MA, 1977–1985

Radhakrishnan, Sir Sarvepalli, Hon. OM, DLitt, Hon. FBA 1950–1953

Spalding, Anne C., MA, 1997–2000. (Chairman, 2000 to date)

Spalding, Elizabeth de C., MB, MRCP, DCH, 1978–2000

Spalding, J. M. K., DM, FRCP, 1953–2000, (Chairman, 1971–2000)

Spalding, K. J., MA, 1923–62

Spalding, Mrs N. M. E. 1923–1957

Stallybrass, W. T. S., OBE, MA. 1928–1948

Thacker, Professor T. W., MA, 1953–1984

Veale, Sir Douglas, CBE, MA, 1950–1973 (Chairman, 1950–1953)

Secretaries of the Spalding Trust

K. D. D. Henderson CMG, MA, 1953–86

E. D. A. Hulmes (Assistant Secretary) KCHS, MA, BD, DPhil, 1974–85

H. L. Dennison MA, 1986 –87

Mrs Catherine (Kate) Kornicki MA, 1988–95

Mrs Tessa Rodgers BA, 1995 to date

Notes

In 1953 K. D. D. Henderson began to serve the Spalding Trust single-handedly as Secretary, soon adding to his responsibilities the work of co-ordinating the activities of the newly-founded Union for the Study of the Great Religions. This took up a considerable amount of his time and energy. The work involved extensive overseas travel and long periods abroad away from home. With the effective demise of the Union this part of the work ceased but there was still a good deal to do. Henderson was starting to talk about retirement, so he approached the present writer informally in 1972 to see if I might help him. I was working in Oxford at the time and agreed readily. My immediate superior, Sir Walter Coutts, sometime Governor-General of Uganda, gave me permission to add this part-time appointment to my existing duties. In 1974 I was invited by the Trustees to act as Assistant Secretary to Henderson. The idea was that when he decided to retire I would be well prepared to take over.

It soon became apparent that immediate retirement was not on Henderson's his mind. He enjoyed the work. His mind was sharp. His general health was good, although he suffered from arthritis. A hip replacement operation in Oxford had helped him to regain mobility, although he still walked with some difficulty, aided by a stick. His mood was buoyant and there was no reason why he should give up the work of which he was the master. This suited me well because my visits to the United States for lengthy periods were increasing. The Henderson house at Steeple Langford remained the Trust's base, with KDDH directing operations.

Henderson eventually retired as Secretary in 1986, a year after I was invited to become a Trustee. The new Secretary was Harry L Dennison, whom Henderson suggested for the post. Henderson had been associated with Dorset House, the Oxford School of Occupational Therapy, where Dennison worked. It was there that the two men met. Dennison was an Oxford graduate, well qualified in every way to act as Secretary, and he was about to retire from Dorset House. In due course he was appointed to succeed Henderson. Working from his home, he kept meticulous records of the Trust's activities. He died suddenly in 1987.

The Chairman, Dr J. M. K. Spalding held things together for a short period, during which six possible candidates were considered. In 1988 the choice fell on Mrs Catherine O Kornicki, an Oxford graduate, a Canadian by birth, and the wife of a Cambridge don. 'Kate' Kornicki was an ideal choice. Her enthusiasm for the work of the Trust was infectious and her administration was efficient in the highest degree. It was through her good offices that the Trustees were able to hold their Annual General Meetings in Robinson College, Cambridge, after many years in which the meetings were held at the Spaldings' house, 'Shotover Cleve' in Oxford. She worked assiduously for the Trust for seven years before asking to be relieved of her duties as Secretary.

On 22 March 1995 her successor, Mrs Tessa Rodgers, was interviewed and appointed. At the end of the Annual General Meeting held in 22 April 1995 in Robinson College Mrs Kornicki and I met briefly in order for me to collect several boxes of Trust papers from her. I had been asked by my colleagues to store them. We met in the car park under the College and I put the boxes into the boot of my car. We said goodbye. She was in excellent spirits. It was the last time I saw her. A few days later she took her own life in the History Department building in Cambridge. Her death was a tragic loss to her husband, her young children, her family and to all who knew her. Dr Elizabeth Spalding, Dr John Spalding, Dr Carmen Blacker and Dr Michael Loewe attended the memorial service in Robinson College Chapel on behalf of the Trust. Mrs Tessa Rodgers has continued to serve the Trust as Secretary with diligence and efficiency.

Select Bibliography

Arberry, Arthur J., 1969, (General Editor), *Religion in the Middle East* (2 volumes), Cambridge University Press.

Dillistone, F. W., 1975, *Charles Raven: Naturalist, Historian*, Theologian, Hodder & Stoughton, London.

Gopal, Sarvepalli, 1992, *Radhakrishnan: A Biography*, Oxford University Paperbacks, Delhi

Henderson, K. D. D.

——, 1953, *The Making of the Modern Sudan: the Life and Letters of Sir Douglas Newbold*, Faber & Faber.

——, 1965, *Sudan Republic, Nations of the Modern World*, Ernest Benn Limited.

——, 1976, 'Francis Younghusband and the Mysticism of Shared Endeavour', the Inaugural Younghusband Memorial Lecture (11 May) World Congress of Faiths, London.

——, 1977, 'Is Religion Necessary?', in Occasional Papers 1976–1986, edited by Edward Hulmes, Farmington Institute for Christian Studies, Oxford, pp. 11–15.

——, 1987, *Set Under Authority: Being A Portrait of the British District Officer in the Sudan under the Anglo-Egyptian Condominium*, 1989–1955, Castle Cary Press, Somerset.

Lago, Mary, 2001, *'India's Prisoner': A Biography of Edward John Thompson (1886–1946)*, University of Missouri Press.

Livingstone, Richard

——, 1943, *Education for a World Adrift*, Cambridge University Press.

——, 1943, *The Future in Education*, Cambridge University Press.

Matilal, Bimal K., 1977, 'The Logical Illumination of Indian Mysticism', An Inaugural Lecture delivered before the University of Oxford on 5 May 1977, Clarendon Press, Oxford.

Radhakrishnan, Sarvepalli, 1952–53, *History of Philosophy Eastern and Western* (ed.), George Allen & Unwin, London,

——, 1961, *The Hindu View of Life*, George Allen & Unwin, London.

Spalding, H. N.

——, 1939, *Civilization in East and West: An Introduction to the Study of Human Progress*, Oxford University Press.

——, 1950, *A Poem of Praise*, Basil Blackwell, Oxford.

——, 1952, *In Praise of Life*, Basil Blackwell, Oxford.

——, 1958, *The Divine Universe, or The Many and the One: A Study of Religions and Religion*, Basil Blackwell, Oxford

Spalding, K. J.,

——, 1922, *Desire and Reason: Being an Account of the Origin and Development of Intellectual Principles*, Kegan Paul, Trench, Trubner & Co., Ltd.

——, 1947, *Three Chinese Thinkers*, International Series of Chinese Studies, Nanking, China.

——, 1962 *Some Letters to H. on Philosophy*, unpublished typescript, found in his papers after his death. Fifty copies were reproduced with a grant from the Spalding Trust.

Zaehner, R. C.

——, 1953, '*Foolishness to the Greeks*', an Inaugural Lecture delivered before the University of Oxford on 2 November 1953, published at the Clarendon Press, Oxford.

——, 1957, *Mysticism Sacred and Profane: an Inquiry into some Varieties of Praeternaturalism*, Oxford University Press.

——, 1962, *Hinduism*, Oxford University Press.

——, 1963, *The Convergent Spirit: Towards a Dialectics of Religion*, Routledge & Kegan Paul, London.

——, 1970, *Concordant Discord: the Interdependence of Faiths* (the Gifford Lectures, 1967–69), Oxford, at the Clarendon Press.

——, 1974, *Our Savage God*, Collins, London.

Index

(Numbers in *italic* type refer to illustrations in the book)